THE CONCRETE PLATEAU

Studies of the Weatherhead East Asian Institute, Columbia University

The Studies of the Weatherhead East Asian Institute of Columbia University were inaugurated in 1962 to bring to a wider public the results of significant new research on modern and contemporary East Asia.

THE CONCRETE PLATEAU

URBAN TIBETANS AND THE CHINESE CIVILIZING MACHINE

ANDREW GRANT

CORNELL UNIVERSITY PRESS
Ithaca and London

First published 2022 by Cornell University Press

Library of Congress Cataloging-in-Publication Data

Names: Grant, Andrew, 1984- author.
Title: The concrete plateau : urban Tibetans and the Chinese civilizing machine / Andrew Grant.
Other titles: Urban Tibetans and the Chinese civilizing machine
Description: Ithaca [New York] : Cornell University Press, 2022.
Series: Studies of the Weatherhead East Asian Institute, Columbia University | Includes bibliographical references and index.
Identifiers: LCCN 2021061793 (print) | LCCN 2021061794 (ebook) | ISBN 9781501764097 (hardcover) | ISBN 9781501764103 (pdf) | ISBN 9781501764110 (epub)
Subjects: LCSH: Xining (Qinghai Sheng, China)—History—21st century. | Tibetans—Cultural assimilation—China—Xining (Qinghai Sheng).
Classification: LCC DS797.66.X565 G73 2022 (print) | LCC DS797.66.X565 (ebook) | DDC 305.895/4105147—dc23/eng/20211221
LC record available at https://lccn.loc.gov/2021061793
LC ebook record available at https://lccn.loc.gov/2021061794

For Lily Tso

Contents

Acknowledgments

This book project has taken me many years to complete. I have gotten advice and feedback from many people and benefited from the words and encouragements of many more. To begin with, I would like to thank Emily Yeh and Adam Moore, who both suggested to me to undertake this book project when I was still recovering from completing my dissertation. At the time, it sounded very pie in the sky. Turns out it was not only possible, but also a very rewarding experience that let me reengage with my research materials. Adam Moore has also been an unflagging source of encouragement in the book-writing process, mentoring me as I learned to write the initial proposal, converse with editors, and respond to reviewers' comments. I wrote the first draft of this book while a visiting scholar at the University of Colorado in Boulder, where I learned from many people, including Emily Yeh, Tim Oakes, Holly Gayley, Somtsobum, Alessandro Rippa, Siddharth Menon, Duojie Zhaxi, Jessica DiCarlo, Yang Yang, Brenda Chen, Rupak Shrestha, Joshua Shelton, Keller Hartline, Andrew Violet, Sam Tynen, Dawa Lokyistang, Drolma Kyab, Mike Dwyer, Carole McGranahan, and others. Please forgive me if I forgot to include your name on this list.

I developed parts of the book during talks at the Department of Geography and the Center for Asian Studies at the University of Colorado. I presented a version of chapter 2 at the Tibetan Landscapes workshop at the University of Copenhagen in 2018, where I benefited from the insights of Trine Brox, Jane Caple, Stephen Christopher, Galen Murton, and Nadine Plachta. The book also draws from insights gained from Charlene Makley, Andrew Fischer, Nancy Levine, Jarmila Ptáčková, James Leibold, Gerald Roche, and Ben Hillman at sessions of the conferences of the Association for Nepal and Himalayan Studies in 2017, the Association for Asian Studies in 2019, and the International Association for Tibetan Studies in 2019. I would also like to thank Nancy Levine and Elizabeth Leicester for hosting me at a panel on Tibetan urbanization at the University of California Los Angeles in

2019, and Youqin Huang and Tom Narins for hosting me for a book talk at the Confucius Institute of the University at Albany in 2020.

Portions of chapter 5 were previously published in the *Annals of the American Association of Geographers*, reprinted here in revised form by permission of the American Association of Geographers, www.aag.org. Portions of chapter 3 are derived from part of an article published in a special issue on urbanization in Tibet in *Critical Asian Studies*, published in 2018, copyright the Committee of Concerned Asian Scholars. I am grateful to be able to publish reworked versions of these articles as chapters.

More generally, I would like to thank Rinchen Tso, Tsemdo Thar, Tselo Thar, Rinchen Jyid, Dobi Shadru, and Konchok Gelek for helping make portions of this book possible, and to Nancy Levine, Julia Cassaniti, Chen Chen, Brian Miller, John Agnew, and Ali Hamdan for their various comments and assistance on aspects of the book and the book-writing process. Thanks to Katherine Graber for helping me at the Billy Graham Archives and to Clare Jones for helping me navigate the world of publishing permissions. I would also like to give a big thanks to Jim Lance at Cornell University Press, for being such a positive editor and for empowering me to continue on with the process. Thanks as well to Jennifer Savran Kelly and Glenn Novak for their careful reading during the copyediting phase. At the Weatherhead East Asia Institute, Ariana King provided assistance and support for getting the book into their series. The three book reviewers Jim and Ariana found for the manuscript provided invaluable insights that pushed me to improve the work, to rethink and sharpen its arguments, and to make it a better narrative. Thanks to you all.

The summer of 2020 was a summer of pandemic and manuscript revision. I would like to thank Suzanne Chapin-Donalson for hosting Laura, Lily Tso, and me during the very long month of June, which turned out to be a pivotal time for me to reengage with the manuscript. Risking acknowledgment cliché, I would like to thank Laura Brown for everything. This book would have been impossible without her close reading skills, mastery of the Chinese language, and love and encouragement.

Finally, the research for the book was conducted with US federal government funding from two Department of Education programs: Fulbright-Hays and the Foreign Language and Area Studies program. These programs provide important skills training for American students as well as invaluable exchange opportunities between the US, China, and many other countries. This book would not have been possible without these programs, and I hope the text and its findings speak to the continued importance and necessity of them.

Note on Transliteration

I have used the Tibetan and Himalayan Library (THL) phonetic transcription guidelines for transcriptions from the various topolects of Amdo Tibetan. Because the THL system is set up for transcribing Standard Tibetan, I have adjusted it in certain cases when the Standard Tibetan transcription differs markedly from Amdo Tibetan—for instance, Jamtso instead of Gyatso. For proper nouns and other significant terms, I have put the Wylie transliteration in parentheses or brackets after the marker "Tib." for Tibetan.

For Chinese, I have used the Hanyu Pinyin romanization system. When translating a proper noun into English, or when highlighting a Chinese term for its significance, I have placed the Hanyu Pinyin spelling in the text in italics or set it off in parentheses or brackets after the marker "Ch." for Chinese.

Besides those of public figures and published writers, all names of people in this book are pseudonyms. Some locations and names of places within Xining have also been modified to protect anonymity.

Introduction

Building the Concrete Plateau

"It's like a hotel room," my friend Dege Metok said with a laugh. We peered out of one of three newly installed windows in her apartment onto the unpainted concrete skeleton of the neighboring building. From the twenty-third floor we had a panoramic view of eastern Xining City and the surrounding construction activity. Below us, workers trundled wheelbarrows filled with wire and buckets of plaster. As they made their way into the buildings, they navigated thin wooden planks that kept them above the mud engulfing the site. Now that primary construction was complete, these workers were giving interiors to the new apartment units. Though Dege Metok had purchased the apartment we were standing in, she was decorating it not for herself, but for future tenants. After investing 180,000 Chinese yuan in 2013, she hoped to rent out the apartment at 1,000 yuan per month while the property appreciated in value. Then she planned to sell the apartment to fund her child's education at a university that would, she hoped, be located somewhere abroad.

Although this dream placed the apartment in a transnational itinerary, she also had desires for it linked to her Tibetan Buddhist practice. When Dege Metok did not have enough space to build a shrine room, called a *chö khang* in Tibetan, she decided to hire a Sichuanese woodworker to construct, between two cabinets above a door, a small nook for this purpose. Now, in the interim before renters arrived, she could make offerings to a small Green

Tara statue. On a different afternoon on the opposite end of the city, as I left a friend's apartment, I turned the corner and was nearly knocked over by a neighbor carrying a tray of smoldering incense and *torma*—molded barley flour sculptures. Momentarily, I felt like I had been transported to the passageways between earthen-walled farmhouses in a Tibetan village. In reality, I was moving among towering high-rise buildings in a new property development in Qinghai Province's buzzing metropolis. As I discovered, Tibetans were leaving all sorts of marks in the city, creating apartment shrines, businesses, and restaurants, and making subtler modifications to the urban landscape that were easily missed by those not attuned to noticing them.

What I was encountering were not vestiges of the rural in the city, but an emergent Tibetan urban assemblage that coexisted alongside Han Chinese and Muslim urban forms while also incorporating places and practices from across the Tibetan Plateau. In Xining, Tibetans were assembling materials, bodies, memories, and deities in an urban landscape thick with political possibility. Within Ziling—the Tibetan name for Xining—this assemblage could be encountered wherever Tibetans built and maintained places. Despite a political context of illiberal authoritarianism, urban redevelopment in China has allowed for new places to be staked out and claimed in an expanding and increasingly market- and consumer-oriented city. As new residential neighborhoods, business centers, and urban parks have been developed and opened, Tibetans have come to see Xining as a Tibetan place, even if it is a place that carries the risk of economic exclusion and cultural assimilation, a threat that Tibetans frequently glossed as "turning Han." This book argues that Tibetans were not merely resisting or staving off an assimilatory national urbanization project; they were instead participating in state-guided urbanization by engaging in urban place-making practices that worked to bolster not only Tibetans' individual aspirations, but also those of a wider Tibetan community.

Xining City has been rebuilt during the twenty-first century with shopping centers and high-end residential districts that are both, in terms of layout and architecture, unmistakably Chinese and similar in national developmental ambitions to new world-class urban districts across the globe. Moving to Xining, Tibetan migrants have been confronted with a dilemma: if they pursue the urban dream promoted by government policy and valorized in national media, they face the steep cost of cultural assimilation. Compared to their co-ethnics in the towns of Xining's hinterlands, Xining Tibetans were more likely to live in housing communities dominated by residents whose linguistic, religious, and sartorial practices differ from those usually found in Tibetan communities. But the city has also provided opportunities for purchasing apartments near friends and family, opening businesses that bring Tibetan tastes and handicrafts into the city, and creating places, public and private, where Tibetans can gather. Indeed, Tibetans have been actively involved in the creation of a subaltern city that ultimately challenged the project of the Chinese civilizing machine, the name I give to the process of state-led urban development that reassembles the people and places of China's peripheries by attempting to remake them in line with the party-state's visions of Chinese material and spiritual civilization. By engaging in a micropolitics of place-making, Tibetans rerouted state attempts to mute local politics and asserted themselves as a community that belongs in China's urban future.

Xining City has been an ideal site to investigate the effects of authoritarian practices of urbanization on minoritized and marginalized populations in general, as well as on Tibetans in particular. Xining is the largest city in, and the capital of, Qinghai Province. Richly diverse, this province contains "autonomous" prefectures and counties for the state-recognized ethnicities of the Tibetan, Mongolian, Tu, Hui, and Salar. Qinghai is not, however, an Autonomous Region like Xinjiang, Inner Mongolia, or the Tibetan Autonomous Region, and because of this, Xining's urban landscape has been developed in line with national urban models that reflect the cities of Inner China (Ch. *neidi*), with few accommodations for "ethnic flavor." Therefore, the politics of place play out in an urban environment within which the city's diverse peoples must rely largely on personal and community initiative to make places that break from the civilizational schema of Chinese urbanization. Xining also differs from Lhasa, the capital of the Tibetan Autonomous Region and a city with a large Tibetan population. Lhasa's tumultuous political history, famed religious institutions, and high-profile uprisings have contributed to that city becoming a major security and surveillance concern for the People's Republic of China. Lacking the intense symbolic significance of Lhasa, Xining perhaps shares more affinities with Chengdu, another city with a substantial Tibetan population. Chengdu, however, is both much larger than Xining and has a more concentrated Tibetan population. While Tibetan places in Xining have been less conspicuous than they are in Lhasa or Chengdu, the city does have a considerable Tibetan past and present. Studying it is key to understanding the growing importance of the urban geopolitics of place in China's peripheries.

In 2017 the State Ethnic Affairs Commission designated Xining a Demonstration City for Progress in Ethnic Unity, a model zone where a diverse population of Tibetans, Han Chinese, several Muslim groups, and other ethnicities were getting along well with one another. At that time, a *Qinghai Daily* article referred to Xinghai Road, a residential area near downtown

Xining, as exemplary of a mixed-ethnicity "happy housing community and happy family."[1] Yet Xinghai Road had gone viral on social media in 2014 for very different reasons. After the 2014 Kunming Railway Station mass-stabbing incident in Yunnan Province, the local Xinghai Road police station demanded that Tibetan monks and "Xinjiang people" staying in a housing community under its jurisdiction register at their office immediately. A photo of this posting circulated on social media, provoking Tibetans to accuse the police of ethnic discrimination. The police station eventually apologized.[2] In this light, Xining can be considered a demonstration city, not only for how authorities manage ethnicities amid a redeveloping urban landscape—with suspicion, propaganda, and assimilatory programs—but also how subaltern populations face these pressures and innovate to make their own places in the city. Peripheral places serve as both laboratories and liabilities for the states that view themselves as these places' centers.[3] They are not, however, only places of politics and possibility for the states that manage them, but also for the people who dwell within them.

Making the Concrete Plateau

Located at an altitude of just over two thousand meters above sea level, and containing a population of just over two million people, Xining is the largest city in Amdo, a large Tibetan cultural region on the eastern Plateau. Along with Kham, also in eastern Tibet, and Ü Tsang, which is farther to the west, Amdo forms an integral part of the three regions in the spatial imaginary of Tibet known as the Chol Kha Sum, a space that coexists but is not coterminous with the administrative divisions the PRC has established on the Plateau.[4] Separated from the Xinjiang region by the Kunlun Mountains to the north, Amdo also contains many formidable mountain ranges that divide several of Asia's major rivers to the south and southeast, such as the Bayan Khala that separates the Yellow River from the Yangtze River. While the river that flows through Xining is a tributary of the Yellow River, the uneven topography of the Plateau means that many of its rivers never leave the highlands. Instead, their waters pool into salt lakes whose frozen surfaces are scraped in the winter to yield a salt harvest. A hundred kilometers west of Xining is the massive salt lake of Tso Ngön Bo (Ch. *Qinghai hu*). During the summer months, tourists mix with pastoralists on its shores and the spacious grasslands that encircle it. Weaker water sources feed the parched Tsedam basin, located four hundred kilometers northwest of Xining, where agriculture is difficult and the population sparse. Where grass grows in sufficient abundance, pastoralists herd yaks and sheep across the uplands of the Plateau, moving to higher-altitude pastures in the summer and to lower encampments in the colder months.

Much of the population of Amdo is concentrated in lower-altitude river valleys to the south and east of Xining. In these places, farmers till valley floors and piedmonts, where swaths of yellow rapeseed flowers alternate with waves of wheat and barley. Historically, mountainous terrain has disconnected the villages in these fertile valleys, while wide river valleys have formed corridors of lowland connection, and narrow mountain passes have made transportation across massifs possible. More recently, state-directed bridge- and tunnel-building efforts have opened the valleys and peaks of Amdo to relatively smooth and horizontal highway travel. The vernacular landscape, however, remains defined by its verticality. Buddhist monasteries ascend hillsides, and the minarets of mosques rise above villages in silhouette against clear blue skies.

On the steep slopes that surround Xining, I encountered Muslim men practicing archery for sport and Tibetan monks tending to the small Buddhist temple atop South Mountain Park. The valleys below are today filled with high-rise buildings. In the city's old eastern quarter are important sites for the city's Muslim and Tibetan communities. During my stays in the city, male Muslim worshippers would unfurl prayer rugs on one of the quarter's main avenues every Friday, diverting urban traffic. Around the neighborhood's mosques, shopkeepers sold plucked chickens, rugs, shawls, caps, butter, and a wide variety of breads and dried fruit. Tibetans were also in significant numbers in this portion of the city and in particular near the Tibetan market, where I bought a broad-brimmed Stetson and sat in a teahouse where I watched video CDs of horse-racing festivals and sipped boiled milk tea.

The diversity of these places owes much to the region's cosmopolitan history. In recent centuries the city was a market town for the tea and horse trade, an important administrative center that connected lowland agricultural valleys to upland pastoralist grasslands, a religious center, and a key regional transportation hub. For Tibetans this city is both a place to dwell and a stop on a wider itinerary that includes sedentary farmhouses, pastoral camps, and apartments in Amdo and Kham and also Inner China, where Tibetans are increasingly working, living, and going to school. Moreover, the city is also connected to global trends in media and goods that originate in Korea, Japan, Europe, and North America. Even at the edges of Xining City, donkey carts occasionally jockey with Porsche SUVs for road space. All these places are sites of encounter for different values, desires, and normative pressures; they all figure into the lively world of the Tibetan Plateau.

This diversity of places and connections has been made possible by political and economic developments that have accelerated the transformation of the eastern Plateau. In the early 1950s, the People's Republic of China (PRC) powerfully remade the Plateau landscape as it incorporated it into the fledging communist state. As Greg Rohlf has demonstrated, during the 1950s authorities attempted to convert grasslands and marginal terrain into productive agricultural fields.[5] To this end, the state created military farms and established reeducation-through-labor farms in places as improbable as the hyperarid and alkaline Tsedam basin. As many as one and a half million settlers, including Han Chinese youth and Hui Muslims, migrated to Qinghai from Inner China during China's first and second Five Year Plans. Promised a land of plenty, these migrants embraced their new identities as pioneers in the proud vanguard of socialist progress. But farming conditions were difficult, and the vast majority of these settler colonists decamped and returned home by the mid-1960s.[6]

While state efforts to convert grassland sod into tillable fields were largely a failure, more permanent changes to the region were realized through the imposition of an administrative system and bureaucracy that altered both where and how people lived. The communists pitched tent towns on the Tibetan highlands, converting them to solid structures as they signaled their intent to stay for the long term.[7] These changes inaugurated a new geography for Qinghai Province. From the pastoral highlands to the farming lowlands, previously nonexistent or formerly diminutive seasonal trade towns were made nodes of administration and the command economy. Between the 1950s and 1970s, the Chinese military and participants in the Cultural Revolution destroyed Tibetan monasteries and religious sites. While some monasteries remained intact, new building projects were often executed with the goal of materially and symbolically disrupting and dominating religious space.[8] Only in the reform period of the 1980s would the state and communities reopen and restore monasteries and stupas.[9]

In the twenty-first century, another wave of urbanization entered the Tibetan Plateau, leading to the expansion of large urban centers like Xining, the growth of county towns, the modernization of rural homes, and the resettlement of indigenous Tibetan pastoralists in rows of uniform concrete-and-brick ranch-style houses.[10] As recent research has suggested, the expansion of urbanization has radically reconfigured the geographical foundations of Tibetan social organization, political authority, and governance; it has produced new valorizations of the city, urbanized Tibetan towns, and led to new forms of competition for resources both between Tibetans and non-Tibetans and within Tibetan communities.[11] Whether in large cities like

Xining and Chengdu, or in county towns, Tibetans are living increasingly urban lives.

Scholars have debated how to interpret the power asymmetries that development and urbanization have brought to Tibet. This has been of particular concern in questions of cultural assimilation and how agency is expressed in a context of state controls on religion, cultural commodification for tourism, and the pervasiveness of Mandarin in education and in urban places.[12] Emilia Sułek and Jarmila Ptáčková have argued that studies must reject analyzing urbanization as social and cultural decay and instead pay attention to how Tibetans are negotiating change, for better or for worse.[13] Ethnographers including Jane Caple, Huatse Gyal, and Charlene Makley have demonstrated the importance of focusing on Tibetans' moral worlds to show that agency in an era of upheaval and continuous change is never reducible to a simplified resistance to the state.[14] For instance, Makley has shown how urbanizing Tibetans have used construction projects to shore up community authority, securing prestige and authority for their community rather than the developmental state.[15] Emily Yeh and Andrew Fischer have viewed Tibetan agency as considerably constrained by social and economic structures that set horizons for desires and choices.[16] Rejecting notions of Gramscian hegemony, Adrian Zenz, in contrast, has argued that Tibetan elites have exercised considerable agency in their pursuits of a pragmatic modernization that can help preserve Tibetan language and tradition.[17] Perhaps the clearest form of agency available to Tibetans is outright resistance, often taking the form of ethnic conflict that can be enumerated as incidents of self-immolation, protest, and violent encounter.[18] But while resistance and open conflict have occurred across Tibet, they can't account for the myriad everyday decisions that Tibetans have been making amid ongoing urbanization.

Chinese officials want Tibetans and others whose lives and livelihoods are disrupted by the urbanization processes to focus on the good things that urbanization is supposed to bring, namely increased living standards, convenience in everyday life, and more lucrative work. For Tibetans, the stakes are high: focusing on the bad and acting against state policies can lead to "political problems."[19] Even excessive expressions of ethnic identity, such as building unauthorized Tibetan-style architecture, can become problems that attract the negative attention of municipal authorities.[20] This puts Tibetans in a bind, because if they don't create places where Tibetan languages, cuisines, songs, decorations, and other affective things are prominent, then Tibetanness risks going unpracticed. For these reasons, many Tibetans have feared that the city inherently leads to their "turning Han" (Ch. *hanhua*). Tibetans have therefore shouldered the responsibility of expressing their

Tibetanness in order to sustain it, but to do so in a way that does not result in state suppression.[21]

Ethnic categories are not intrinsic qualities that are active in people at every moment, but must be practiced in order to have significance.[22] The early PRC instituted some ethnic categories, raising them to the level of official state nationalities, or *minzu*.[23] Over time, Chinese scholars have debated policy reforms that would "depoliticize" *minzu*, which is today translated as "ethnicity" to suggest inseparability from the Chinese nation. While such debates were influential, the party-state has only begun to embrace these reforms.[24] Recognizing the constructed nature of *minzu* and ethnicity in general, scholars have also been deconstructing China's recognized ethnic groups and revealing the social fissures and local distinctness within them.[25] Such a focus on forms of molecular difference is important but does not negate the importance of group identities like Tibetan and Chinese, which continue to resonate with and politically animate large imagined communities.[26] This book shows that urbanization has not unraveled Tibetan identity but has actually heightened it as a meaningful category through which Tibetans have challenged Chinese civilizational dominance.[27]

Civilizing Machine

The key argument of this book is that urbanization on the Plateau works as a civilizing machine and that to understand the politics of Tibetanness today, it is necessary to engage with this machine. The civilizing machine is the process of state-led and Sinocentric urbanization that has redeveloped the Tibetan Plateau. It has developed and codified places including Xining City in order to accomplish goals of social, economic, and political transformation. As a civilizing project, the Chinese center both relies on peripheralizations to guide its progression and also continuously generates peripheries through the creation of uneven development. Such a project can, however, be channeled and transformed through the activities of those in the periphery. From the margins of the civilizing machine, Tibetans have worked to assemble an alternative urbanism that fuses a different civilizational project to that promoted by the state.

Civilization and the periphery are closely intertwined in post-reform China. The Chinese term for "civilization" connotes both China's unique cultural tradition and the developmental horizon that China's increasingly world-class urban form is making into an everyday reality. Within Chinese developmental discourse, civilization is further divided into material civilization (Ch. *wuzhi wenming*) and spiritual civilization (Ch. *jingshen wenming*).

While material civilization refers to the tangibles of housing, utility infrastructures, roads, and increased purchasing power, spiritual civilization refers to cultural and emotional content, including the pursuit of a meaningful and contented life. The latter term also draws from a self-consciously Chinese tradition.

Civilization is both a micropolitical and geopolitical technology. It has been promoted in contemporary China both as a mode of urban reform that targets sidewalk hygiene and residents' behavior and as a form of international diplomacy, such as in the civilizational cooperation rhetoric of the Belt and Road Initiative.[28] Because the very idea of civilization rests on an opposing understanding of a relative absence or paucity of itself, discussions of civilization can easily slip into questions of comparative cultural value and refinement. This is true in the normative Chinese city, where non-Han ethnic groups are continuously exposed to assimilatory pressure. As the world-class city is nationally a marker of civilization, the city produces and spatializes new valuations and distinctions that hinge on stereotypes about backwardness and lack of human quality (Ch. *suzhi*), two things that do not belong in China's officially recognized "Civilized Cities," which are further explored in chapter 3. Such stigma can fall disproportionately on Tibetans and other marginalized urban groups and gain currency among urban residents as they work to make sense of their place in the city.

As a geopolitical project, there are continuities between the current Chinese civilizing mission and past practices of peripheral pacification and transformation. Imperial Chinese political cosmographies were intentionally geometric; the center dominated a hierarchy of cultural and political order and also retained the possibility of drawing external barbarians to the center and assimilating them.[29] In the ancient nonary model found in the Chinese classical text *The Tribute of Yu*, nine states form a civilized center beyond which concentric zones demarcated areas of diminishing agricultural production and political control that ended in a periphery of wastelands and barbarism.[30] Generations of Chinese writers and statesmen have drawn from this model when portraying the Chinese periphery as zonal, with more civilized and assimilated "cooked" barbarian peoples residing in regions under state administration and untamed "raw" peoples living further afield.[31] Today, the Chinese center continues to develop and "civilize" its periphery.

There is also continuity in attempts to realize the civilizing project through urban space. This includes not only notions of urban planning as a form of order, but also cities as places of modernization where China could reassert its central position and resist being peripheralized by Western imperialists. In the late nineteenth and early twentieth centuries, Chinese scholars and officials sought to develop a framework for the emerging Chinese nation by drawing from the technical accomplishments of Western civilization, while also grounding their cultural and political project in Chinese civilization.[32] Prasenjit Duara has described how the modern East Asian notion of civilization was "affirmed in the West before it was confirmed in Asia," where Western economic and political progress was supplemented with an Eastern moral sensibility. Geopolitically, Chinese intellectuals hoped that the outlining of an Eastern progressive civilizational undertaking would ward off colonial encroachment by allowing for a Hegelian recognition of the Eastern state-subject. Micropolitically, they hoped that it would moderate the potentially deleterious influence of Western behaviors and cultural practices.[33] From the late-Qing "internal civilizing mission" that modernized urban police forces to discourage foreign intervention to the Nationalists' New Life Movement that synthesized a rejuvenated Confucian morality with Western standards of clothing, hygiene, and behavior, urban spaces would become sites where both geopolitical and micropolitical state objectives were pursued.[34] While civilizational discourse initially became muted under the communists, it would soon return as a political project during the PRC's reform era.

In the 1980s the national Spiritual Civilization campaign promised more political autonomy for citizens. While this campaign began in villages, in the twenty-first century it has come to dominate urban landscapes.[35] Contemporary cities have become places where the state actively seeks to cultivate "civilization" and "happiness" by polishing urban appearances, making city districts attractive to capital, and molding urban subjectivities to meet national guidelines for polite and appropriate behavior and responsible citizenship.[36] In China's peripheries, the traditional opposition between civilized and uncivilized has persisted even as political ideologies changed over the course of the twentieth and twenty-first centuries. As Stevan Harrell has argued, "asymmetrical dialogues between the center and the periphery" have continued to take place as different civilizing projects have been deployed in China's borderlands. In their twenty-first-century regional development program, the Open Up the West campaign (Ch. *xibu da kaifa*), state planners categorized mostly non-Han ethnicity areas as the regions of China's West most in need of intervention to rectify their peripheral backwardness and low *suzhi*.[37] Indeed, China's efforts to alleviate the perceived defects of its western periphery have sustained a narrative in which Han Chinese migrants construct material and spiritual civilization far from the core and metropole of Inner China. Tom Cliff has argued in his ethnography of Korla City that the construction of cities in Xinjiang as self-consciously civilized places serves as a "statement of intent" of the nation's plan for future transformation of the region into a core-like place while also steeling Han migrants' resolve to do the work of transformation.[38] Notably left out of the center's "asymmetrical" narrative are the voices and interests of the indigenous peoples of the areas being targeted by the Chinese civilizing project.

Despite China's long history, elaborate cosmographical explications, and complex bureaucratic administration, its civilizing projects haven't occurred in a vacuum. The current project both coexists with an alternative Tibetan civilizing project and is vulnerable to appropriation and challenge owing to its need to dominate and transform.[39] The two aspects of civilizational policy, the material and spiritual, are presented in state discourse as supplemental to each other, but they can also be in tension. For example, in the context of modern European social development, Norbert Elias called the "civilizing process" the continuous need for European nobility and the rising middle classes to cultivate themselves in ever more sophisticated ways.[40] Elias argued that in Germany, the superficial nature of the civilizing process created a backlash and desire for an alternative civilizational project—*Kultur*—rooted in inward cultivation.[41] Civilizational projects can help articulate counter-civilizational projects as disagreements arise over what counts as cultural superiority. As discussed above, in modern China this in part played out through the rejection of Western values for an Eastern moral sensibility. I argue that this tension has also played out on the Tibetan Plateau, where Chinese and Tibetan civilizing projects continue to encounter each other.

Other scholars have studied urban development through the relationship between the Chinese center and its western periphery. Cliff and Yeh have shown how state-led development in China's western periphery has supported the political and social project of the PRC, drawing the periphery closer to the Chinese center, and Andrew Fischer has argued that state-led development brings to Tibet a structural transformation typified by economic dependency and exclusionary urbanization.[42] This book takes a different approach to the previously mentioned authors by emphasizing that center/core and periphery can be topologically collapsed through processes of uneven urban development, and that this collapse can be politically productive. As urbanization extends across the Tibetan Plateau, it folds peripheries into cores within variegated urban spaces. As AbdouMaliq Simone has argued, "the 'urbanization' of relationships amongst things entails a speed and intensity of diverse positions and practices of inhabitation that can't be stably represented in clear categories."[43] Urbanization breaks down straightforward geometries of center and periphery while also placing into juxtaposition and thereby troubling categorizations of rural and urban, civilized and uncivilized. Such a diversity of places complicates the discursive link between the material and spiritual aspects of the civilizing project and gives rise to a subaltern urbanism that grows and changes alongside the project of state-led urbanization.

On the Tibetan Plateau, the civilizing machine acts as an urban assemblage that draws places, things, and people together to create a new type of Chinese urban space and population. The production of this national urbanism, despite its civilizing intentions, is not totalistic. As Manuel DeLanda reminds us, assemblages allow us to move beyond an essentializing focus on a totalizing interiority of relations and toward contingent wholeness and a recognition of the capacities and possibilities of assembled parts and their exterior relations.[44] The concept of the machine as assemblage highlights how emergent relationships between things, ideas, and values can produce new social arrangements. Studying development in India, Vinay Gidwani has argued that when development, as a machine, is "plugged into a nation-state assemblage, development is operationalized as a technical apparatus for improving the Nation's well-being."[45] Urbanization as a civilizing project in China has similar ends; but as an ever-changing assemblage, the urban cannot be reduced to the state projects that have initiated it. The civilizing machine is not only used by the developmentalist state as a technical and social tool, but is also productive of unintended effects that the external relations of its parts, such as people and places, make possible. Assemblages are always in the process of becoming, so while the civilizing machine works on and through Xining's Tibetans as urban residents, Tibetans retain place-making capacities that allow them to shape their own material presences, homes, and notions of belonging in Xining and beyond.[46]

In what Simone has called the messy "cityness" of urban neighborhoods, Tibetans are articulating an urbanism that challenges China's civilizing project. This is a politics in flux, without a firm vision or outcome, and it is a politics that occurs within and through places. It occurs despite the political context of an authoritarian government and draws from the creative possibilities of the periphery. Urban assemblages involve competition, dispute, and valuations of "others." On a daily basis, Tibetans in Xining use personal networks to learn about new opportunities and threats to their businesses and plans, to cooperate in schemes to improve their children's prospects, and to rework the very materiality of the urban environment to create a sense of belonging for their sometimes precarious-feeling existence. They use the city's resources to create places that reinforce a Tibetan identity and sense of place, as well as generate Buddhist merit. As Tibetans select what things to assemble into their urban worlds, their inputs into the civilizing machine produce an alternative urbanism that has sustained a Tibetan civilizing project on the Plateau as a form of counter-civilization that calls into question the state-led civilizing machine's developmental project in both its material and spiritual aspects.

The desires fostered by the state-led civilizing machine—for development, for consumer goods, for stability, for a unified national identity—have also been challenged. For Félix Guattari, desiring-machines are inherent to socio-technical machines such as the city; they "manifest and mobilize the investments of desire that 'correspond' to the conscious or preconscious investments of interest, the politics, and the technology of a specific social field."[47] While many contemporary social scientists that follow the assemblage thinking of Deleuze and Guattari have chosen to ignore or jettison its psychological dimensions, I contend that listening to Tibetans while taking seriously their dreams and desires also invites us to consider how similar socio-technical assemblages can host different investments and valuations and affect minds in different ways.[48] For instance, as discussed in chapter 4, the materialism and superficiality of the city can be counterpointed with Buddhist concerns about leading a meritorious life. This doesn't mean that Tibetans' desires must be totally opposed to those encouraged by the civilizing machine, but that these desires must be understood as its channelings or modifications, gingerly embraced in some moments, rejected in others, and often bringing anxiety about how to move forward.

The Urban and the Politics of Place

The approach of this book is to bring together assemblage thinking with the politics of place in order to highlight the geopolitical and micropolitical aspects of the civilizing machine. The literature on the politics of place in liberal democracies has emphasized the role of political rhetoric and macroeconomic transformations in influencing place-based expression, which often manifests through electoral politics.[49] In such contexts, the politics of place can also play out at the urban level, such as through zoning and the naming and design of urban places from neighborhood streets to museums.[50] Even when hotly contested, places have the potential of changing through political participation. By contrast, in illiberal states urban development has favored the monumental and spectacular, giving marginalized urbanites little input in planning processes. For example, Natalie Koch has shown how authoritarian governments have used planned capital cities to project geopolitical imaginaries of regional wealth and stability.[51] These imaginaries have been used to enroll citizenries into national urban development projects that allow little room for alternative place-based expression.

Scholars focusing on what they have called urban geopolitics have explored cities as targets of violence in conflict-torn states.[52] From this perspective, urban violence has had a major role in decentering the nation-state and national border as key sites where geopolitical struggle occurs; this research has also highlighted the experiences of the people whose urban worlds are subject to continuous violence.[53] Scholars of urban geopolitics including Stephen Graham and Sara Fregonese have used the term "urbicide" to describe the destruction of cities in these conflicts and to conceptualize how this violence is deployed.[54] A focus on conflict and urbicide travels with some difficulty to the context of an increasingly urban Asia, where urban construction has overshadowed destruction, even amid massive evictions and dislocations during redevelopment. I argue that the geopolitics and micropolitics of place in Xining have occurred then not only through moments of resistance amid destruction, which would be subject to rapid state suppression, but also through everyday participation in urban creation.

Understanding the politics of place, according to John Agnew, requires analyzing the uneven economic conditions of the places where people live, work, and form communities.[55] The materiality of places matters, as do the durable yet mutable senses of belonging that are perpetuated in locales of everyday interaction. Global shifts in political economy and changes in national policy can, at scales down to the household and urban neighborhood, disrupt long-standing political allegiances and entrench others. Moreover, they can lead to the establishment of new social solidarities and expressions of place. These elements of the politics of place are also in effect in Xining City, where there are few avenues for liberal-style participatory politics or opportunities for contestation. In contemporary China, the government tightly controls what sorts of places—residential, commercial, or other—can be established and used toward what ends.

Land-use reforms and the shift from socialist housing provision toward commercial real estate have increasingly spatialized capital and class across China.[56] Looking at contestations over land use that emerged at the turn of the last century, You-Tien Hsing has argued that administrative territory should be added to the economic and social aspects of the politics of place.[57] Municipal governments' manipulation of urban territory can dispossess long-standing residents, pushing them to the urban periphery as central districts are sold at profit to land developers, a phenomenon that has also occurred as towns and cities in Tibetan regions annex farmland and convert it to urban residential space.[58] Municipalities' search for capital, like their attraction of national and international companies such as the American coffeehouse chain Starbucks and the Japanese casual outfitter Uniqlo, attests to the degree that newly developed urban zones are increasingly open to transnational flows of goods, architectural design, and capital.

In her studies of global cities, Saskia Sassen has suggested that globalization does not remove politics from urban places, but reconfigures politics around new networks of governance and social mobilization that can cut across the national containers within which cities are located.[59] Cities in authoritarian states are not divorced from globalization, and authoritarian governments that have joined global capitalism to nation-building developmentalism have found urbanization to be a powerful political tool to create governable spaces and populations. Spectacular urban zones attract mobile capital and publicly perform national unity and developmental success. Urban redevelopment can also disrupt regime-threatening political solidarities by mowing over troublesome neighborhoods and dispersing their inhabitants.[60] In some Chinese cities, urban residents have been able to contest urban redevelopment through petitioning and legal action.[61] For ethnic groups in China's western periphery, however, protests and legal contestation always carry the risk of inviting further state repression. I argue for the importance of attending to less visible and less coordinated expressions of the politics of places. While municipal governments surveil and control public spaces and can curtail political activities within them, locales of interaction persist in the city's intimate interiors and in subtler place-making activities such as those found in markets and parks.

Although this study shares an affinity with conflict- and contestation-oriented studies of the politics of place under conditions of rapid development insofar as it attends to both macro-level geopolitical narratives and the micropolitics of urban place, existing scholarly approaches cannot account for the situation on the Tibetan Plateau, where geopolitics is playing out not just through destruction and resistance to it, but also through a state-led civilizing project that redevelops places in order to transform China's ethnic periphery. Tibetans participate in a generative assemblage of newly made and remade places, infusing material places with their own civilizational supplement.

Living and Researching

On a cold and dry afternoon in March 2014, all the foreign students at Qinghai Minzu University (QMU), including me, were called into a large lecture hall to hear a special presentation. The director of the International Educational Exchange Center, Mr. Lao, was in a scolding mood. Using Mandarin Chinese instead of the English he typically reserved for friendly chats, he reprimanded the students for showing up to classes tardy or not at all.

Next, he pleaded with us not to take photos of things that were "not pretty" (Ch. *bu piaoliang*) on our vacations. As Mr. Lao explained, over winter break a student had gone on a trip to Lhasa and taken some unflattering photos that were posted online. These images had been shared over social media and even among some of the Exchange Center staff, and now Mr. Lao was facing pressure to keep his students in line.

He emphasized the good and pretty things that we ought to be noticing and photographing, such as the spectacular post-earthquake reconstruction of Kyegudo, the municipal seat of Qinghai Province's Yulshul Tibetan Autonomous Prefecture. Mr. Lao asked us rhetorically about the source money for the earthquake rebuilding: "Where did it come from?" The answer of course was from the Chinese government and people. Then he asked us to think more deeply about what we chose, as foreigners, to focus on: "What place doesn't have some unsatisfactory things?" I looked around the lecture hall, which I had never been in before. Our claustrophobic classrooms had broken chairs and peeling paint, but this special meeting was held in a newly finished building with comfortable tiered seating—it was a pretty place reserved for big events. And sure enough, staff were taking photos of us watching the presentation.

There was more. Mr. Lao then told us that he was also receiving pressure from the Public Security Bureau. Some QMU students had broken their travel restrictions by revisiting the same villages several times in a month. These students had been skipping class and even lying about where they were going on the travel forms that we were asked to turn in whenever we left Xining. Mr. Lao asked, "Why would you want to see the same place over and over again? It doesn't make any sense, does it?" We couldn't go just anywhere, he told us. The school permitted us to travel on weekends and during breaks for leisure and to see beautiful sights.

Mr. Lao's pleas were couched not only in terms of relieving the pressure on him, but also in the spirit of helping out the whole school and ourselves as well. If none of us were in trouble, the school could continue to host us, and we foreigners could continue to come and pursue our projects in the city. And all of us had projects. Among the American and South Korean students were evangelical missionaries who proselytized among Qinghai Province's population. Other students were practicing Buddhists who used Xining as a base from which to pay visits to monasteries where they had built relationships. Others, like me, were pursuing research projects. Mr. Lao's instruction was clear: keep our bad photos (and negative thoughts) to ourselves and abide by the most important rules. If we did this, we could carry on our business as usual.

Compared to the students who were reprimanded for their constant traveling, I was relatively stationary. I spent most of my time in Xining, which, in accordance with the logic Mr. Lao was voicing, had the "prettiest" built environment in the province, due to its continuing reconstruction. Unlike in other cities, such as Lhasa, dramatic photos of a continued security crackdown couldn't be taken and then subsequently embarrass appearances of government benevolence. I first came to Xining City in 2007 as a volunteer English teacher, and I spent one year teaching English to students at Qinghai Normal University, one of three large universities in the city. My time at the school was split between courses for Han Chinese English majors and courses for the university's separate English degree program for Tibetan students. These classes were more or less ethnically segregated owing to the organization of the university's majors. I was struck by this social and spatial division, which only became clearer in the aftermath of the March 2008 unrest in Lhasa and across Amdo. Rumors spread of violence in towns outside Xining, of monks' arrests, and of Tibetans being forced to sign denunciations of the Dalai Lama. I found the state of events frightening, and it opened up for me many questions about the relationship between the city and its hinterland.

The relationships I built in Xining in 2007 and 2008 and during subsequent summer trips grounded this project. I maintained contacts with Tibetans I had befriended during this period, and they helped me locate many of the people I interviewed for this project over its seventeen months of primary research in 2013–2014, 2015, and 2017. Working with two assistants, I interviewed Tibetans from a variety of places, including Xining City, Haidong City, and the five Tibetan autonomous prefectures of Malho, Tsolho, Tsoshang, Golok, and Yulshul.[62] Some of the interviewees were relatives or acquaintances, but we also used a snowball method to find more participants. We asked interviewees about their contacts: coworkers, friends, and neighbors. In this way we conducted fifty semi-structured interviews with Tibetans, Han Chinese, Hui, and Salar Muslims living in Xining City.

These interviews allowed me to gather information about housing, type of employment, size of household, reasons for migrating to the city, and attitudes toward the threats and opportunities posed by urbanization. We conducted many of the semi-structured interviews in offices, stores, and occasionally apartments. Others were done at coffeehouses such as the city's Greenhouse Café, in restaurants, and even over the glossy and cramped tables of KFC. I learned to never record interviews anywhere near the restroom hand dryers if I intended to transcribe them later. Given the multilingual environment, we used many languages in the interviews. When my interlocutor knew Chinese, I led the conversation and asked for help with clarification. When we spoke Amdo Tibetan, my assistants helped interpret the conversations.

Beyond these interviews, I engaged in participant observation over the course of my year and a half in the city. I lived in two different apartment complexes in the eastern end of the city, where I attended school. I often traveled to other parts of the city and conversed with neighbors, shopkeepers, and friends. One of my neighborhoods was a relatively new development with a large mechanized gate. At a glance it might be taken for a gated community, but it was porous at the front entrance, where the guards chatted and watched TV, and in the back, where compound walls opened into a thicket of brush that led to the Huangshui River. A large grizzled dog barely contained in a bent cage was, however, effective at keeping me away from that rear entrance. My second apartment was in a retirement community for state employees from a nearby Tibetan autonomous county. This much smaller housing community was watched over by a friendly couple who lived in the gatehouse. Inside, old Tibetan women set up chairs in the sunshine, where they counted prayer beads and turned Tibetan prayer wheels. I was always out of place in these neighborhoods as a white male foreigner. At times I wanted to be inconspicuous so that I could satisfy the researcher's conceit of grasping things as "they really are" without altering the scenario. At other times I wanted the opposite, that my novelty would open doors to new connections and conversations. My positionality—in race, gender, and nationality—influenced both what I was capable of seeing and hearing and the ways others presented themselves to me. As a result, this book is a necessarily partial view of urbanization in contemporary Tibet.

In addition to regular contact with neighbors, acquaintances, teachers, fellow students, and friends, I spent time at Xining's Tibetan markets, at dancing squares, and at festivals inside and outside the city. I took field notes of curious interactions and notable events in the city and in my neighborhood. It was these experiences that helped me make sense of the context within which Tibetans create their city. During my research, the city was constantly changing. New roads were paved, new shopping malls opened, and the People's Armed Police (Ch. *wujing*) set up guard stations after the deadly Kunming stabbings mentioned above. These events influenced what people did in the city and where they did it, and also altered the sometimes-tense fabric of urban ethnic relations. Because urban assemblages consist of more than people, I took photos, recorded sounds, and jotted down notes about lighting and smells in public and semipublic spaces, such as building corridors. I discussed these with Tibetans, as well as their own decorative choices in private places.

Finally, I also read books and media in multiple languages in order to flesh out the history and memory of places and to better understand contemporary debates over urbanization in Tibetan society. I did this both during my initial research period, when I would scroll through Weixin, a popular social media application, and peruse the latest publications of the provincial press at Xinhua Book Store, and remotely during this book's write-up period, when I checked the online portals of newspapers like *Qinghai Daily* and read historical works on Xining and its hinterland. Because I was interested in popular understandings of and debates about urbanization, my analysis also includes film and music videos and the writings of widely read Tibetan authors who engage with the themes of urbanization.

Overview of the Book

The book begins by looking at the circular migrations of people and goods that bring the Tibetan Plateau into the city and take the city onto the Plateau. Drawing from writings on planetary urbanization and circular migration, I examine urbanization as an explosive process that is incorporating ever more rural populations and land into an expanding urban form. Urbanization has been a promoted state policy and is reflected in the constantly changing statistical categories of the "urban" and the "urban population," which I demonstrate have been continuously recalibrated as the urban has become a privileged site in post-reform China. Nonetheless, these statistics still don't capture the nature of rural and urban co-penetration. I focus on Xining's Tibetan markets to reveal how Tibetan entrepreneurs have lived across the rural-urban divide, both remaining highly mobile and facilitating the movement of goods and migrants between these two milieus of Tibetan life. The stories of urban migrants suggest the existence of a regional modernity in which Tibetans use urban resources to pursue their individual and community goals, while working to distinguish these aspirations from those promoted in Chinese president Xi Jinping's "Chinese Dream."

Chapter 2 examines how municipal authorities and popular writers have sought to narrate and commemorate Xining's urban infrastructure within a history of Chinese peripheral pacification and a mythology based on tourist-friendly Kunlun folklore. A regional political, economic, and religious hub for centuries, Xining contains material and immaterial heritage that has been marshaled into different historic and cultural narratives. I explored these narratives during my fieldwork, searching the urban landscape, popular bookshops, and social media for interpretations of Xining's past and asking urban Tibetans what they knew about the city's history, I found that although the civilizing machine has recoded the material landscape of the city, Tibetans participated in the politics of place by offering alternative urban pasts that they could still read in the redeveloped urban landscape.

Chapter 3 focuses on the role of civilization in the civilizing machine as policy and practice. In the twenty-first century, municipal authorities have continuously remade Xining City in line with national urban standards that are themselves influenced by global world-class urban models. Urban authorities have participated in urban practices and competitions, such as that for the "Civilized City" designation, which seek to reform citizens' hygiene and bodily practices, as well as transform urban aesthetics to make the city more appealing for middle-class living and more distinctive from its Chinese urban peers. The chapter shows that urbanization's moving bar of "civilization" discriminates against Tibetans and Muslims by devaluing their neighborhoods and stigmatizing their bodies. Some Tibetans also critiqued state policies as superficial and ineffective for changing citizens' urban behaviors and treatment of one another. Yet the partial success of the civilizing machine in creating a desire among all ethnic groups for the high-quality lifestyle promised by the Civilized City has meant that the aspiring Tibetan urban middle class may criticize state policy without fully rejecting the affordances of the civilizing machine.

The civilizing machine has, however, also been subject to social and cultural criticism that links its technical and material aspects to moral decline. Chapter 4 examines Tibetans' critiques of the urban, which stemmed from both experiences of ethnic stigmatization and a rejection of urbanization as bad for Tibetan livelihoods, society, and Buddhist personhoods. Plugging their own ethical and social capacities into the civilizing machine, some Tibetans rejected Xining City as itself intolerant, superficial, and conducive to deceitful behavior. I argue that by engaging with and critiquing the aesthetic of redeveloped urban spaces, Tibetan urbanites and artists have participated in a politics of place that devalues Chinese urban civilization. I also show that urban Tibetans have used the countryside as a resource with which to stem the urban's negative normative and moral effects. Interlocutors stressed that their hometowns were milieus where language, morality, and other unconscious dispositions could be instilled into Tibetans at a young age; they strategized to send their children home for periods of time to acquire these dispositions.

Chapter 5 shows how Tibetans have created an alternative urbanism through place-making in urban territories that I argue have promoted a "neutral" ideal Hanness. While municipal territories have restricted Tibetans' urban place-making practices, Tibetans have also channeled territorial restrictions and sensibilities, carefully adjusting them so that they do not appear out of place and draw the nervous attention of non-Tibetan neighbors, housing community managers, or authorities. Through decorating their apartment doors, building apartment shrines, and constructing religious structures, urban Tibetans have brought forth an affectively intensive urbanism that is sensibly available to other Tibetans. Through a discussion of the works of the writer and director Pema Tseden, the chapter also explores the difficulties and dilemmas of bringing animals, co-creators of Tibetans' rural multi-species environments, into the city. The careful paths that marginal place-makers must tread between disturbing dominant sensibilities and fulfilling their own desires reveal the complex subtleties of the politics of subaltern place-making.

Chapter 1

Circulations and Dreams on the Urbanizing Plateau

One morning, after I returned home from Amdo Tibetan language classes, my phone rang. It was my friend Jamyang. He was in Xining and could meet me in an hour. When we had talked a few days before and discussed getting together sometime soon, he was several hours away at his home in Chabcha and had no plans to come to Xining, so it surprised me that Jamyang had unexpectedly arrived in town and was hailing a taxi to come to my home as we spoke. This wasn't the first time Jamyang had called me on short notice to meet; he had an unpredictable work schedule.

Jamyang's business was construction contracting. From the early-to-mid-2010s, the contracting work he engaged in shifted from road building in his home area of Chabcha, a mostly agrarian county southwest of Xining, to installing solar panels in the arid landscapes of the Tsedam basin. He rarely knew what he would be doing before the work started. Through word of mouth or phone notifications, he would learn about a construction bid on a work project and then rush to Xining to enter his name in the bidding. He would try to put in the lowest bid he could afford but was often outcompeted. Joking together, we referred to him as the boss (Ch. *laoban*), making light of this deal-making and his authoritative position as a leader of a group of workers who included family members and day laborers from Chabcha. For Jamyang this was a significant improvement from several years before, when he had worked for another boss and spent his nights sleeping in the side room of a shared Xining office. In those days, he labored under the sacks of cement and other materials he shouldered up and down the office building's stairs as his boss worked out contracts.

Months after Jamyang's unexpected visit, I paid him a visit in Chabcha. Over plates of *ganbian mian*—pulled noodles served with a beef sauce, shredded carrots, and hot pepper—Jamyang explained to me that he was unable to get a contract the day he contacted me in Xining because he was outbid by a Han work team. He had been down on his luck lately and out of work for weeks. Indeed, almost any time I was able to meet with him it meant that he was without work, without a contract. The unpredictable, on-and-off work also affected Jamyang's older brother, who was his business partner, and the dozens of Tibetan construction workers who carried out manual labor for them. These men and women were recruited through advertisements pasted on the walls of Chabcha's central streets and via smart-phone messaging. This contingent work was but one of many types of employment that put Tibetans into migratory circulation around and even beyond Qinghai Province. It also facilitated Jamyang's translocal lifestyle—he had owned property in Xining in the past, and during my period of field study he both owned a small apartment in Chabcha and was rebuilding his house in his natal village with concrete and bricks. I would often wonder: was Jamyang living an urban life, given his experience in the city of Xining and his regular residence in the town of Chabcha? Or, considering the amount of time he spent doing construction-related work under the often-searing highlands sun, was he living a rural life?

This chapter suggests that the answer is both. The rural and the urban interpenetrate on the eastern Tibetan Plateau, creating an assemblage of places and people that collapses geographical distance and folds the rural and urban together. Peoples, goods, and ideas from rural areas can be found within Xining City, in markets, shops, and in peripheralized places, such as Jamyang's temporary office-home. Likewise, urban goods and the modern cosmopolitan imaginary that the urban fosters have entered Xining's hinterland through commerce and transportation infrastructure. These processes are facilitated by the Chinese state's promotion of the urban in its developmental policy. The state-led process of urbanization has resulted in more cities and towns and in the extension of the urban beyond formal administrative boundaries. At the same time, the circulations and practices of Tibetans as they pursue income, housing, and their individual and community goals blur the rural-urban distinction.

The rural and the urban are topics of constant attention in contemporary China, in media, in policy discourse, and among Tibetans whose living environments have been either urbanizing or who have been themselves increasingly laboring in urban places. The Chinese state has its own definitions that delineate the rural from the urban, which are further investigated below. In my research, Tibetans also differentiated between rural places such as farming and pastoral areas, and contrasted them with cities and urban towns. This chapter is informed by these classificatory and imagined understandings, but it also examines how the two spaces of the rural and the urban, despite their separation in developmental discourse and everyday discussions, are in practice closely connected. The "urban Tibetans" discussed in this chapter and throughout the book comprise people who spent a good deal of their time in Xining, typically living, working, or going to school there. Rather than offering a formal definition qualified by length of stay or labor embeddedness in urban areas, my conceptualization of urban Tibetans includes not only long-term inhabitants of the city or recently arrived renters, but also people who find themselves spending enough time in cities and towns that they consider themselves influenced by urban life and actively differentiate themselves from those they view as primarily living in agricultural areas.[1] Indeed, they all inhabit a Plateau that, in practice, is not neatly divided into urban and rural places.

The increasing reach of the urban as a material space and basis for economic organization on the eastern Tibetan Plateau can be understood through what Henri Lefebvre has called urban implosion and explosion—the process by which economic activities are concentrated into cities and then extended up to and beyond their formal boundaries.[2] Working from Lefebvre's ideas, Neil Brenner has argued that contemporary urban typologies have perpetuated a bounded-city thinking that distracts from the reality of an interconnected, exploded urbanism. For him, the urban is a "concrete abstraction" with planetary reach that escapes planners' and statisticians' attempts to contain it through taxonomies.[3] In this view, the conceptual boundaries between city and town, and town and country, break down as urban processes of production, capital accumulation, and labor and environmental exploitation penetrate the whole of planetary space.

State-led urbanization policy, which relies on both top-down planning and its entanglements with Chinese capital, has made tracing urban extension on the Tibetan Plateau topographically complex. On the ground, the situation is also topologically complex. Applying John Allen's work on topological space to Tibetan regionality, Stéphane Gros has argued that topologically breaking down the hyphen in Sino-Tibetan borderlands works to merge "the internal and the external [and] creates possibilities for emerging social forms and events."[4] A similar focus on topology and nonlinear spatial connection, rather than on linear topographical urban extension, can be brought to bear on the rural-urban divide. The civilizing machine has remade Xining and its hinterlands not only through urban extension, but also through a breakdown of how the urban and the rural interface materially and socially.

For urban Tibetans like Jamyang, the rural and urban coexist in a relational simultaneity, in which an "exterior" rural is also co-present inside built-up urban sites, and urban materials and ideas can likewise be found in villages and grasslands. Through a discussion of Chinese urban policy and its rural-urban classificatory system, the following section explores the explosion of the urban into the rural on the eastern Tibetan Plateau and in particular the Huangshui valley, where Xining is located. The next section discusses the lived experience of circular migration. Stories of Xining's Tibetan markets and businesspeople demonstrate the interpenetration of the rural and the urban in Xining in terms of mobility and goods. The final section shows how urbanization has influenced Tibetans' personal, familial, and community pursuits. Contrasting Tibetans' dreams with the national middle-class project of the Chinese Dream, I argue that Tibetans have invested the possibilities that the urban civilizing machine's circulations afford with their own desires and projects.

Recalibrating the Urban

China's 2014 national urbanization plan, called the New-Type Urbanization Plan, aimed to achieve an urbanization rate of 60 percent across the country by the target year of 2020.[5] This goal followed from several decades of Chinese policy that facilitated urban growth and recognized urbanization rates as measures of economic and social developmental progress. What has counted as urban has been, however, continually in flux under the PRC. In official statistics, what places and populations are urban has changed over time. State planners and statisticians have made adjustments to account for changes in where people work and dwell, their frequency of circulatory migration, and for the nature of what places should be recognized as "urban." Under the New-Type Urbanization Plan, which followed from years of erosion of a geographically defined rural-urban labor system, urban clustering has been promoted across the country, continuing an extensive urbanization into formerly rural areas that is also being intensively concentrated in particular places through the promotion of high-density settlements that are intended to improve quality of life and land-use efficiency.[6] The rural has thus become increasingly urban.

Scholars including Kam Wing Chan have shown how China's urban statistical definitions have been adjusted over time to better capture the de facto urban that administrative boundaries and *hukou*, China's household registration system, don't fully account for. Recognizing the limitations of these statistics, policy makers and statisticians in China have continually sought a "more accurate" measure of the urban.[7] This is in part because market reforms over land sales have encouraged local government authorities to collaborate to annex rural land for use-right sales and commercial development, often beyond the designs of central policy makers.[8] It is also because official policy discourse has elevated the urban over the rural as more developed and advanced, and uses this binary difference as justification to facilitate developmentalist projects.[9] The Chinese state's push for more urbanization and the mutable nature of its rural and urban classification schemes illuminate how Tibetan places have come to be in closer circulation with Xining City, as well as how Tibetans' own experiences have followed a topological interpenetration of the rural and urban.

The roots of contemporary state typologies date back to the early People's Republic of China. In the first national census of the PRC, conducted in 1953, statisticians divided the country into bounded rural and urban areas. Similarly, over China's first several censuses, populations were enumerated based on whether they lived within rural or urban places, the latter being municipalities and towns. With some exceptions, to be urban was to be within the bounds of an urban administration, and to be rural was to be within a rural administration.[10] This changed in the reform era; when China's labor market became more mobile, urban places began to annex collectively owned rural land, and townships and counties were allowed to scale up to towns and cities to promote rural-urban integration and industrial and commercial development.[11] Statisticians adjusted their definitions and instruments in order to keep pace with an increasingly urban country.[12] In the post-reform period, this can be seen in the changing rules for distinguishing between urban and rural properties (Ch. *chengxiang shuxing*) and in shifting definitions of the urban (Ch. *chengzhen*) and the rural (Ch. *xiangcun*).[13] By the sixth census of 2010, techniques such as remote sensing allowed for better delineation of census tracts and differentiation of extensive urban-style settlements. For that census, the definition of urban included a variety of places that evaluating officials could observe (Ch. *keguancha*) as built up. Urban places were defined as those linked to "contiguous built-up" areas (Ch. *shiji jianshe lianjie*), which can refer not only to land being used for industry, storage, and housing, but forms of public infrastructure including bridges over water, "void" land located between industrial facilities, and villages into which built-up areas have expanded.[14] These evaluations have used visual (Ch. *jingguan*) methods to capture how extensive urbanization has reached beyond urban administrative categories.[15] In Xining, for example, Chinese data scientists have used Landsat remote sensing imagery to reveal the extension of "impervious surfaces" (Ch. *bu toushui mian*), a measure of the extent of urbanization. Cement and asphalt have thus become indicators of the urban itself, and tracking their distribution a tool for guiding future urban policy.[16]

The extension of the urban is, however, statistically different from the growth of the urban population. For the 2010 census, the urban population was calculated as all those living six months or more in any city, town, or otherwise built-up area, minus the locally registered population with urban *hukou* that had left these places for six months or more. From this, the urbanization rate for any administrative unit could be calculated as the ratio of "permanent" urban population to the total population.[17] In line with these standards, the sixth census has enumerated a record national urban population, heading toward the policy goal of a 60 percent national urbanization rate and the developmental level associated with the "new style urbanization" (Ch. *xinxing chengzhenhua*) that the state is seeking to foster.[18]

National trends in urbanization have affected the Tibetan Plateau. In Tibetan areas, populations are increasingly living in "built-up" urban places, and Tibetans' pursuits of income and urban resources have increasingly brought them to places where they can be counted as members of the urban population. Within pastoral areas, the New Socialist Countryside and other programs modernize housing and concentrate populations along roadways in conspicuously built-up settlements, often under the guise of poverty alleviation and environmental protection.[19] Scholars have, however, suggested the unevenness of such resettlement attempts. For example, Jarmila Ptáčková has argued that the number and size of housing projects reveal little about the actual mobility or income of settled populations. The degree of urbanization of populations varies depending on their continued access to grasslands and the availability of other forms of labor.[20] Households have also adopted strategies in which older family members stay in the settlements, middle-aged family members graze animals, and the youngest adults work in urban areas to generate cash income.[21] Pastoralists' attitudes toward resettlement have also been conflicted. In some pastoral places in Amdo, Tibetans desire new housing and higher incomes, even if settlement life turns out to be difficult; and Tibetan households have faced pressure to relinquish their lands.[22]

Similar patterns can be found in farming areas. Duojie Zhaxi and Wang Shiyong have shown that Amdo farmers are increasingly engaged in the pursuit of nonfarm supplementary labor in urban areas. Furthermore, Tibetans engaged in urbanizing labor such as construction work also contribute to the state-subsidized urbanization of the countryside by using their earned income to reconstruct their rural houses to meet state-stipulated building standards.[23] Competition for high-status housing in the countryside has driven rural-urban circular migration as farmers earn cash income to finish completing houses whose costs are not fully covered by state subsidies.[24] Rather than simply being urbanized, or becoming "rural voids" abandoned by both state developmental policy and villagers seeking to escape poverty, rural places have remained important to the lives and livelihoods of Tibetans.[25] Migrants have pursued new avenues for income through selling off livestock, engaging in or renting out land for caterpillar fungus picking, seeking compensation for former lands and housing, obtaining state subsidies for building houses, and engaging in sideline labor.[26] The rural and urban are in upheaval, their peoples, goods, and typological attributes breaking out of the definitional boundaries that claim to contain them.

Nonetheless, Tibetan places have been subject to administrative urbanization and placement into the shifting urban typology of the PRC. Ben Hillman and Charlene Makley have illustrated how Shangri-La and Rebgong have been urbanized as authorities resourced local culture and developed the towns as tourist attractions. This has included the conversion and incorporation of peripheral rural land into urban administration and land use.[27] Emily Yeh and Mark Henderson have shown that the state has "scaled up" urban places in the Tibetan Autonomous Region in the post-reform period, a phenomenon indicative of the privileged position that administrative cities (Ch. *shi*) and towns (Ch. *zhen*) have in state policy. From state planners' perspectives, urban places are viewed as having a greater capacity to attract investment, house a skilled population, and settle conflicts over land rights with neighboring administrative units.[28] In the Qinghai Provincial Urban System Plan for 2014–2030, provincial authorities have aimed for an overall provincial target of 60 percent urbanization by 2020, in line with the national goal and slightly above neighboring western provinces' urbanization estimates.[29]

The Qinghai Provincial Urban System Plan is coordinated in a four-level structure that connects the "central city" of Xining with four "regional cities" (Ch. *quyu zhongxin chengshi*), eight "small cities" with lower populations and administrative levels, and finally, 110 "small towns" with smaller populations. The resulting vision is a merged, integrated, and developed new-style urban space that extends into the rural periphery, incorporating and scaling up Tibetan areas into differentiated tiers of state-classified urbanization.[30] Xining has become one piece in an increasingly urban Plateau; the city shares its eastern boundary with the province's only other prefecture-level city (Ch.

diji shi), Haidong Shi, which authorities scaled up to that administrative level in 2013.

As Xining itself has grown outward and become more urban, its Tibetan population has grown. While the PRC's earliest Xining urban plans focused on the city's urban core, successive plans have increasingly extended the city across Huangshui River tributary valleys.[31] Xining's municipal government set an urbanization rate target of 75 percent for 2020—a rate that the 2020 seventh census reported as being accomplished at 78.63 percent, a significant increase over the 49.94 percent the Xining Statistical Bureau reported for 2000 and the 56.58 percent reported for 2010.[32] Tibetans are an increasing part of Xining City's four central municipal districts, which have had nearly total urbanization rates in recent years.[33] The enumeration of the Tibetan population in these districts has increased both with urban growth and densification, and in response to the statistical adjustments described above. According to the Xining Statistical Bureau, 8,885 Tibetans lived in the four core districts in 1997. This number jumped to 21,641 in 2000, and then to 41,501 in 2012. An overall Tibetan population of 123,563 for all of Xining's administered districts and counties was recorded for 2012.[34] Between 2010 and 2020, the combined permanent population for Xining's non-Han ethnic groups grew at a rate three times that of the Han, to account for 28.57 percent of the population.[35] Even if these statistics can't fully capture the fluidity of Tibetans' circulations between Xining and other places, the eastern Plateau's "central city" is clearly an increasingly significant milieu and place of dwelling for Tibetans.

The eastern Plateau has become increasingly "urban" as Chinese authorities have recalibrated statistical definitions to account for de facto urbanization and continually redeployed the rural-urban distinction to meet developmental goals. While urban and rural places have remained an abstract, if mutable, dichotomy in terms of state administration and planning, urban and rural spaces are more integrated than ever in terms of material development and mobility of labor. Ultimately, Tibetans have come to live in a world where the urban and rural are both close at hand. The following sections explore how Tibetans live in this urbanizing environment as they realize their own employment paths and cosmopolitan dreams.

Bridging the Rural and the Urban

Tibetans' circular migrations complicate rural and urban typologies, joining Xining and its hinterland together in a continuous flow of people and goods. These circular migrations, encouraged by state urbanization policy, have reshaped Plateau landscapes and economies. As Vinay Gidwani and K. Sivaramakrishnan have argued, circular migrations help to create an "emerging space of work [that] is regional—neither exclusively local or nonlocal, nor exclusively rural or urban."[36] Tibetan entrepreneurs have helped forge this emerging space, their economic pursuits promoting regional circulations that are both topographically extensive and topologically connected at sites throughout Xining City.

One such site that bridges the rural-urban divide is Xining's Tibetan Market. There, entrepreneurial migrants sell modern manufactured goods from Inner China that are useful to Tibetans, such as stereo equipment and luggage, as well as modernized traditional Tibetan goods for domestic and devotional use. During my fieldwork between 2013 and 2015, Xining's Tibetan Market was an enclosed multistory structure that housed dozens of independently operating stores. Markets in Amdo have long brought together people from different ethnic and religious backgrounds and livelihoods: farmers, pastoralists, and long-distance traders. As the missionary ethnographer Robert Ekvall explained, Muslim traders in Amdo during the early twentieth century had long-term relationships with their Tibetans clients, from whom they would receive live animals, wool, hides, and salt in kind for manufactured cloth, cookware, weapons, and luxury foods.[37] In Xining, nearby Tongkor, and other market towns, Tibetans would stay in Muslim-owned hostels, where they obtained food and lodging for themselves and their animals in exchange for a portion of trade proceeds.[38] Although such private trade went dormant during the socialist period, it reemerged in the 1980s under new guises, in particular as an earlier incarnation of the enclosed Tibetan Market.

When I first arrived in Xining in 2007, the Tibetan Market (Tib. *bod gi khyom ra; bod mi khrom*) was an important urban entrepôt that facilitated the movement of urban manufactured goods to the Tibetan countryside. Located in the East District just southwest of the train station and across from the city's now razed central bus station, the market was at the northeastern edge of the city's historic Muslim quarter. The market grew rapidly in size over the course of the 1990s, transforming from a cluster of restaurants and shops to an expansive array of stores that sold clothing, jewelry, Buddhist statuary, *thangka* paintings imported from Nepal, ornamental carpets featuring the Potala Palace (manufactured in southern China), electronics, video CDs of popular Tibetan musicians, and Stetson-style hats.[39] The proximity of the businesses allowed for the easy conversion of grasslands products such as caterpillar fungus into capital that could secure these manufactured goods useful for life outside the city.

Because of its key location next to Xining's aging transportation hubs, this Tibetan Market did not survive twenty-first-century urban redevelopment. In 2010 the Xining Municipal Government General Office issued a notice that it would be seizing the land the market was on as part of its comprehensive plan to build a new Xining train station. The scheme included both tearing down the old market and compensating property owners there for the land that would be taken (see figure 1). The scope of the demolition and relocation program covered 1,956 households over an area of 126,300 square meters. Those who left received either cash to purchase new housing or subsidized housing away from the site, with extra cash incentives available for those who moved quickly.[40] Shopkeepers, both primary lessees and secondary tenants, as well as those who had made improvements to stalls and stands under the market canopy, were given compensation for their properties. Leaseholders had the option to renew the lease in an as-yet-unconstructed replacement market slated to be completed within three years or to break their lease and move on with a refund.[41]

Facing uncertainty, enough Tibetan shopkeepers migrated from the old market to a new one to reconstitute a new Tibetan Market. I frequently visited this new market in 2014, where I sat for in-depth interviews with shopkeepers in the multistory market also known colloquially in Chinese as the Small Commodities Market (Ch. *Xiaoshangpin*). Located down a narrow alley off a congested street east of the new train station, the new market had shops that sold the same wares as the old market, as well as Han Chinese businesses selling curtains and sundry goods. Shopkeepers sold a multitude of products to their modern Tibetan clientele, including upholstered car seat covers with Tibetan designs and ornate wooden boxes for *tsampa*, the Tibetan roasted barley staple. This more concentrated market retained, if less discernibly, some of the patterns of the old Tibetan Market and earlier market towns; it continued to link Xining to its hinterland in circular migrations.

The shopkeepers I interviewed in the new market sold products including cell phones, customized posters and print material, synthetic fur-lined *chupa* robes to wear on holidays, and tents. Zontar was a twenty-eight-year-old from Rebgong who had been living in Xining for about a year when I interviewed him. He had learned computer design and printing skills first in his hometown and then in Xining as a part-time employee of a friend's store. Eventually he started working for his uncle, who rented store space from Muslim landlords in the old Tibetan Market. In the evening Zontar, his brother, and two other relatives had slept on the second floor of their old store. When the market was torn down, his uncle began searching for a

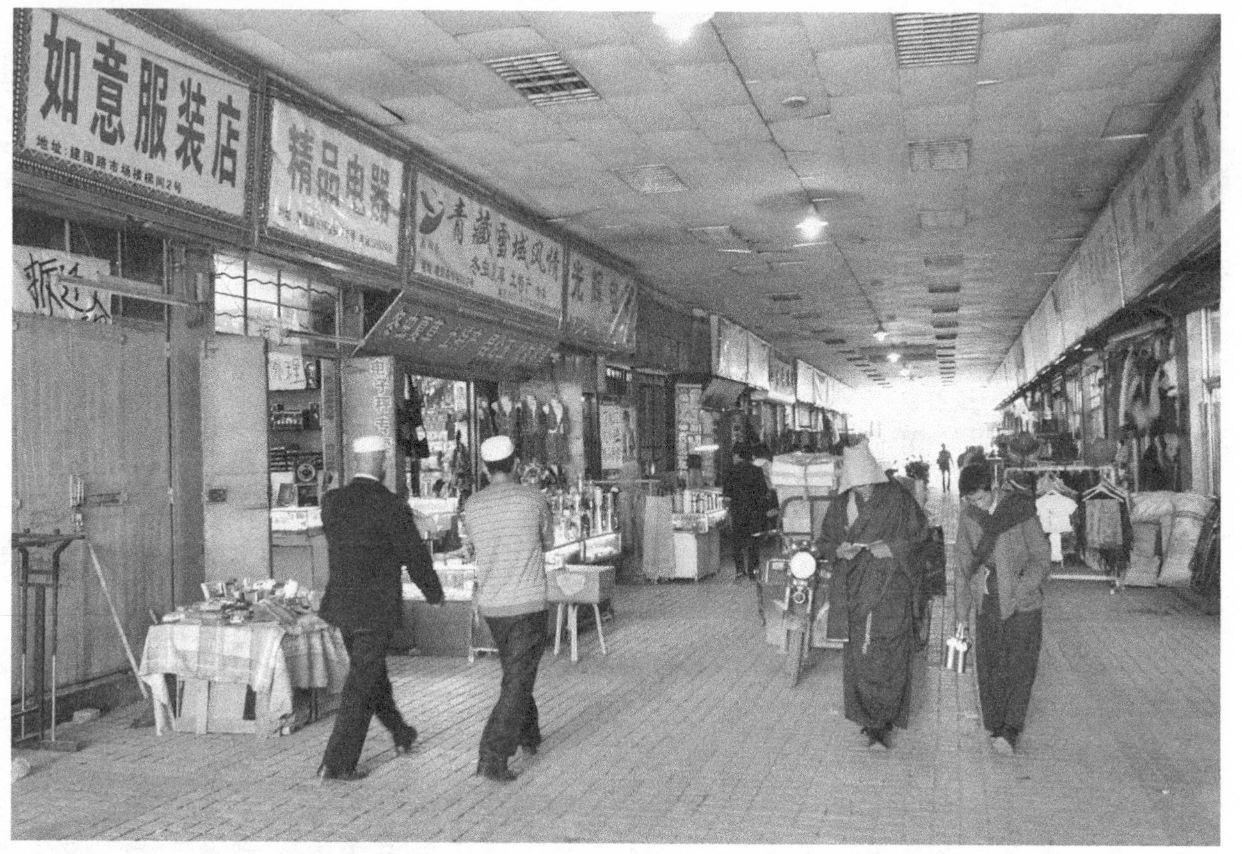

FIGURE 1.1. Last days of the "old" Tibetan Market.
Photo by the author, 2013.

new location. Because the new Tibetan Market had yet to be constructed, he and other shopkeepers from the old market had to find a building to house a transitional Tibetan market. These shopkeepers signed a five-year contract with the Han Chinese building owner to create what would become the new Xining Tibetan Market.

Business had its ups and downs. At first the shopkeepers were confident that word of mouth would popularize this market. By early 2014, however, Zontar and the others were less enthusiastic about the new location. He grumbled about poor business and told me that others were dissatisfied too. The old market was much better for business because the shops were all on one floor near a major road where people could easily stroll about. In comparison, the new market "had too many floors and is all indoors." Its off-the-main-road location made the market hard to find, and its verticality discouraged window shopping. Construction on the train station had closed off the main route of entry from the west, making the market difficult to reach by foot or by vehicle. After paying its bills, Zontar's shop averaged a monthly profit of 5,000 yuan (Chinese renminbi). The shop did better during winter than in summer, when its pastoral clientele was busy herding and searching for valuable herbs and caterpillar fungus on the grasslands of Yulshul and Golok.

I interviewed another young man, named Jinba, in the market while he sewed tents. The walls of his store were covered in images of canvas tents of various shapes and sizes. Their different shapes and trims were modeled to recall the styles used in Tibetan locales such as Chabcha and Golok, as well as serve their different functions. Ornately decorated tents were made for religious festivals and community assemblies, and simpler, plainer enclosures were crafted for pastoral work. The largest tents looked palatial, resembling multistoried dwellings. As he sewed strips of red and yellow trim together, Jinba told me that he had been living in the city for only a few years. Most of the shop's work was done in a factory employing twenty people, who lived in an older housing compound at their workshop near South Mountain. The market store was essential, however, because Jinba could take orders and demonstrate the company's handiwork to visitors. Starting from a price of 2,000 yuan per tent, at 100 yuan per square meter for the canvas material, the tents had been selling steadily over the summer. They would pop up across the Qinghai grasslands on summer pastures, at religious events, and at horse racing festivals. Within Xining, urban customers even pitched them on top of South Mountain for the annual urban Tibetan Festival (Tib. *bod tshogs*), where Tibetan businesses and organizations sponsored tents for employees and their friends and families.

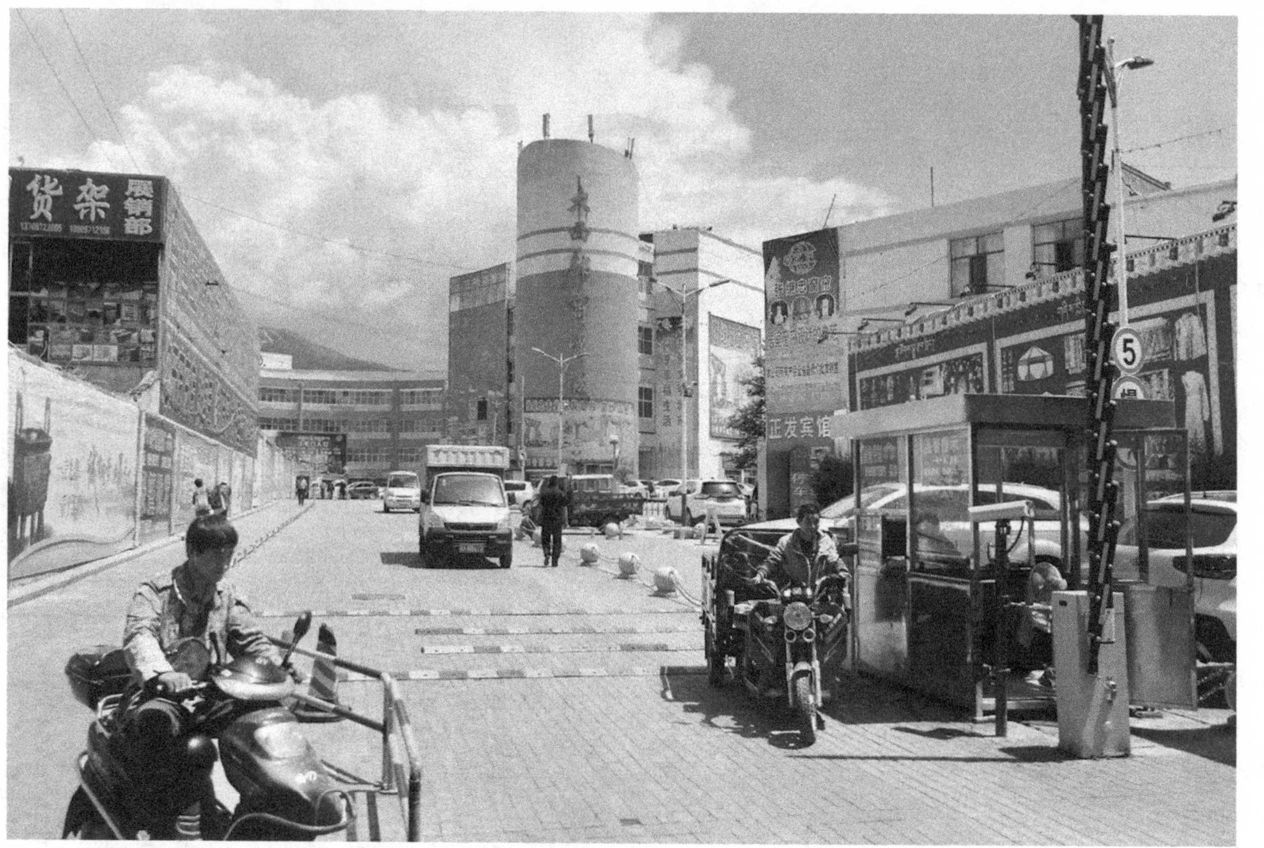

Figure 1.2. The multistory building (*center*) with a round tower houses the new Tibetan Market, which many shopkeepers migrated to during 2012 and 2013. This market was more concentrated and harder to locate than the older market.
Photo by the author, 2017.

Figure 1.3. Tents on top of South Mountain during the annual Tibetan Festival.
Photo by the author, 2018.

In the mid-2010s, the Tibetan Market remained a site where the rural entered into the city. Rural customers purchased manufactured goods to take back to their villages and pastures, and sellers were themselves often recent rural-to-urban migrants. Yet Tibetans weren't the only ones taking advantage of Xining's pivotal trade location to sell seemingly Tibetan things to Tibetan people. Non-Tibetans also play a part in producing and marketing goods for Tibetan consumers, competing with Tibetans while also shaping Tibetan urban consumerism.[42] At Xining's furniture and white goods emporium called North Mountain Market, Sichuanese woodworkers sold carved and painted Tibetan-style interior decorations. These colorful designs were recognizably Tibetan and could be found in some of Xining's Tibetan-owned stores and restaurants. Several of the Tibetan shopkeepers I interviewed were concerned that such practices took opportunities away from Tibetans. While this did not stop their co-ethnics from purchasing goods from these stores when other options were unavailable, my Tibetan friends felt that Tibetans' deserved position as purveyors of their own cultural products was being undermined.

Nevertheless, Tibetan entrepreneurs were resourceful and flexible, looking for ways to make a profit in the city despite the difficulties imposed by urban redevelopment and interethnic competition. As the Tibetan population of Xining grew and became increasingly deconcentrated across the city, entrepreneurs followed their potential customers. Shopkeepers in the Tibetan Market discussed moving elsewhere after the new train station was to be completed, including to sites still under construction nearby and to other parts of the city. Mobile dairy and bread vendors took advantage of urbanites' desire for convenience by bringing Tibetan staples directly into urban neighborhoods. Every morning starting at seven, the street below my second Xining apartment was converted into a teeming market, which would disappear shortly before noon. No matter the weather or the season, the street would fill with peddlers of vegetables, fruit, meat, seafood, clothing, toys, and appliances. While Han Chinese dominated the market, it also included three Tibetans vendors, all specializing in breads. I frequented the stand of one vendor from a village outside Rebgong; she lived in a small apartment a half kilometer away with her husband, children, and older sister. They rented their apartment as well as a store at the foot of their apartment building. There, her older sister baked bread in two large ovens, while her family members traveled around the city selling the bread at regular markets and outside the front gates of housing communities.

As in bakeries the world over, the master baker—in this case, the family's older sister—slept on a cot in the store, waking up at two o'clock in the morning to begin work. She would bake three hundred loaves, including one hundred large ring-shaped loaves and two hundred smaller round loaves. Family members would then sell the large loaves for ten yuan and the small ones for five yuan. They made enough of a profit to be able to continually expand the scale of their business, selling *tsampa*, butter, and yogurt from Tsekhok, a pastoral region near Rebgong. Tibetans I knew were happy to have these products increasingly accessible in the city. For instance, they deemed the ring-shaped bread called *goré nachu*, or *Rebgong goré*, superior in taste to the round loaves Muslims sold at window bakeries across the city, even though the *goré nachu* baked in modern city ovens was held to be inferior to those baked in earthen village ovens. Likewise, several yogurt sellers advertised their products as unadulterated (Tib. *slad med*) and sourced from yaks, called *dri*, on pastoral highlands. The rural origins of these products distinguished them as safer than the processed foods that were frequent subjects of adulteration scandals. Accounts of the rashes and hospitalizations allegedly caused by tainted products were continuously circulated over social media during my fieldwork and helped drive a market for purer products.

Business operations in Xining not only drove the circular movement of products between the city and its hinterlands—they also drove further circular migration through increased labor demand. As mentioned above, Jamyang had lived in a Xining office with his colleagues, who would sleep there for days or weeks at a time before returning to the countryside to carry out construction projects. Zontar and Jigmé Tendzin, an entrepreneuer discussed further below, both lived in housing near the Tibetan Market. Zontar lived with his brothers and two fellow villagers, and Jigmé Tendzin lived with his uncle and three of his brothers. They rented housing whose chief virtue was its proximity to the market; their neighbors were mostly Han and Muslim whom they rarely saw or interacted with. Furthermore, the businesses of Jigmé Tendzin and Jinba both hired workers who also rented housing. The family operations of bread and yogurt sellers also relied on family and village connections. The regular delivery of fresh yogurt demanded long drives between Xining and areas with livestock, as well as frequent overnight stays in the city. In one case, yogurt was delivered by a village government truck directly to a store in an urban produce market. The proximity of rural places and the seasonality of business filled and emptied out apartments at different rhythms, indicating a population more fluid and circular than statistics indicating near-complete urbanization rates for the central urban districts of Xining suggest.

Housing and education could also drive such migrations. As rural Tibetans worked to secure investments, comfortable housing, and educational opportunities for their families, they utilized urban resources. Wangchuk was born into a pastoralist family in Nangchen, a part of Yulshul Prefecture, but he never learned to herd because his family instead wanted him to pursue a college education. When we talked, Wangchuk was in his late twenties and lived in an apartment that his father had purchased near Xining's Second Hospital. This location was chosen on the advice of his relatives, and the capital used to purchase it came from wealth generated from the Tibetan grasslands.[43] In good years, such as the 2010–2012 period after China's stimulus-fueled economic rebound and just before the onset of Xi Jinping's anticorruption campaign, Wangchuk's family could make up to 100,000 yuan.[44] The money from these sales had been applied toward purchasing the apartment Wangchuk lived in, a spacious 115-square-meter unit that had cost his family a total of 805,000 yuan.

Wangchuk's family had also used caterpillar fungus money to build a large hotel in Nangchen where Han visitors would stay in the summer. As Wangchuk described them, these lodgers occupied a position between friend and customer. They came year after year from cities including Chengdu, Shanghai, Guangzhou, and Shenzhen and spent significant amounts of money to buy these treasured fungi directly at the source. The wealth generated from these relationships had been so substantial that when we met in 2014, Wangchuk owned the latest iPhone model and a new Hyundai car. He even had his expansive Xining apartment all to himself when his family was occupied with doing caterpillar fungus or hotel-related business, which was most of the time.

But the emptiness of his apartment was uncommon among my interlocutors. Sometimes during interviews, children would peak at me from behind sofas and hallway doors. They could be the children of my participants, but just as often they were relatives' children living in Xining in order to attend school there. Other relatives came for shorter periods of time. Apartments filled with people during the winters, as older relatives sought to escape intense high-altitude cold and parents sent children to attend supplementary education over winter vacation. I met pastoralists who had come to Xining to stay at hotels for weeks at a time, selling fungus, visiting car dealers, and accompanying sick relatives who had come to visit one of the city's many hospitals.

The urban and rural interpenetrate in Xining, but this doesn't mean the rural is simply being consumed through topographical urban extension. Xining's Tibetan Market, in its many guises, has been a place where the rural and urban encounter and cater to each other, merging in the reinventions of Tibetan entrepreneurs and the circulations of consumer goods. Entrepreneurs have also pursued a deconcentrated Tibetan market across the city, where some sell manufactured goods to rural Tibetans and others market grasslands and farming goods to a more general urban clientele. Whether they own or rent their housing, Tibetans have also driven further circular migration as they welcome employees, fellow villagers, and family members to come to Xining to stay with them while they pursue work, comfort, or education. The result is a topological complexity in which it can be difficult to define and clarify where rural and urban goods, livelihoods, and spaces begin and end.

Cosmopolitan Dreaming

On the urbanizing Plateau, circular migration has provided resources for Tibetans' cosmopolitan dreaming. K. Sivaramakrishnan and Arun Agrawal have argued that emerging regional modernities can challenge notions of homogenizing globalization that neglect the intermediate scales and identities that contour economic and social development.[45] The extensive space of the urbanizing eastern Plateau has created a Tibetan regional modernity that challenges Chinese national mediations of urban modernity. Urbanization, as a key venue for the obtainment of modern technical skills and fashionable goods, has accelerated these remediations of modernity; a "migrant cosmopolitanism" has taken shape that has allowed for the subversion of the social hierarchies promoted through urban development without completely rejecting all things urban.[46] Focusing on the experiences of Tibetan urban migrants, this section highlights urban Tibetans' cosmopolitan aspirations by focusing on their personal, familial, and community goals, their embrace of entrepreneurialism to contribute to the Tibetan community, and their difficulties in obtaining their cosmopolitan dreams given the social and ethnic hierarchies implicit in the civilizing machine and the challenges of finding secure work.

During my fieldwork, I would ask Tibetans about their plans for the future and whether they thought they could realize them. A topic that frequently came up was the Chinese Dream. In the mid-2010s, Chinese citizens were being encouraged to imagine their future within the framework of the Chinese Dream, part of the party-state's spiritual supplement to material development. In late 2012, Xi Jinping introduced the concept of the Chinese Dream, an ideal toward which all Chinese people could collectively strive as they realized higher levels of national development and wealth; working together the Chinese could make their country stronger and more prosperous. In this way, Chinese Dream rhetoric has drawn a clear line connecting economic development, social development, and national revitalization.[47] Chinese publicity departments quickly appropriated the term for use in their propaganda, and by the summer of 2013 Xining was covered with posters and banners that carried variations on slogans including "China's Dream, National Rejuvenation, My Dream." In addition to collective attainment, propaganda also stressed individual success, often featuring images of young, smiling middle-class families living in modern urban housing. In areas of Xining with denser populations of Muslims and Tibetans, publicity departments blended the promotion of ethnic unity (Ch. *minzu tuanjie*) with these collective and individuated aspirations; the local state encouraged ethnic groups to align their goals with those of the national Chinese Dream.

While expressing agreement with the individual and familial aspects of the Chinese Dream, my research participants rejected its stress on a national collectivity, instead substituting a regional Tibetan collective. I interviewed Tsondru, a young man whose *hukou* was registered in Xunhua, a farming area in Amdo. He worked in telecom infrastructure construction and told me that among his office coworkers there was saying: "The Chinese Dream is to take the wrong road."[48] This was because while government officials (Ch. *guanfang*) had embraced lofty Chinese Dream rhetoric, they were in practice idle and corrupt, squandering money on pricey food and engaging in graft. He was strongly dismissive of the dream's personal relevance to him: "The Chinese Dream is about progressing the country, but my dream is to progress [Tib. *khong 'phel*] my own family by earning more income." Tsondru rejected the national community promoted by the Chinese Dream, but he tacitly agreed to the individualized middle-class pursuits it endorsed; he had recently purchased a sizable new apartment in the city's newly built New Lake District.

In the Tibetan Market, one floor below Zontar's print shop, there was a cellphone store run by the charismatic Jigmé Tendzin. Only twenty-five years old, the Chabcha-born Jigmé Tendzin had his own business, which he had relocated from the demolished Tibetan Market, signing a three-year contract for the new space. He had earned an associate degree in management from the prestigious Nankai University in Tianjin and was confident that this degree gave him an edge in business. Tibetans, he said, lacked a business environment and were poor at bargaining. With his business knowledge, Jigmé Tendzin was finding success. To help with his bustling store, he had hired several female Tibetan shop assistants he found through online job solicitations. He had also decided to open a second store that specialized in clothing in another stall in the market. While he hadn't purchased an apartment or transferred his *hukou*, he had recently bought a new car and was paying off his loan on it. Jigmé Tendzin told me that his *milam* (Tib. *rmi lam*), or dream, was to have stores that sold Tibetan-language electronics of all types, which were at that time difficult to obtain. "I don't think," he said with a smile, "that this is the Chinese Dream." Echoing a concern widespread among Tibetans that Tibetan-language digital communication generated suspicion among China's primarily Mandarin-reading security organs, Jigmé Tendzin thought that Tibetans would have to pursue the goal of Tibetan-capable electronics on their own.

One of the most important motivating factors for entrepreneurs like Jigmé Tendzin was to make cultural contributions to contemporary Tibetan society. As Françoise Robin has argued in her analysis of the entrepreneurism promoted by Tibetan financier and poet Gangshun, the recent generation of young Tibetan businesspeople is consciously incorporating Tibetan culture (Tib. *rig gnas*) into their products, designs, and handicrafts.[49] Zontar's shop had a massive printer that rolled out colorful glossy posters. His print designs blended traditional patterns, portraits of and quotations from famous religious figures and authors, and stunning photos of Tibetan landscapes. "I design for everything," he told me, "I do it for companies, homes, schools, and shops. Every design has a specific meaning, and there are different designs for each place. You just tell me what you need, and then I will design it." He had acquired his skills working at another print shop run by a non-family member, and he saw his art as a means to preserve and contribute to (Tib. *phan thoks*) Tibetan culture in the city. Despite the financial risks involved, it was his *milam* to make the shop bigger and more successful. Zontar blended business acumen, technology, and aesthetics to fuse his personal and community aspirations.

I also interviewed Jamtso, a twenty-five-year-old woman born in Nangchen, a pastoral region in southern Yulshul Prefecture. She had grown up in urban places including Xining and a county town. Her goals were primarily for herself and her family: "The Chinese Dream is to be relatively well-off [Ch. *xiaokang*]. It is too big. Education reform, medical reform, all of these public reforms. What a mess. But my dream, it is just a personal [Ch. *geren*] dream." Jamtso was considering opening a clothing store when she was older. Seeing that Tibetans in Yulshul no longer wore the traditional dress they once had, she wanted to promote new fashionable styles of Tibetan clothing. Still, she told me that it wasn't necessary for people such as herself to dress in a Tibetan manner if they lived in the New Lake District, a newly developed portion of western Xining. This was because that place "belongs to the modern, to the urbanized. It has a new culture." Likewise, Zontar accepted this "new culture," self-consciously pursuing its urban style. Rather than purchase the

Tibetan clothing marketed at the Tibetan Market where he worked, Zontar stressed that he bought his own clothes downtown, in the big chain stores where the styles were "more fashionable." Circular migration produced cosmopolitan tastes that Tibetans were both reworking for their communities and incorporating into their personal styles.

Consuming fashionable styles of clothing, studying or traveling abroad, learning a foreign language, all of which are typical practices and aspirations for young urbanites in contemporary China, couldn't guarantee that Tibetans were accepted into the national community as equals. Social hierarchies embedded within the civilizing machine meant that dream-pursuing Tibetans could still be reminded that they were out of place, that their horizons could not be as extensive as those of many of China's other national urban citizens. I met Tashi at a café on a heavily trafficked side road in Xining's South Mountain district, where he was living and working. Tashi was one of a handful of my research participants who spoke fluent English. He was born in an agro-pastoral community in Tsolho Tibetan Autonomous Prefecture, where Yellow River tributaries cut long farming valleys through the high grasslands.[50] His village had been resettled and lost its farming fields, but Tashi said that this made little difference to his family's economic situation, as his mother was a medical researcher. He had earned his BA in another western Chinese province but had returned to Qinghai to work at an NGO that helped poor Tibetans get primary and secondary education.

Tashi told me how his English skills had helped him build community when he was new to Xining and living near the Tibetan hospital. There in the evenings, he would sometimes relax with hospital staff on the roof of the housing compound where he rented a room. He would teach them English phrases, and they would teach him about Tibetan medicine in exchange. When he later moved to a larger apartment with his cousin farther away from the hospital, he no longer interacted with his neighbors, who were now mostly Han: "Not many people are willing to talk. They are afraid of me. Maybe I am a thief, right? When I was in Lanzhou I rented a room near the downtown, and it was the same. Nobody was willing to talk. They were scared." Tashi assumed that Han Chinese in the city didn't feel comfortable talking to strangers, and that, moreover, his looking and speaking Tibetan likely intimidated them.

Fears of Tibetans as potentially violent or engaged in crime can contribute to estrangement from and stigmatization by Han Chinese urban neighbors.[51] But what bothered Tashi much more were the social hierarchies that resulted in the belittling of his education: "When I was in Kumbum monastery, I used English to speak to some foreigners about the monastery's history. One

Chinese person approached us and said, 'Oh, Tibetan people can *also* speak English.' It's like they are thinking 'How can Tibetan people speak English?' " Tashi recounted with relish the pithy comeback he had delivered in Chinese: "So I said to them, really I said this: 'We can't only just speak English, but we can also speak Japanese!' " Though Tashi only knew a few phrases in Japanese, he made the case to these condescending eavesdroppers that not only he, but the "we" of a wider Tibetan community, had linguistic skills that connected them to a world beyond their home areas and even China. "They think that Tibetans can't study abroad or don't have the abilities needed to study abroad, but for [Han] Chinese people to do it is completely normal," Tashi told me with growing agitation. "If you say that you are Tibetan and you studied abroad, they are surprised. They don't think Tibetans have that kind of power." When people understood that Tibetans were educated, they were less afraid, he said. For instance, his Han landlord trusted him because of his college education and NGO employment. For Tashi, the promise of the Chinese Dream was that all fifty-six of China's nationalities could share the same dream to do things like study abroad and live in the city. It was the presumed inability, in the eyes of some Han Chinese, to be distinctly Tibetan and cosmopolitan in a modern mode that pained Tashi. Despite the skills Tibetans like Tashi had gained through their regional circulations and taking up of urban occupations, they still risked being seen as somehow incapable of accomplishing nationally shared aspirations.

As Tibetans navigated urban lifestyles and pursued their dreams, they could be acutely aware that national priorities were often misaligned with what was best for Tibetans. Rabten, a fifty-year-old female employee of a state-funded research organization that supported women's social and economic development, told me, "[Xi Jinping] says 'national rejuvenation' [Ch. *minzu fuxing*], but what nation is he talking about? What nationalities? China has fifty-six of them. What will this rejuvenation make them become?" Rabten was concerned that Tibetans might not reap the benefits of economic development, and so made a clear distinction between her dream and the Chinese Dream: "I have a different dream. It relates just to Qinghai. Here in Qinghai we Tibetan women and children should get more involved in enterprises and businesses. There are some really exceptional, outstanding people [who could work in such enterprises]. I think that it is really a shortcoming that so few women are involved." Rabten's goals, similar to the goals of other Tibetan women's empowerment activists in Amdo, are both cosmopolitan and locally situated insofar as they are influenced by national and global rhetorics of development and also oriented toward helping a regional Tibetan community.[52]

Rabten saw Tibetans as being at a structural disadvantage to obtain the community-wide development they sought. She saw this as part of Tibetans' general inability to properly use the resources they ought to be able to access: "From the perspective of economic development, Qinghai is quite backward. There are many aspects to this problem. First, Tibetans don't really know how to use capital resources when we have them. Second, our nationality has too few skills and capabilities to do business. Third, the government thinks that all resources belong to it and not to ordinary people. Tibetans don't understand that these things could be ours." She explained that caterpillar fungus, *thangka* paintings, and underground mineral resources were "really controlled by other ethnicities," alluding to Muslim middlemen in the fungus market, to Han Chinese private companies that had been capitalizing on *thangka* art, and the Han-dominated state-owned enterprises that had extraction operations throughout Tibetan areas.[53] In this view, Tibetans were not currently prepared to position themselves in an economy increasingly dominated by outside private initiative on the one hand, and state expropriation of Tibetan resources on the other.

I met Dekyi in her apartment in the North District, where she had been living for nearly twenty-five years. She worked for a well-known transnational cosmetics marketing firm and told me that she was the first Tibetan to hold such a position. She was very successful in her career, earning tens of thousands of yuan a month, part of which she was using to support her family members and to contribute to temple construction in her hometown southeast of Xining. Dekyi also wanted to extend both this work and the beauty benefits it provided to more Tibetan women; her goal was to establish a network of saleswomen across Tibetan towns, so that each large town would have its own cosmetics vendor. While such a plan certainly adheres to the business model of her industry, she stressed that she was customizing her approach for the Tibetan community, which she saw as losing its culture (Tib. *rig gnas*) under Chinese influence from urban areas. When we spoke, she was in the process of hiring Tibetan staff to translate cosmetics advertisements into Tibetan. She also planned to conduct Western-style business training sessions that she emphasized were markedly different from and superior to those usually run by Chinese businesses. As Dekyi's example shows, in fostering a regional modernity, Tibetan businesspeople can actively work to bypass the national scale, localizing the global and creating assets that can be used to stave off the assimilatory pressure of the civilizing machine.

The successes of the Tibetan entrepreneurs I interviewed were well-earned, but they could also be fleeting, as business was risky. Many young college-educated Tibetans I befriended or interviewed felt pressure from their parents and had been counseled by their lamas to secure government work, which, as I was frequently told, would allow them to attain "peace of mind" (Tib. *sems bde gi*). Like other members of China's aspiring urban middle class, Tibetans have seen government work as a guarantee of economic security and a stable, middle-class future.[54] People who obtain official work are often well positioned to help their family members by, for instance, obtaining bank loans to buy housing. In this way, these positions provide peace of mind to entire families.

Across Tibetan regions and China as a whole, the public job allocation system (Ch. *fenpei*) that guaranteed stable work under socialism has been steadily dismantled over the reform period, pushing more Tibetans to enter into the competitive private labor market. As Andrew Fischer and Adrian Zenz have argued, despite an uptick in *fenpei* positions in Tibetan areas following protests and unrest that began in 2008, the overall number of available positions is insufficient for the number of Tibetan college graduates who want to secure such work.[55] Because these public jobs privilege college education and are largely clerical, most are found in urbanized areas.[56] In order to get and keep such positions, Tibetans are put into circular migrations between their home areas, cities with colleges where they study and prepare for government work, and the government seats, such as county towns, where they often end up working.[57]

One type of government employment that is particularly desirable because of its benefits is that of the civil servant (Ch. *gongwuyuan*). Norbu, a twenty-five-year-old man from Xunhua who had recently begun work as a police officer in Xining, explained to me the advantages of being a civil servant: "It is a stable job in which you can keep your salary your whole life, even after you retire. Your salary is stable, and you will have additional insurance and other subsidies on top of your earnings. If you get a loan, there will be no problem for you. With civil servant work you can feel satisfied and there is no stress [Tib. *sems 'khur med*]." Norbu contrasted this sort of work with other public institutions (Ch. *shiye danwei*), including teaching and hospital work. In those types of work, health insurance and housing costs are deducted from the worker's salary, and workers receive a smaller pension after retirement. Government work was helping young people like Norbu, whose duties included processing *hukou* applications, to see and plan their futures more clearly. Having only recently gotten this job and moved to Xining, Norbu was planning to transfer his *hukou* to the city and become a permanent urban resident, just as soon as he and other new officers were offered the discounted apartments promised by his work unit.[58] To qualify for the best positions, Tibetans had to take civil service examinations. As the geographer Duojie Zhaxi has argued, everyday familial pressure to secure public work has also encouraged college-educated Tibetans unable to secure public posts to migrate to Xining, where many engage in lower-paying service-sector work.[59] For these Tibetans, the pursuit of employment that would offer peace of mind has become stressful in and of itself.

Jamtso, the woman who wanted to open a clothing store, had lived in Xining for nearly twenty years. Her parents sent her to Xining at a young age in order to set her up to be successful in the civil service examination. She had developed a critical perspective on Tibetan students' near single-minded determination to become civil servants: "Ninety percent of my classmates have taken the civil service examination. My best friend, it is her dream to become a civil servant, but she is going crazy preparing for the exam. All she does is read." Jamtso had witnessed many of her friends fail the test over and over. She felt that compared to Tibetans, the Han Chinese were much more flexible in what they prepared for. They took the civil service examination, but they also took examinations for more specialized positions, such as those related to law. And if this didn't work out, they were happy to look for private-sector work, which, according to her, most Tibetans avoided. Jamtso saw herself as fortunate that she had some relief from the pressure of securing civil servant work. She had a job writing and doing communications for an Inner Chinese–based NGO engaged with post-2010 Yulshul earthquake disaster relief. Furthermore, her mother was a government pensioner, and her father made money from selling caterpillar fungus. Economic security within a family can put younger Tibetans in a better position to both pursue their individual dreams and to contribute to their community in novel ways.

Circular migration has fostered a regional modernity among eastern Tibetans who have used the education and business acumen they have acquired to fashion cosmopolitan aspirations that are not mirror images of state-fostered desires, such as those promoted in Xi Jinping's Chinese Dream. While the civilizing machine has directed individual and household goals toward a shared goal of national development, Tibetans have used urban resources to help themselves and their families. Moreover, Xining-based entrepreneurs have created and distributed products to assist a Tibetan community that is increasingly interested in fashions associated with urban modernity and new technologies that can be customized to Tibetans' tastes and dispositions. While such entrepreneurial pursuits can bring stress and are not easily manageable without household financial support, where they are successful they contribute to a Tibetan regional modernity whose reach extends beyond any urban administrative boundaries.

In Xining City, circular migrants' movement between rural and urban places has been catalyzed by urban extension: the topographical expansion of urban places across valley floors and on grasslands, where new settlements and urban developments are increasingly linked through new road infrastructure in a comprehensive provincial urbanization plan. The state retains its rural-urban binary as part of a developmental model through which it valorizes and promotes urban expansion as a measure of economic and social development. While rural Tibetan places have been subsumed or up-scaled into municipalities and towns whose inhabitants are encouraged to collectively pursue the Chinese Dream, Tibetans have been using resources provided through urbanization to realize their own projects.

Whether working in itinerant construction jobs, in goods markets, or as government workers, Xining's Tibetans were hardly rural visitors to the city or the fully urbanized permanent residents that statisticians and policy planners have been at pains to locate in their urbanization forecasts. Urban Tibetans like Jamyang were continually circulating between the countryside and urbanized areas for work and for family. Their purchase or rental of urban houses drove more circular migration as family members, fellow villagers, and employees also came and went for labor, education, and other reasons.

Urbanization is not merely extensive or a "continuum" that state categorizations fail to capture; it is also topological.[60] As built-up urban areas have become important sites of livelihood and dwelling, circulations of people, goods, and ideas have confounded the administrative and material boundedness of the urban and rural as naturally opposed abstractions. Topographical extension of the urban into the rural has facilitated the topological emergence of the rural amid the urban, such as in the case of commodities like *Rebgong goré* and Tsekhok yogurt being sold from the backs of motorized carts in locations across Xining. The rural and the urban have also come together through cosmopolitan appropriations of modern technologies and styles for Tibetans' use, which can work to promote individual and community aspirations as distinct from those of a national-scale collective. These circulations of people and goods thus give Xining and its hinterlands an emerging regional modernity that is necessarily distinct from that found in other parts of China, while also having continuity with historical regional trade and the boundary-spanning exchange and resourcefulness that have shaped the Tibetan Plateau more generally.[61] The next chapter explores circulations of a different sort: those of historical figures and technologies that brought civilization and political order to Xining City and have been, to varying degrees and through various methods, memorialized for urban inhabitants.

Chapter 2

Remembering Xining

> The true essence of Leandra is the subject of endless debate. The Penates believe they are the city's soul, even if they arrived last year; and they believe they take Leandra with them when they emigrate. The Lares consider the Penates temporary guests, importunate, intrusive; the real Leandra is theirs, which gives form to all it contains, the Leandra that was there before all these upstarts arrived and that will remain when all have gone away.
>
> —Italo Calvino, *Invisible Cities*

When the writer Gu Zhizhong rode into Xining on the back of a donkey in the early 1930s, he and his co-travelers passed through three narrow gorges. For Gu and his eastern Chinese companions, all members of a Qinghai study mission investigating the potential of the region for development, this portion of their trip through the region was tense.[1] In these gorges they feared attacks from the ferocious barbarians of the west—Tibetans.[2] While Xining wasn't the most pleasant destination, it provided security, well-stocked inns, and respite for the anxious investigators.

For foreign travelers of the nineteenth and twentieth centuries who passed through Xining, there was little to celebrate. The American missionary Victor Plymire bemoaned the torrential rain and mud he encountered in his travel to Xining up the narrow valley of the Huangshui River, and the American travel writer Paul Theroux described the city as battered by a rapidly shifting climate of "rain, dust storms, blinding sunlight and snow."[3] Theroux's assessment of Xining City in the 1980s did not include an encounter with bandits—he arrived by train—but he wrote about the city in negative terms nonetheless. His description of its "square brown buildings on straight streets, surrounded by big brown hills" resonates with the comments of French explorer Fernand Grenard one hundred years before, who wrote that Xining's buildings were "more remarkable and more imposing for the vast extent of their inner courts, which follow one another in long rows, than for the effect of the architecture, which is heavy and as it were crushed under excessive development of the roofs." Grenard did, however, see some redeeming features in the city's natural environment, offering that "the insignificance and ugliness of the human constructions are atoned for, in a certain measure, by the beauty of the site."[4]

Outsiders have long described Xining as a place with few memorable traits, seeing it as a stepping-stone or gateway on itineraries to Lhasa or more significant nearby places, such as architecturally stunning monasteries and lively market towns located elsewhere in the crisscrossing river valleys of the eastern Tibetan Plateau. Xining was regarded as a base for further exploration, a waypoint on journeys elsewhere. In 2007 one of my responsibilities at Xining's Qinghai Normal University was to teach English to Han Chinese from the lush farming regions of Sichuan and Chongqing. Early in our first semester together, I asked students to write travel recollections of their journeys back to Qinghai at the end of the summer. In essay after essay students lamented leaving their homes to come to this wild place "as bald as an old man's head," where windblown loess settled in chalky dun residues on their desks and dormitory beds.

While Xining hasn't meant much to these sojourners and reluctant students, the relative comfort of the city as a well-provisioned place has made it a tolerable outpost of Inner China on the Tibetan Plateau both in the past and present. Indeed, the Chinese name of the place itself derives from a historical frontier garrison that would grow to become a hub of the Ming dynasty's famed tea and horse markets and a regional administrative center for all mainland Chinese governments since. Viewed in this light, Xining is an urban and infrastructural extension of China. I argue in this chapter that urban places in Xining can work to assemble and narrate the city through what I call a chronotope of pacification. In the enunciation of this assemblage, particular urban places are remembered insofar as they speak to a temporality of peaceful and subordinate connection to Inner China.

But this is not the only city Xining can be. Names, materials, infrastructural legacies, and memories all play a role in the composition of Ziling, the Tibetan city. Though this city is less apparent to an outsider not attuned to its presence, it is well known to the city's Tibetans, who assemble parts of it together through their speech and imagination. As Gastón Gordillo has argued, material sites, in their ruination and in recollections of their past prominence, have the capacity to gather communities and their collected memories in constellations that may be otherwise suppressed.[5] This chapter draws from this insight; it also argues that toponomastics, the inquiry into place names and their origins, is an important practice in assembling the Tibetan city amid the Chinese city.

As Robbie Barnett has demonstrated in the case of Lhasa, Chinese urbanization has remade Tibetan cities, bringing new built forms and creating new foci for social gathering and political authority.[6] Urbanization in Tibetan regions can threaten architectural heritage and disrupt traditional Tibetan geographies of pilgrimage and power, reorienting cities toward Inner China. The transformation of contemporary Lhasa, with its iconic sites such as the Potala Palace and the Jokhang Monastery, is clear to urban dwellers and visitors alike. In comparison, Xining's transformation away from its historical Tibetan legacy may appear less remarkable. The city and the valley within which it rests have an eventful urban history, however, of which Tibetans have played a significant part. This chapter will shed light on how Ziling, the Tibetan city, is preserved and practiced amid the changes brought by the civilizing machine.

The first two sections focus on narratives and memorialization practices that place Xining within the political and developmental ambit of China's civilizing center and mythology. These narratives are realized through two main sources: writings in provincial publications that introduce readers to the history of Xining and its hinterlands, and commemorations approved by municipal authorities for urban public spaces. The latter includes toponyms and dromonyms (road names), as well as historically themed park displays. These memorial practices work to place contemporary Xining into circulation with the Inner Chinese lands to its east. These practices depend on the selective use of infrastructure, which I define, following Brian Larkin, as "built networks" that reinforce connections, material and symbolic, to particular centers of power. Historical and mythological narratives are realized in the urban environment by building new infrastructures and by raising the profiles of old infrastructures.[7] Following this is a discussion of Tsongkha, the Tibetan region that includes Ziling, and how it has been assembled as an important place both through religious circulations and through stories about places and their names that recall a history of local Tibetan religious, commercial, and urban centrality.

Remembering the Chinese City

Visitors to contemporary Xining encounter a city that has a readily apparent long and continuous Chinese heritage. The urban landscape is replete with toponyms, commemorative sites, and parks that render self-evident the city's deep connection to the rest of China in both space and time. Charlene Makley has emphasized the importance of chronotopes as "historically loaded idioms" that reveal ongoing dialogue and contestation between the authoritative time-spaces of Chinese state rule and Tibetan local and monastic institutions.[8] Focusing on chronotopes draws our attention to how past time interacts with the present and the role that time and space play in articulating particular kinds of stories, such as those of the city and the spatial relations it sustains. Mikhail Bakhtin argues that some chronotopes homogenize time by narrating particular events as ultimately inconsequential compared to the emplotments that drive the narrative.[9] Such narratives highlight the unchanging nature of key relationships despite the passage of eventful biographical time. The narrative elision of durations of what are ultimately insignificant events allows for the emergence of an "extratemporal hiatus" in which the key relationship is shown to be immutable.

Chinese civilization has this kind of enduring relationship with Xining; while official and popular historical accounts do offer chronologies of changing rule and alternating conquest, their rhetorical stress on continuity and the unchanging nature of center-periphery relations presents an urban temporality outside biographic time—eternal and essentially unchanging, despite evidence of social unrest and political discontinuity.[10] The rendering of the extra-temporal hiatus is made possible through the exercise of editorial power by authors, urban authorities, and developers, by their selective memorialization of the urban landscape and subsequent narration of China's imperial past into the present.[11] The city emerges as an outpost of stability that for thousands of years has secured regional trade, brought developmental progress, and sustained inter-ethnic peace. Through infrastructures such as walled garrisons and logistical networks such as caravan routes, the center kept the periphery close.

Xining is one of the ancient Inner Asian cities that Piper Gaubatz has called a "frontier of control" created by Chinese dynasties to attain security through the establishment of military garrisons and administrative centers.[12] These cities also served as infrastructures in what Larkin has called an "architecture of circulation" that enables particular political and social orders to function.[13] As a form of both symbolic and material infrastructure, cities in the frontier of control were built according to urban forms patterned on a Sinocentric urban ideal. For Paul Wheatley, the quadrilateral form of the traditional Chinese city, with its high walls and axial roads, allowed for the application of a "cosmic image" based in canonical texts in which "the future was viewed as an endless repetition of the past."[14] Such canonical "repeatable formulas" were a form of cosmic infrastructural standards. By deploying them, rulers could center and order cities and their hinterlands.[15] While in practice early frontier cities deviated from cosmic and geomantic infrastructural standards, they retained their pretensions as civilizing outposts that sustained and symbolized the center's pacification of the periphery.[16]

Urban toponymy also reinforced these infrastructures, enunciating their civilizing power. Uradyn Bulag has argued that the Ming dynasty names for Ürümqi and Hohhot articulated the civilizing capability of the Chinese city to transform the barbarian frontier. These cities were named Dihua and Guihua, which meant, respectively, pacification and cultural transformation.[17] The first Chinese name that bookends Xining's history in the *Xining City Gazetteer Urban Establishment and Construction Annals* is Xiping Ting, or Western Peace Prefect, which was established in 111 BCE.[18] After centuries of changes in political and administrative geography, the Western Peace site would eventually take the name of Xining Zhou, or Western Tranquillity Prefecture, under the Song dynasty.[19] The modern urban name of Xining City thus reveals its role in the historic project of frontier pacification.

Explanations about just what the city was pacifying can be found in recent works of urban memory, which elaborate on memorialized features of the urban landscape. The multivolume *Old Xining* (Ch. *Lao Xining*), a work of popular history written by Jin Yude, an author, editor, and member of several state educational councils, uses Xining as a vantage point to offer a Sinocentric history of the municipal core and its environs. During my research, Jin Yude's books were found in Xining's airport and in bookstores and gift shops across the city. They read as gazetteers that include explanations of the toponyms and famous figures that color Xining's past, while also incorporating them into the chronotope of pacification. Though Jin acknowledges the vicissitudes of Xining's political and demographic history, his narrative arc begins with Xiping Ting, the Western Peace Prefect, and the gazetteer itself focuses on places strewn across the much larger administrative space of contemporary Xining. He argues that "research into the source and development of Xining's toponyms helps people retain memories" of the city as it expands and old sites are lost to redevelopment.[20]

For readers, the most accessible sites are those with material bases in the city. They invite the urban resident or tourist to verify the city's ancient past by witnessing it firsthand. When I worked as a teacher at Qinghai Normal University in 2007, I would pick up my international mail at the post office next to New Peace Square. On my way there, I strolled past a weed-covered hill that for months I assumed was excess soil from recent construction work.[21] When I finally entered the park that surrounded the hill, I learned it was actually the largest and most conspicuous ancient site in the city. Called

Tiger Mount (Ch. *Hutai*), the hill was an earthwork built in the short-lived Southern Liang Kingdom (397–414 CE), one of China's historical Sixteen Kingdoms, for the purpose of mustering soldiers and cavalry. The Southern Liang's rulers met memorable ends, one dying from wounds sustained by falling drunk off a horse and another from poisoning.

Jin Yude suggests that something about the place encourages people to ponder the past, and he quotes Ming and Qing poets who gazed from the western walls of Xining onto the mount, which then dominated their view of the valley. They imagined resting on its grasses and conjured up images of indigenous peoples worshipping at the site. Their writings, Jin attests, have allowed for future visitors to experience the reverberations of past humans and horses gathering at the site. By 2005 Tiger Mount had been engulfed by urban expansion, and the historical site was transformed into the Southern Liang Tiger Mount Ruins Park. This park, Jin Yude suggests, had become "a go-to attraction for Xining urban residents' leisurely sightseeing," where visitors enjoyed the "lush turquoise grass" growing on the hill, a statue of the ruler Rutan that recalls Sixteen Kingdoms iconography, and sculptures of several large cauldrons (Ch. *ding*) also associated with ancient Chinese culture.[22] An inscription at the site recounts the military history of the Southern Liang Kingdom, ending with the statement that subsequent generations have recognized the kingdom's education system and interest in enlightening its urban inhabitants. Connecting this story to the Jin dynasty (266–420 CE), the inscription suggests an enduring relationship with Chinese civilization. Lyrical writings of poets, the conversion of the site to a historic park, and the kingdom's enrollment into Chinese history all activate the trope of the chronotope of pacification for urban denizens.

Also narrating the regional past through park space is a shaded pedestrian walkway along Establish the Country Avenue in the East District that commemorates twelve "Historical Personages of Hehuang" with statues and engravings. The first notable is the fifth-century BCE nomadic Qiang headman Wuyi Aijian, whose inscription credits him with developing the Huangshui area by turning hunters into farmers and pastoralists, but only after experiencing firsthand the Sinified culture of the ancient Qin state (897–207 BCE) east of the Tibetan Plateau. Aside from Deng Chunlan, an early twentieth-century activist for gender equality in education, the other historical personages of Hehuang are all men, five of whom were born in Inner China. There are two Han dynasty generals credited with bringing garrison farming to the region, several poets, and one Tibetan who was a PRC official. Notable in all these cases is the influence of the Chinese civilizing center through time. Inner Chinese places and the circulation of peoples and practices between them and Hehuang have worked to develop and pacify the region.

The most recent personage in the walkway, as well as on Jin Yude's list of personages, is Wang Luobin, a Beijing-born composer who became famous for collecting the folk music of northwestern China and modifying its style and content to reach a national audience in the mid-twentieth century.[23] As Jin Yude stresses, Wang became famous for doing propaganda work during the war with Japan and for his song "In That Distant Place." Beside the statue of Wang strumming his guitar on the historical walkway rests an engraved stone that discusses the song's links to the composer's experience in Qinghai. The song's lyrics have the imagery of pastoral romance, comparing a Tibetan woman's ruddy cheeks to the red sun.[24] Wang Luobin fits into the urban landscape as a bridging figure who worked between Tibetans, Muslim ethnicities, and the Han Chinese, as well as between Communists and Nationalists, for whom he worked as a media propagandist and a music teacher, respectively.

Ma Qi and his son Ma Bufang are two figures who risk disrupting the chronotope of pacification but who are ultimately narrated into it as transitional figures between a feudal past and modern present. They belong to one of the three Ma families that rose to prominence in the late nineteenth century in support of the Qing dynasty's military campaigns in the region. During this period, differences in doctrine and economic tensions led to Muslim rebellion and communal violence in northwest China. In the 1870s and 1890s, the "Muslim Rebellions" disrupted trade routes around Xining as rebelling communities fortified their villages and cities against Qing armies, weakening the circulations of the center in the region. During these rebellions Xining was besieged, and the Dongguan Mosque burned down three times. Qing armies pacified Muslim rebels through execution or expulsion.[25] Contemporary historical works and urban memorial sites have helped narrate this violent history into a story of political continuity and interethnic cooperation by selectively remembering this Ma family. As Jin Yude recounts, among Ma Qi's patriotic deeds was his participation in the Qing pacification of the Hehuang region during the rebellions.

After the fall of the Qing dynasty in 1912, the Ma family in Gansu and Qinghai supported the Republican government, enforcing China's territorial integrity in the face of foreign encroachment. Jin Yude glosses Ma Qi as patriotically coordinating with central authorities to fight opium, to further education policies, and to work against British plans to cartographically divide Tibet and extend their influence. The tourist-oriented *Book of Qinghai*, a provincial press publication that mixes historical description with cultural explanation in the context of sightseeing, includes a profile of Ma Qi that devotes several pages to his defense of Chinese Tibet against the British.[26] Missing is how, as Uradyn Bulag has shown, Ma Qi and Ma Bufang strategically cooperated with the central Republican government to maintain a degree of political autonomy at a time when the center was dependent on borderland elites.[27]

Ma Bufang is the most famous, or perhaps infamous, Muslim political leader of this period. The chairman of Qinghai from 1936 until the Communist Liberation of 1949, he is known most widely in China as a warlord who disrupted the Long March. Among many Tibetans, he has been remembered for military campaigns that killed Tibetans.[28] In contemporary popular histories such as *Old Xining* and the *Book of Qinghai*, his legacy as a warlord is condemned while certain aspects of his collaborations with Chiang Kai-shek's government are celebrated. Ma Bufang receives praise for helping repel British imperialism in Yulshul and for modernizing projects called the "Six Core Works," which included massive expansion of road infrastructure, afforestation, the reformation of the *baojia* registration system, and the promotion of education and literacy.[29] In the description of these projects, the connection to the modernizing initiatives and institutions of the Chinese center are emphasized time and again.

Yet the Ma family's profile in contemporary Xining is slight. As Susette Cooke has explained, the physical traces of Ma Bufang occupy an uncomfortable place in Xining City.[30] His former residence, built in 1942, is now the "Ma Bufang Residence Scenic Area" and is registered as the "Fragrant Cottage" in Qinghai Province's Register of Protected Cultural Relics. Located near Xining's train station, the site has received mercurial treatment by the authorities, having been opened and closed several times since 2006. In his *Book of Qinghai*, an illustrated work of popular history, the writer Tang Rongyao says that the residence serves as a "historical remembrance" of the region's final feudal rulers, writing that "here there is no longer any feel of the former landlords. Only the old mansion's depth and its solemn and mysterious atmosphere can transport visitors to the time of Ma Bufang and even to the Xining and Qinghai of that time." Yet the museum does have portraits of Ma Bufang and his Nationalist allies. Cooke has argued that the museum's avoidance of the troublesome topic of Ma's battles against Tibetans and communists and its embrace of his Inner Chinese–oriented political connections have sanitized Ma Bufang into yet another famous personage of the Nationalist era, facilitating "a safe Chinese state-centric narrative framework, uncontroversial for state officials or the majority of visitors."[31] Ma Bufang and his father Ma Qi can be commemorated insofar as they supported the military campaigns and developmental policies of the Chinese center, not for the ways they pursued their own regional political interests.[32]

On September 5, 1949, a reconnaissance cavalry unit of the People's Liberation Army entered Xining City, proclaimed the city liberated, and opened the way for the establishment of new China.[33] Over the following decades, communist municipal planners would transform the city's infrastructure and its commemorative urban landscape, both of which would orient Xining and its hinterland toward Inner China and the new temporality that communist liberation created. Xining would be rebuilt with the same rationalist spirit and gridded patterning that inspired early socialist urban development across Qinghai.[34] Urban plans determined locational siting for heavy industry, the train station, and new networks of roads and railways.[35] As Qinghai's administrative center and logistical hub, Xining would draw the eastern Plateau into the circulations of the PRC.

As Xining City expanded far beyond its old city walls to fill out the Huangshui River valley, the city adopted new dromonyms, or street names. The eastern portion of the city, where Ma Bufang's residence is located, gained avenues named "Establish the Country," "The Masses," and "Liberation," as well as "July First" and "August First" to commemorate the founding dates of the Chinese Communist Party and the Chinese Red Army, respectively.[36] The new dromonyms, placed in the same urban district from which Muslims rebels besieged the Qing garrison in 1895, speak both to the infrastructural modernization of the PRC and to the banishment of an inconvenient past of unstable regional ethnic and religious relations.[37] They, along with Tiger Mount, the Historical Personages of Hehuang, and popular historical publications, have worked to realize the chronotope of pacification that narratively locks Xining into circulation with historical and contemporary Chinese centers.

Myth and the Remembered City

Memorializing existing historical infrastructures and creating new memorials for figures and events support a linear temporal narrative, even if the enduring relationship they express appears timeless. In addition to this linear temporality, however, there is another temporality that operates through urban redevelopment: the mythic time of Chinese folklore. In Xining's municipal districts and administered counties, governments and businesses have used mythology to highlight Xining's connection to Chinese civilization. This has both given newly developed spaces an exotic flavor and incorporated them into a storytelling tradition that permeates the landscape with its characters and sites, making Xining inseparable from Chinese civilizational heritage. These myths have provided another enunciatory mode through which the chronotope of pacification binds Xining to the Chinese center.

The deployment of mythic temporality is at its strongest in the use of the Queen Mother of the West (Ch. *ximuwang*). Officials and writers have fused the landscape in and beyond Xining to the Queen Mother and the stories that circulate around her. Tang Rongyao begins the *Book of Qinghai* with the unearthing of a legend about the relationship between King Mu of the ancient Zhou kingdom and the Queen Mother of the West, who resided in Jasper Lake, located in the Kunlun Mountains. Tang acknowledges that the legend is likely unverifiable myth, although he suggests that there was perhaps a real kingdom situated among the mountains and grasslands of Qinghai. There, the Queen Mother could have been a nomadic chieftain, rather than a goddess. Tang uses the myth to narrate the geographical connection between the Kunlun Mountains of the northeastern Plateau and Inner China, and thus Qinghai and the rest of China. Though the ancient documents that could verify the Queen Mother's exact location have "disappeared into the dust of time," he finds traces of evidence across the province in caves and on pottery sherds that date back five thousand years.[38] The Queen Mother is both nowhere and everywhere, existing in myth and fragmentary materials, and the search for her in Qinghai becomes the search for her in China itself.

There are several historical sites in the city where the Queen Mother has a presence, including three massive elm trees that hulk over passersby on West Avenue in downtown Xining. Draped in colorful cloth and protected by thick guardrails, the elms' trunks compete for limited sidewalk space with pedestrians and shops. While municipal accounts differ on the exact age of the trees, they agree that the trees date to the mid-eighteenth century, the same period in which the Qing dynasty established Xining Prefecture (Ch. *Xining fu*) and rebuilt Xining's urban core and the yamen administrative complex.[39] That these trees have survived in one of Xining's busiest commercial areas is an infrastructural miracle, given that their roots are today wedged between building foundations and the tunnel of an underground mall. Material objects like the trees help ground continuity with the city's Sinocentric past and the era of strong central order when they were planted.

The elms also exist in mythical time. A *Qinghai News* article from 2014 recounted the fate of the city's "Eight Immortal Trees" (Ch. *baxian shu*): Long ago, a grove of old trees named after the mythic Eight Immortals grew outside the southwestern corner of the city wall, where a canal entered the city. These trees are both mythical and historical. In a story enriched with Daoist folklore, the Eight Immortals visited Jasper Lake to enjoy the Queen

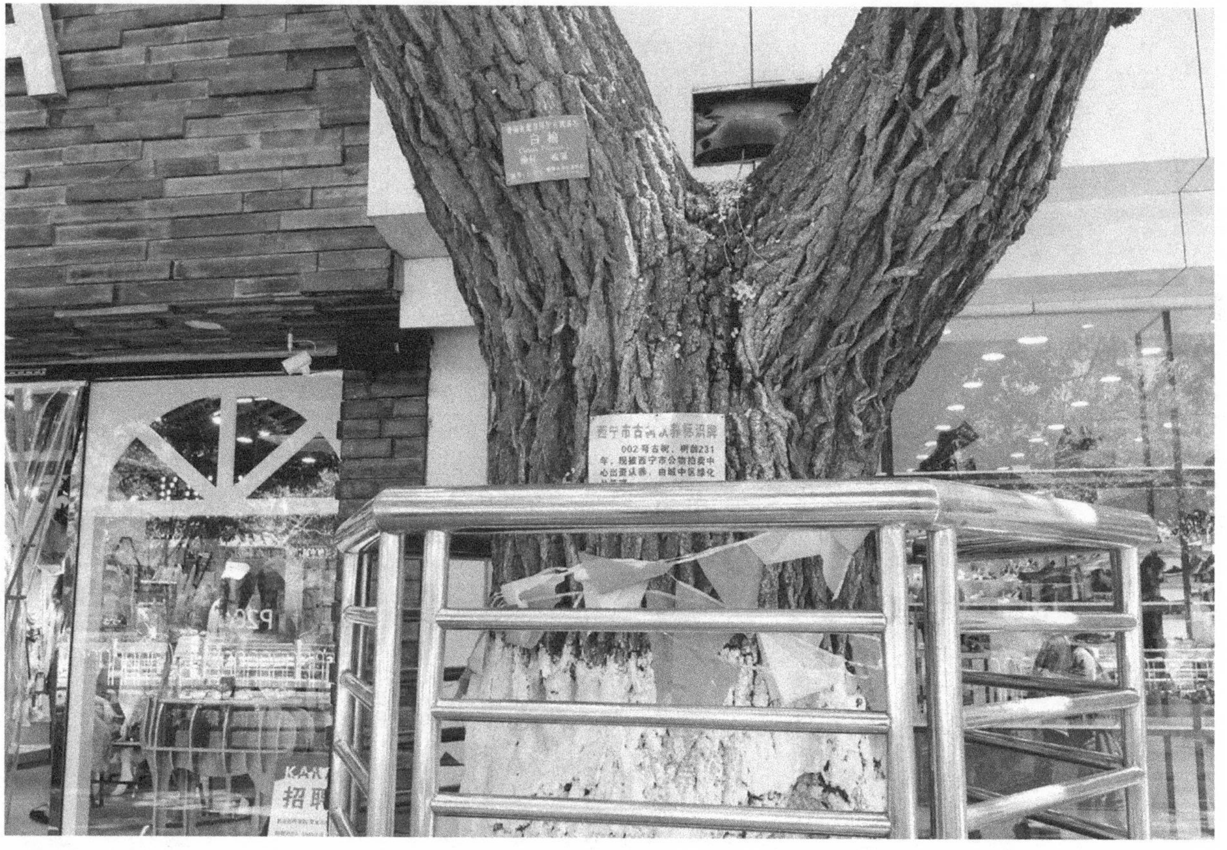

FIGURE 2.1. One of the old white elms located on the Great Crossing shopping boulevard.
Photo by the author, 2018.

Mother's hospitality. Afterward, they rested along the Huangshui River at the base of a great elm they spied from the clouds. The article explains that the historical grove is now all but gone, including four "immortal" trees chopped down during the urban expansion of the early socialist period. The only trees that remained, according to popular legend, are the three elms on West Avenue.[40]

The Queen Mother also dominates the peaks of Xining City. In the story of the Eight Immortals and the Queen, the pungent fragrance of ambrosia left over from a banquet attracted a pair of phoenixes to the forest grove; the mythical beings eventually alighted upon nearby South Mountain. This peak, today an urban park, also has the name Phoenix Mountain. Across the valley from that site, North Mountain is the location of a Daoist temple with a Hall of the Queen Mother. After being destroyed in a fire in 2007, the hall, a "prominent sacred site," was rebuilt to attract tourists and local sightseers alike. In Xining's Huangzhong District, a statue of the Mysterious Lady of the Nine Heavens, who is associated with Queen Mother folklore, has been constructed at "a key site from which Kunlun culture spread." At this tourist site, the Zhamalong Phoenix Mountain, visitors are encouraged to recall the mythical landscape created when the Mysterious Lady melted rock and gave the region a phoenix form.[41]

There is another female figure who grounds the relationship between the Tibetan Plateau and Inner China: Princess Wencheng. A datable historic figure, she was a princess in an alliance marriage between the Tang and Tibetan empires. The many stories concerning her trip to Lhasa to meet the Tibetan emperor Songsten Gampo and her subsequent life in Tibet have passed into legend.[42] Tang Rongyao describes her trip to Sun and Moon Mountain (Ch. *Riyue shan*)—today a popular tourist attraction located in Xining's Huangyuan County—as the geographic point at which she crossed from the sphere of Han Chinese culture into that of Tibetan culture. Her reluctance to leave behind the Tang dynasty in its heyday, the strangeness of the changing scenery and culture, and the hardship of her journey west all came to a head for her at this site, where Tang lore suggests the princess broke down in misery. In this melancholy folktale, Princess Wencheng—just like my Inner Chinese students in Xining centuries later—could only survey the bleak landscape around her in sadness.

The princess also figures into stories of the three elms. My friend Dege Metok, a retired teacher who had lived and taught in Xining for over a decade, remarked that "Han people like to say that they are gifts from Princess Wencheng." In this rendition, the trees were planted when the princess passed through the city en route to Lhasa. Of course, that couldn't be true,

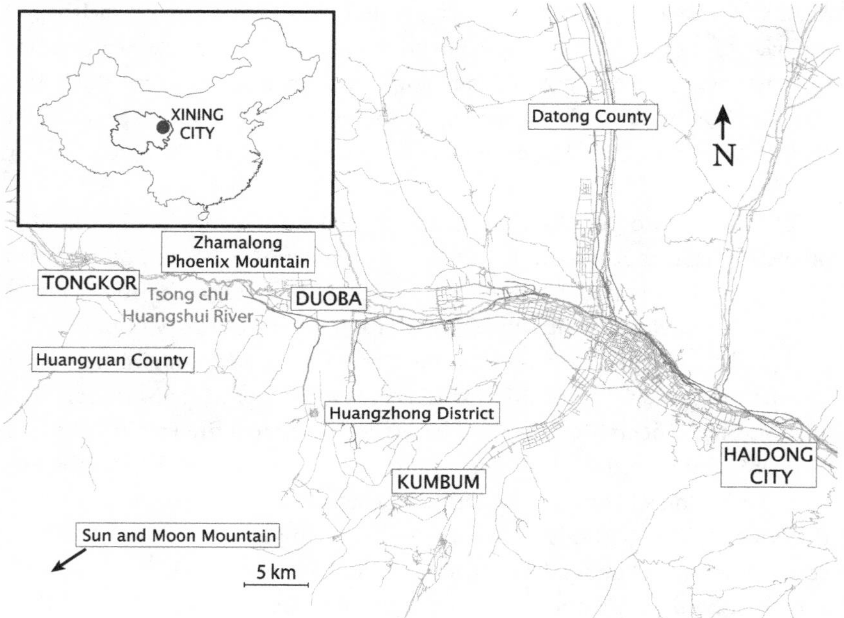

FIGURE 2.2. The Tsongkha or Huangshui Valley is defined by the Tsong Chu or Huangshui River, which flows from Tongkor in the west to Haidong City in the east. Inset map shows location of Xining in China.
Map by the author. Courtesy of OpenStreetMap contributors.

she told me, because they wouldn't still be alive today if it was. This story was just another way that the princess was narrated into the landscape, and, as Dege Metok suggested, it was a self-serving story that Han told Han.

Infrastructures have become sites through which China's mythologies reemerge in the present. Enunciated in memorialized and commercialized landscapes, these mythological infrastructures work to convince tourists, as well as local urban residents, that Xining is inseparable from Chinese heritage. These places work together to assemble a collective memory of Xining City that places it within a particular Sinocentric past. In contrast to male-dominated linear temporalities of political control, mythic temporalities are female dominated and emphasize landscape transformation and cultural connection at the Chinese periphery. They are both part of the chronotope of pacification that ties the frontier to Chinese civilizational heritage. Chronotopic closure is, however, difficult to attain. Even as urban authorities commemorate sites, erect statues, and affix dromonyms to traffic poles, Tibetans are assembling urban places with different temporalities, enunciating a different city.[43]

Remembering a Tibetan City

While I was discussing the history of the city with Dege Metok, she remarked on the striking difference between official history (Ch. *zhengshi*) and "wild" history (Ch. *yeshi*). As she explained it, official history was the controlled form of history that the state promoted in the media and in textbooks, while wild history was what people really think and say, often contradicting official history. Xining's Tibetans had a lot of interest in wild history. More than hearsay, this history was attached to written documents and stories about Xining and its environment that emphasized Tibetan sites and infrastructures. In assembling stories about a constellation of these places, Tibetans brought the memory of a Tibetan Xining, or Ziling, out of the wild.

The Tibetan name for the Huangshui River is the Tsong chu. This river defines Tsongkha, the region of Amdo Tibet that encompasses the headwaters of the Tsong chu near Tso Ngon Lake and Sun and Moon Mountain in the west through contemporary Ziling and beyond.[44] When Tibetans state that Ziling is historically a Tibetan city, they are drawing upon a history of Tibetan activity, secular and religious, in the Tsongkha valley. While Ziling is significant as a Tibetan place in the imaginations of contemporary Tibetans, it has not always been regarded in this way. The nineteenth-century Amdo regional history *The Oceanic Book* mentions Ziling mostly as a passage point for the three great Tibetan polymaths who came to Amdo in the tenth century.[45] Another Tibetan geography from this period, *The Mirror Which Illuminates All the Inanimate and Animate Things and Explains Fully the Great World*, describes Ziling as a Chinese fortress, which it locates by reference to the more significant Kumbum Monastery.[46] As the largest Tibetan monastery in Tsongkha, Kumbum was a much brighter node than Ziling in Tibetan infrastructural constellations.

Kumbum Monastery was established at the site where Tsongkhapa was born. Tsongkhapa, meaning "Man from Tsongkha," is the famed originator of the Gelug teaching of Tibetan Buddhism. His religious teachings inspired a movement that would remake the religious landscape of Tsonghka in the fourteenth century. While Gelug was not the only strain of Buddhist teaching in the region, many Gelug monasteries and branch monasteries can be found both within Xining and in neighboring prefectures and counties. This includes the Four Northern Monasteries, which my Tibetan friends frequently visited.[47] Kumbum, about twenty miles southwest of downtown Xining, is a very popular religious site and tourist attraction. A sandalwood tree there is said to have sprouted from the spot where blood spilled as the umbilical cord between Tsongkhapa and his mother was cut.[48] For Tibetan Buddhists, this tree is a site of pilgrimage with a relevance that far outshines the West Gate Avenue elms, which are steeped in Chinese legend.

While religious sites and circuits of pilgrimage are crucial for understanding a Tibetan history of Tsongkha, I found many Tibetans were also interested in looking into the wilder histories of places within Ziling, uncovering inconsistencies in official histories. Nyima, a Tibetan working as an editor in the city, was deeply interested in urban place names and what they indicated. One afternoon, as we passed the Qinghai Province People's Hospital while taking the bus through the Central District, Nyima told me in a conspiratorial tone, "In the time of Ma Bufang, that was called Qinghai Zhongshan Hospital, but the communists changed the name when they came." He described to me the urban improvements made by Ma Bufang, and then how the communists moved swiftly to take credit for the legacy of his administration: the hospitals, the schools, even the greening and road-building campaigns. Ma Bufang retained the capacity to rupture the Chinese chronotope of pacification, as he was a figure tied to an alternate urban development trajectory that the communists had attempted to co-opt.

Tibetan writers and urbanites were also interested in collecting and recalling Tibetan place origins and names, which often clashed with the Chinese toponyms that dominated street signs, tourist attractions, and media discourse. Just as toponyms are politically important for the Chinese state, they are also important to Tibetans. As Alexander Gardner has shown in the case of the prominent Buddhist scholar Kongtrül's nineteenth-century gazetteer of Kham places, the curatorial collection of place names can assert a distinct geographical identity in contexts of external political subordination.[49] And when the Chinese state elevates certain toponyms over others, as Carole McGranahan has argued, it acts to "reassemble [places] with new boundaries and sensibilities."[50] Today, Tibetans participate in a subaltern urban politics of place when they actively recall and enunciate Ziling's Tibetanness through toponyms and stories of places, socially mapping them onto the redeveloping landscape.

One site where official and wild histories come together is Mojia Street (Ch. *Mojia jie*), located downtown just southeast of the Great Crossing. While living in Xining, I had mostly heard of this place as the go-to site to buy cold noodles (Ch. *niang pi*) during the summer months. Jin Yude explains that the street is named after the Mo family, who in the thirteenth century migrated to Xining from Inner China. According to the Mo clan records, the family was publicly acclaimed for rebuilding the city's fortifications.[51] During the time of my fieldwork, Mojia Street was a tourist attraction, rebuilt to draw foot traffic to a pedestrian street marked off from traffic by ornamental wooden gates. A large embossed fresco at the site titled "Picture of Life in the Ancient City's Mo Family Ancestral Hall" recalled an earlier period of gustatory delight, depicting a halal beef noodle shop and a liquor store packed with bottles and pots. While the fresco, and the contemporary shopping street, celebrated regional diversity, they were also rooted in their strong Inner Chinese heritage.

But there is another Mojia Street. Tselo, who worked for a Tibetan-language television station, stressed to me that Mojia Street was originally Tibetan. He told me that the street was once the location of the Tsongkha Monastery where the Buddhist sangha would meet for meals called *mang ja*, a near homonym of Mojia. Jin Yude's *Old Xining* also includes an account of another thoroughfare called Mojia Road (Ch. *Mojia lu*), located near a now-vanished Buddhist temple. Jin offers it as the original "mang jia" but never explicitly states that the homonym is Tibetan. Another popular account of Mojia Lu in the urban booster book *Story of West District* also skirts the Tibetan history of the site.[52] Regardless of the monastery's true location, memories of the *mang ja* make suspect the dominant historical narrative of the Mojia Street site.

Tselo was a professed enthusiast of geographical knowledge, so when we sat down for an interview, he took me on a tour of other "wild" urban toponyms. Tselo said that at one time Tiger Mount rose above a large body of water. The name of this now-vanished water persists in the current Chinese street name Leng hu, or "Cold Lake." As he explained, *Leng* was a transcription of the first syllable in the Tibetan Lu Tso, or Serpent Deity Lake (Tib. *klu mtsho*). Long ago, Tiger Mount formed a platform from which people could participate in *chöba* offering ceremonies performed to placate wrathful lake-dwelling serpents. More generally, scholars have argued that such demon taming is part of the practice and rhetoric of the Tibetan Buddhist civilizing project.[53] The example of Serpent Deity Lake similarly suggests that Tibetans had been civilizing Ziling. While talking with Tselo, I realized that there was a much more elaborate history of Tibetan places in this valley than public commemorations and popular texts were enunciating. I asked Tselo where he had learned of all these names, and he insisted he had seen them in books and in magazines available in the bookstores of the Tibetan Market.

These Tibetan publications, written by local scholars and intellectuals, contain articles that provide historical explanations for Tibetan toponyms. One topic of concern these authors engage with is the name Ziling. Acknowledging the toponym is often assumed to be derived from the Chinese "Xining," several authors have rejected this etymology and provided alternative explanations. One argues that "Ziling" is derived from the sound of the hubbub (Tib. *zi zi ling ling*) that once arose from the Tsongkha valley floor. Another explanation is that the two syllables of Ziling are from two surnames that were once common among the Tibetan inhabitants of the region.[54] These articles are printed in government-approved publications and are not suppressed. The ideas they espouse, however, have not become enunciated in the urban landscape. Therefore, their audience is limited to educated readers of Tibetan journals and scholarly publications.

Nonetheless, other media forms have spread knowledge of the Tibetan city to a wider audience. Dobi Shadru, a well-known writer and the former director of the Qinghai Tibetan Research Association, has published extensively on the Tibetan history of Amdo. This has included writings on the eleventh-century Tsongkha kingdom, which was centered in Ziling, in periodicals including *Tso Ngon Tibetan Research* and *Amdo Research*.[55] Dobi Shadru has also helped popularize understandings of this Tibetan history through a map he designed that has reached a wide audience over the social media platform Weixin.[56] In his work of historical cartography, Dobi Shadru has detailed Tibetans' political, religious, environmental, economic, and demographic presence, offering an alternative urban history that highlights a Tibetan heritage.

While the Dobi Shadru map is ostensibly about the Tsongkha kingdom, it is not restricted to any one time period, language, or terminology. It uses the Tibetan terms "Ziling" and "Tsongkha kingdom," as well as the Chinese "Qingtang," to draw all these places together and emphasize their Tibetanness. While initially the map might appear anachronistic, placing later structures within the city, the writings of Dobi Shadru draw connections between older Tibetan sites and the later structures, suggesting continuity between the earlier era and still-existing places such as Hongjue Temple in the downtown. The map shows the location of several fortresses, including that of the Tsongkha king Jiaosiluo. The city walls encompass urban residences for the Tsongkha nobility, visitors' hostels, and a trading center in the location of the current Tibetan Market. Outside the walls are a large number of religious sites and many fields for pasturing horses. The map also corroborates the slippery toponyms that Tselo had told me about, such as the *mang ja* offering street and a site called Plain of One Hundred Thousand Serpents (Tib. *klu 'bum thang*) just north of Tiger Mount.

Dobi Shadru carefully and deliberately assembled the places on his map. The selective juxtaposition of Chinese toponyms next to Tibetan names suggests phonetic similarities and invites the map viewer to conclude that Chinese toponyms are transcriptions of Tibetan names that have more distinct meanings—for example, the Tibetan Doba Khar Okma or "Lower Valley Fortress" for the Chinese Duoba, an untranslatable toponym for a town located along the highway from central Xining to Huangyuan County.[57] The pictorial composition of the map is also important. The inclusion of a diminutive West Peace Prefect in the lower right-hand corner, outside the Qingtang city walls, decenters and diminishes Chinese control of the Tsongkha valley.

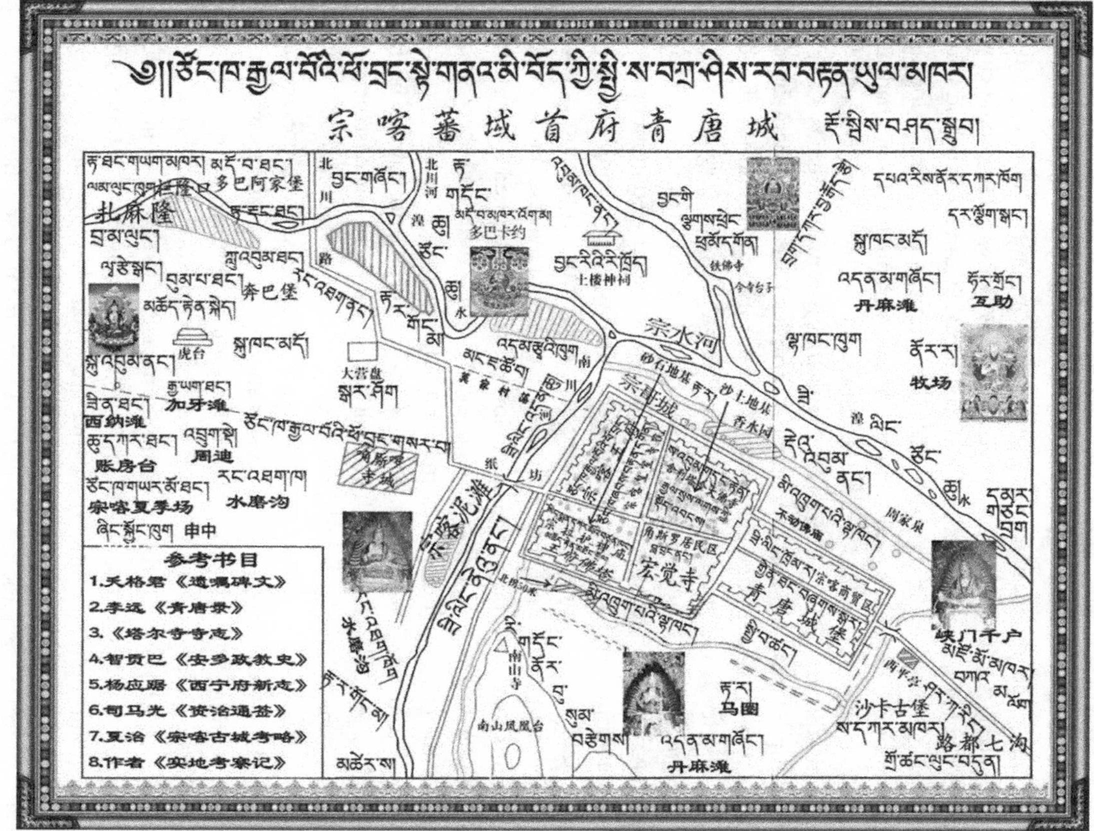

FIGURE 2.3. Dobi Shadru's map titled "Palace of the Tsongkha Kingdom, the Early Tibetan People's Community Land, and Tashi Rapten Fortress." It lists both Tibetan and Chinese toponyms.

Source: Dobi Shadru.

One of the weediest fields in Xining's wild history is the position of the city of Qingtang, which centers the map of Dobi Shadru. Located roughly at the site of Ziling's walled core, Qingtang was the capital of the Tsongkha kingdom for a century. Bianca Horlemann has suggested that the Chinese name "Qingtang" may stem from the Tibetan term "Yu Khang," or "Turquoise House," referring to the blue-green glint of tiled roofs.[58] The confederation that Jiaosiluo established lasted several generations and was continually embroiled in conflict with both the Tangut and Song empires.[59] His capital city was divided between the families of Tibetan political elites in the west and a diverse trading community in the east.[60] This city is difficult to materially locate in contemporary Xining, as evidenced by the cartography of Dobi Shadru, which uses the Chinese walled city as the infrastructural basis for Qingtang.[61]

In contemporary Xining, there is one site that is remembered as an architectural relic of Qingtang. Municipal authorities have monumentalized a long section of the rammed-earth wall that runs through the south of the Central District as Qingtang City Historic Ruins Park (Ch. *Qingtang cheng yizhi gongyuan*); the Chinese *yizhi* suggesting both a historic site and a ruin. In addition to colorful flowers, stone footpaths, and exercise equipment, the park has inscriptions that commemorate the old city of Qingtang that was abandoned after the Ming entered the region in the fourteenth century and established their garrison slightly to the north of the old walls. One inscription explains that the Xining Municipal Government established the park in 2006 in order to "rescue" (Ch. *zhengjiu*) Xining City's ruins and serve as a witness to the city's political, economic, and cultural history.

A friend told me that the municipal government had not always been interested in rescuing the ruins. The wall had been slated for destruction prior to its conversion into a park. It was only after protestation and lobbying by the Qinghai Tibetan Research Association that the site was preserved. Although Tibetans pushed for the preservation of the remaining wall, its commemoration would be part of the Sinocentric chronotope of pacification. This is indicated both by the Ming-style brick wall mock-up added to the site's entrance and the set of three maps in the park that illustrate the "evolution of Xining's urban form."[62] In just three maps, two thousand years of urban toponyms and boundaries are assembled together, starting with the ancient Western Peace Prefect and ending with contemporary Xining City. Although the park does provide a separate embossed map and history of the Qingtang-era divided city, the overall effect is to place that city within the *longue durée* of historical Xining. This contrasts sharply with the cartography of Dobi Shadru, which reframes Xining's history around the Tibetan Qingtang.

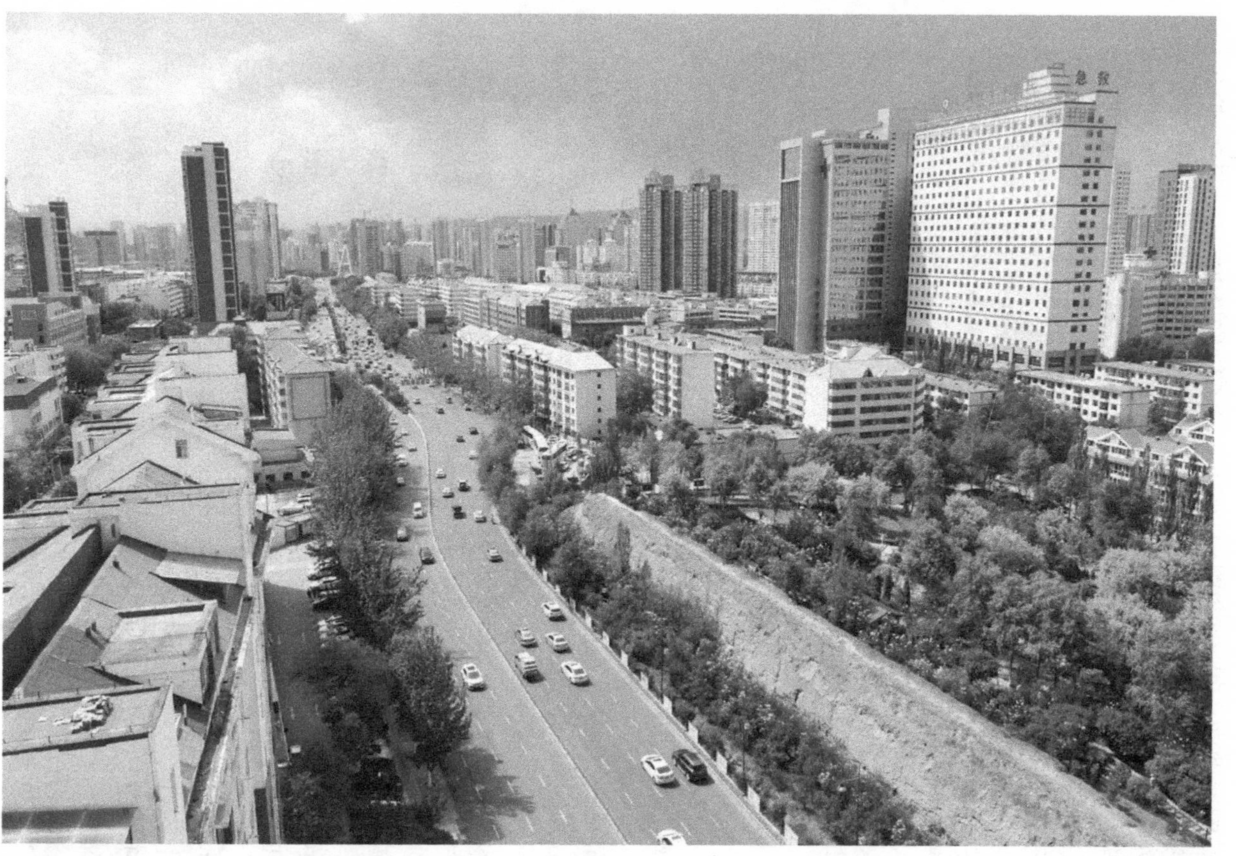

Figure 2.4. The Qingtang city wall is located between Qingtang City Historic Ruins Park (*right*) and the heavily trafficked Kunlun Avenue.
Photo by the author, 2018.

While the remaining Qingtang wall has been preserved, other areas that contribute to Tibetan urban memory were in the process of being destroyed and redeveloped during my fieldwork. When the missionary and suspected fabulist Évariste Huc passed through Xining in 1840, he noted that it was "of a very large extent, but its population is limited, and itself, in several parts, is falling into absolute decay."[63] He quickly moved on to other sites, including Tongkor (Tib. *stong skor*), which he described as a bustling center of commerce and intermingling languages. The town sits at a crossroads of trade routes and would become a center for the Amdo wool trade at the turn of the twentieth century.[64] Today the town's trading past is being used to draw tourists, and the use of the exotic-sounding Dange'er, another transcription, is used to promote the old town and shopping street. While Nyima encouraged me to visit Tongkor, stressing its past as a "Tibetan city," Dege Metok told me it was a waste of time because everything there was fake.

When I finally visited Tongkor in 2018, an elderly Tu shopkeeper whose family had moved from Huzhu to the town in the 1960s told me that the old-looking Confucian Temple and government structures were all selective restorations: none of them were original, save two stone blocks that held up a reconstructed gate. The rest, he said, had been destroyed during the Cultural Revolution. Nearby signs notified local inhabitants of an impending reconstruction project. The urban development authorities were calling for a redevelopment of the old "shantytown" (Ch. *penghu qu*), and some of these buildings, with their locally renowned wooden door decorations, bore the character *zheng*, denoting state requisition of land for planned redevelopment. The new plan would preserve some of the old housing stock while modernizing the district's commercial amenities. While Tongkor continued to vanish, the memory of it as a Tibetan place with a Tibetan name and trading center that once surpassed that of Xining lived on.

Urban redevelopment under the civilizing machine has led to the destruction of some old urban infrastructures and the reconstruction and renaming of others. These processes have unfolded over a landscape rich with history and legend. Stories told about places, ranging from explanations of local toponyms to the origin of trees and earthen walls, have emplotted urban places within particular narrative temporalities. Official commemoration and popular storytelling both enunciate the material environment, making meaningful urban assemblages' endless kaleidoscope of possibilities.[65] They make the city a cohesive place from its many places and pasts. They also allow for many cities to be copresent simultaneously.

This chapter has argued that there are three types of memory-making practices at work in Xining that codify the urban in different ways. The first

FIGURE 2.5. An old residential alleyway in Tongkor prior to its partial demolition and reconstruction. Photo by the author, 2018.

practice is a chronotope of pacification that relies on a narrative of uninterrupted Chinese historical dominance in Xining and its hinterland, a kind of extratemporal hiatus. This chronotope relies on histories of material sites in the city, some of which are turned into parks, as well as commemoration of historical personages and events. As toponyms, dromonyms, statues, or gazetteer entries, people and places are marshaled to serve a narrative of political and infrastructural connectivity with Inner China. The second practice is also part of this chronotope, but uses the temporality of a mythology that binds Xining to China's legendary landscape. Related commemorations may work from toponyms or features in the natural environment; they seek to re-enchant the region for commercial purposes and to secure its status as an integral part of shared Chinese folk traditions. In both practices, China bestows order and civilization to its western periphery.

The histories and legends in books, monuments, and stories corroborate one another only imperfectly, if at all, as in the case of Xining's West Gate Avenue elms. This opens a fertile space for "wild history" to enter into the urban imagination, where it can loosen the dominance of official histories and the publicly commemorated landscape. For my Tibetan interlocutors, this third enunciatory practice was important to assert that Ziling had a distinctively Tibetan past. In the illiberal context of the Chinese frontier city, commemorative naming is unable to "open a space for the contestation of collective memory" in deliberative forums.[66] Instead, Tibetans draw upon different parts of a shared material assemblage to enunciate a subaltern urbanism that coexists with the dominant heritage imaginary. Working from an authoritative but less privileged scholarly tradition, Tibetan scholars have studied regional toponyms and fixed them to material sites. These findings have circulated in articles, through conversation, and over social media. Additionally, cosmic infrastructures that work to civilize the landscape for Tibetan Buddhism, such as Serpent Deity Lake, and towns that once outshone Xining, such as Tongkor, all play roles in the narration of Ziling and the Tsongkha valley as a Tibetan place.

By assembling memories of Ziling, Tibetans have created a subaltern urbanism that challenges the codifications of the Sinocentric civilizing machine. By so doing, they reroute the state's contemporary valorization of the urban as an essentially Chinese developmental project to show that the urban is not external to Tibetan history and civilization. The next chapter explores how urban Tibetans have navigated urban redevelopment projects increasingly promoted as self-consciously "civilized" and optimized to transform Xining's urban inhabitants.

Chapter 3

Civilized City

Xining has many qualities that make it a Tibetan city: its considerable Tibetan population, its Tibetan markets and businesses, and its repertoire of materialities and toponyms that have been assembled into a Tibetan Ziling. For many Tibetans who come to Xining, however, it is the city's concentration of resources and promise of good living that makes it an attractive, and even necessary, place to dwell. Xining's position as a center for politics, economics, and education has been reinforced in twenty-first-century provincial and municipal urbanization plans. These plans have not only created Xining as a center—they have created Xining as an expanding and shifting series of centers. Within the administrative city, urban redevelopment has produced relative cores and peripheries among the city's districts, with hierarchized economic and social values attached to them. This uneven developmental process has had significant outcomes for Tibetans, who don't want to be left out of the resources and social status that urban centers provide. As Jamsto discussed in chapter 1, certain districts were more associated with the "urban" and the "modern." These were the places Xining's Tibetans, and urbanites in general, wanted to be.

The redevelopment and reordering of the city's spaces have occurred along with shifts in population governance and urban aesthetics that have brought Xining in line with national urban aspirations while also working to distinguish the city as culturally unique. This chapter explores how different programs of civilizational development have been deployed as material and aesthetic practices with important outcomes for where Xining's Tibetans live and work. Moreover, the accompanying revaluation of intra-municipal spaces has peripheralized and devalued neighborhoods associated with minoritized ethnic groups. As a result, these groups, including Tibetans and Muslims, risk exclusion from middle-class urban citizenship unless they gain experience with and are assimilated into the bodily and aesthetic order created by the state-led civilizing machine.

Twenty-first-century Xining has participated in several competitions and initiatives that have sought to improve the quality of the urban environment and the etiquette and health of the urban population. In this sense, the civilizing machine works as a biopolitical machine that transforms the spaces and rhythms of everyday life. Ash Amin and Nigel Thrift have understood urban "biopolitical machines" as coordinating "material and routines [that] settle and habituate distinctive regimes of social order and authority . . . in ways that make the regimes seem natural, necessary, ordinary."[1] Planners and developers have worked together to rebuild Xining and other Chinese cities as standard-bearers of happiness, civility, and development. In contemporary propaganda and urban management, these motifs have emerged as slogans, behavioral guidelines, and seductive architecture and landscape aesthetics that make the realization of China's models of urban civilization a seeming necessity for social and economic progress.[2] Slogans like "If I am civil, Xining is civil; if I am honest, Xining is honest; if I am beautiful, Xining is beautiful" are more than empty rhetoric; they reveal the underlying logic and goals of municipal practices that aim to assemble places and bodies into the civilized city, remolding urban citizens' subjectivities so that they can assist in the project of the state-led civilizing machine.

As Carolyn Cartier has argued, through these practices "the party-state continues its attempts to control social behavior and create a future nation of uniformly 'civilised,' ideologically homogenous and modern places—a Chinese version of the 'world class' city."[3] As part of the discourse that justifies urban redevelopment to achieve economic and social progress, "civilization" undergirds how China's growing number of urban residents seek to conduct themselves, distinguish high-quality places, and become responsible urban citizens. Xining is the relative center of the urban civilizing project on the eastern Tibetan Plateau; within Xining, relative centers of civilizing have also emerged. My interlocutors imagined their own position in the city, and their own trajectory in securing the trappings of their middle-class dreams, within the landscape of this ever-shifting material and social geography. They also pushed back against some of the logic and practices of the policies that created these geographies, even as they participated in them.

This chapter demonstrates how the politics of place has played out as Xining has become a "civilized city." The continuous redevelopment and proliferation of "centers" is intertwined with the project of civilized urbanization insofar as certain places came to be seen as having high quality and high levels of civilization, and others as lacking these qualities and therefore less desirable. The following section explores the civilized-city campaign and its role in providing practices that cultivate urban civility, such as discouraging uncivil behaviors like jaywalking, shouting, and spitting. The next section discusses the importance of "centers" for business, hospital access, and other public goods and services, and how urban Tibetans' lives have been shaped as Xining's centers have changed. Following this are several sections examining how a form of aesthetic urbanization based on notions of ecological civilization and local ethnic culture has added value to urban residential places in Xining. Authorities have distilled the diverse landscape and peoples of the eastern Tibetan Plateau into a unique aesthetic. By unifying the design of the urban landscape, urban planners have dampened alternative possibilities for ethnic expression and the politics of place.

Governmentality, the Urban Middle Class, and the Civilizing Machine

Recently, scholars have explored the intercity competition and policy sharing that have contributed to a boom in visually spectacular urbanization in Asia and beyond.[4] In addition to erecting aesthetic centerpieces that demonstrate national economic prowess and political strength, urbanization has been used by state authorities to create "milieus of intervention" in which, as Aihwa Ong has argued, spectacular new material environments have become sites for neoliberal governmental practices that foster productive and responsible citizenship.[5]

Through domestic intercity competitions and international urban knowledge and policy transfers, Chinese municipalities have striven to create exemplary environments for raising economic and social developmental levels.[6] Models of political practice have circulated with the careers of officials and experts, moving from city to city and across regional boundaries. Innovation and success in one place can lead to a model being deployed more widely elsewhere.[7] Urbanization in an authoritarian state doesn't operate simply in a top-down fashion, however; there is overlap between liberal and illiberal urban governmental practices. Illiberal governmental practices found in China's urban environments overlap with those in liberal states that share similarities such as a consumer economy and neoliberal self-governance dynamics. Populations in cities across the world are subject to governmental practices that seek to shape their behaviors while also empowering people to shape one another.[8]

The various civilizing projects that have been carried out in twenty-first-century Xining are cut from the cloth of urbanization projects that are designed to create spectacular urban landscapes and to cultivate the bodies and minds of the urban citizenry. For example, Xining has competed with other Chinese cities to be nationally recognized as a "civilized city" (Ch. *wenming chengshi*). Key to becoming a civilized city is the correction of citizens' bodily behavior and the cultivation of a landscape that encourages better behavior.[9] Michel Foucault's explication of the "two poles of development" that have emerged to become key parts of modern governmentality is instructive for examining the civilizing machine's power over urban life, including not only individual citizen's bodies, but also the overall urban social body.[10] These two poles are the anatomo-political and biopolitical, and they both play a significant role in the post-reform Chinese city.[11] In the former the governmental focus is on "the body as a machine: its disciplining, the optimization of its capabilities . . . its integration into systems of efficient and economic control."[12] In the civilized city, this has been manifested in the pedestrian bridges and waiting areas that aim for the internalization of "civility" in urban public behavior, as well as more coercive measures such as the erection of traffic median fences that obstruct jaywalkers' paths.[13]

The other pole is biopolitics, which has focused on the regulation of "the species body" and investments in its biological success.[14] Security mechanisms that strengthen social security and reduce risk to life improve the general level of health throughout the population and "optimize a state of life" across the urban "field of intervention."[15] Rebuilding an urban environment with more modern facilities and cleaner neighborhoods is a biopolitical practice that, in tandem with the anatomo-political cultivation of a more courteous population, makes the city more livable, raises the quality of the urban population, and enables a form of self-government that reinforces state interests.[16] As Xining's mayor Zhang Xiaorong stated in an interview he gave after Xining was awarded the designation of a National Civilized City in 2017, "As people participate in the process of building a civilized city, they themselves work to better the environment around them and to make better the disposition and spiritual face of the city."[17] As empowered urban "participants" (Ch. *canyuzhe*) in the realization of a new, improved city, members of the urban population join their bodies and capacities to the assemblage of the civilizing machine.

Also important for the realization of the civilized city is the coding into its urban landscape of spiritual and aesthetic forms of Chinese civilization. These both make the city attractive to capital and allow it to become a place that facilitates the development of a high-quality population focused on economic production, participation in the private market, and respectable and responsible social conduct. The concept of the civilized city is part of a certain self-imagining that Chinese leaders have increasingly promoted in the post-reform period. As Ann Anagnost explains, the term *wenming*, or civilization, calls attention to a specific version of Chinese modernity that emphasizes refinement of "human quality," or *suzhi*, and its ability to bring about social development and economic growth.[18] In government rhetoric and in popular usage, *suzhi* is something that a place or person can have in high or low amounts or lack altogether; it indexes a teleological modernization project within which Chinese civilization is both an ongoing process of the cultivation of quality and the apogee of social progress and refinement.

Like all forms of urban redevelopment, "civilized" redevelopment is an uneven process that produces spatial winners and losers. Civilized cities are valorized as the most refined places in China's territorial administrative hierarchy, and when they emerge on the eastern Tibetan Plateau—a region that in Open Up the West campaign rhetoric has been associated with poverty and backwardness and with lacking urbanization, consumerism, and *suzhi*—the civilizing mission of the Chinese state comes into sharp relief against its developmental other.[19] Not only can rural bodies bring uncultivated behaviors into the city, but urban districts and neighborhoods with high concentrations of Tibetans and Muslims can come to be stigmatized as vestiges of backwardness incompatible with modern urban civilization.

Civilized urban development privileges some urban places and peoples over others. Even as these divisions occur, a myth of shared social mobility in contemporary China has pushed the aspirational category of the middle class into the forefront of urban lifestyles. Following the insights of E. P. Thompson, Li Zhang has argued that the emerging Chinese middle class (Ch. *zhongchan jieceng*) is a subjective category that does not rigidly correspond to a statistical reality. It is a condition toward which Chinese people increasingly aspire and which is understood to be obtainable in urban places.[20] The middle class is not a bounded category of wealth or income, but is relative to rural places and a less prosperous past. Li Zhang has used the term "the spatialization of class" to describe the geographical sorting of urban residents based on their purchasing power. Urbanites can obtain the relative position of the middle class through participation in the commodity housing market. As urban socialist legacies have been demolished and cities rebuilt within the land markets of contemporary municipal territories, people's work and housing are increasingly separate, and well-positioned urban residents can select where they want to live through the buying of private property in areas thought to be safe, convenient, and likely to benefit from rising property values.[21]

The state's allowance of the formation of a "middle class" in private housing communities has been a deliberate attempt to create urban subjects who self-govern as they prioritize economic stability and family success but, as Luigi Tomba has explained, remain "politically docile" and are "willing to participate in an ethical and moral community in the name of social stability, consumer rights, and [middle-class] virtues."[22] Private housing communities are part of a state effort to generate middle-class neighborhoods that potentially all members of society can eventually enter into.[23] This governmental vision implicitly acknowledges that economic development will be spatially and temporally uneven. Furthermore, its economic focus presumes that national standards of consumerism and morality can simply be absorbed by urban populations participating in these urban spaces. Yet as the spatialization of class raises the value of middle-class neighborhoods, it devalues neighborhoods of the urban poor and, in particular in Xining, those of non-Han ethnic groups that are already associated in developmental policy with a lack of quality. Whether engaged in public or private work, Tibetans aspiring to be middle class in Xining face unique social challenges because of their status as a peripheralized ethnicity in China.[24]

Xining as Center

In the early 2010s, the Yulshul-born businessman Kelsang and his colleagues decided to take advantage of the good market conditions in Xining and open a downtown luxury goods store. Over the summer of 2017, I spent several long days at their shop. There, Kelsang explained to me that location in large cities was a necessity for their business because it allowed efficient access to retail services and the city's large market. He described Xining's good conditions in this regard as a result of Chinese officials' emphasis on top-down planning and systematic creation of unequal opportunities through development. "I consider this to be the problem," he told me, blowing the steam off of his mug of green tea. "People in the government like to say 'center.' They say political center, economic center, cultural center. Whatever kind of center. Everything is focused on this place—the center. So, they take all of the opportunities and monopolize them into just one place." The result was a clear problem, and one that Kelsang acutely felt when he considered opening stores in smaller Tibetan towns closer to his home place. "There are no opportunities in other places. There is no way you can live in other places." Though he considered it, it just wasn't feasible to do business outside officially supported "centers."

Beijing, Kelsang told me, was the key center in the country for economic opportunities, education, superior health care, and a host of amenities. For Tibetans, cities like Chengdu, Xining, and Kyegudo (the urban seat of Yulshul Prefecture) were centers of various sizes that attracted many people in search of access to such resources. But these centers didn't simply grant opportunities; they were actually the results of poor planning that compelled people to migrate to them: "In the cities [Ch. *chengshi*] there are very few opportunities for work. [Newly arrived migrants] think that if they just stay squatting in the street, then work will come to them. They don't think they have to go out to find it. Then they are hungry and must go out again to find another place with opportunities." Drifting from center to center, some Tibetans, like construction workers, labored to profit from these places' redevelopment. Better off were businessmen who had enough means and information to prepare and plan for municipal redevelopment, like the shopkeepers in the Tibetan Market discussed in chapter 1.

Kelsang's perception of the "center problem" in Xining reflects an element of urban planning found throughout the PRC that has been amplified as China's cities have increased in number and areal extent. The Chinese state has continuously engaged in administrative rescaling and the rebalancing of regional economies as various levels of government have attempted to raise their developmental level.[25] China's cities are made in blueprint long before they are built. The development of the city of Xining has been outlined in urban master plans (Ch. *zongti guihua*) that both locate and rank the cities' urban centers and outline axes of development that prefigure urban expansion and transportation circulation. For example, in the early 2010s, Xining's urban layout and land-use plans for 2020 included three city centers (Ch. *chengshi zhongxin*) and ten area centers (Ch. *pianqu zhongxin*).[26] The bigger the center, the more developed it would be and the more desirable for business, transportation, and urban citizens' other practical concerns.

Kelsang's coworker Gyeltsen was also from Yulshul. He had lived in Xining for a decade, which he calculated by counting the number of New Years he had spent in the city. Like Kelsang he was a homeowner in Xining. He had an apartment near South Mountain, which he shared with his uncle and other relatives. Both of these men had business training they had acquired through development workshops rather than degree programs. They had chosen to open their store in Xining in part because the market in Yulshul was too small, and the market in Chengdu too saturated. Chengdu has a sizable Tibetan commercial district, which, as Trine Brox has observed, has emerged as a central place for that city's Tibetan population. This is due to a variety of factors, including its transportation connectivity to Kham, the city's concentration of Sichuan Province's best medical care, and its access to customers ranging from Tibetans to Han Chinese Buddhists and foreign tourists.[27] But with these opportunities have come high rent and competition. As Gyeltsen put it, "The requirements for living in Chengdu are too great." Xining was a better choice because its property was more affordable, its market was less competitive and therefore more accessible, and regional urban development was concentrating opportunities in its redeveloping spaces.

Jigmé Tendzin, the owner of the cell phone store located in the Tibetan Market discussed in chapter 2, told me that he thought Xining was a great place to do business because the market attracted many Tibetans who were otherwise purchasing Mandarin-language cell phones, which were available in the many smaller shops across the city and in smaller towns. He saw Xining as having market potential, and he hoped to open more Tibetan-language electronics stores there in the future. Although he liked the more open cultural climate in Xining, he wanted to move back to his home in Chabcha to be closer to his family and friends, but felt that the market back home was insufficiently developed for good business. Just as Kelsang and Gyeltsen chose Xining over Yulshul, Jigmé decided on Xining over Chabcha.

Gyeltsen had plans to open up more stores in Yulshul and in other parts of Xining. When I spoke with him, he was eyeing the market in Xining's New Lake District, a recently redeveloped subdistrict located in the West District. The New Lake District was a new, up-and-coming area that entrepreneurs I spoke with were certain would soon have the most lucrative market opportunities in the city. As he explained to me, "At the moment the best place is near New Tranquillity Square, where the Starbucks is located." For Tibetan entrepreneurs, locating the best places to make money was an ongoing process. The Limeng Commercial Alley Pedestrian Street, where a Starbucks opened during the course of my fieldwork, had only become popular over the last several years. It received a lot of foot traffic and was packed with crowds clutching branded shopping bags and high-end milk teas. Gyeltsen thought it was crucially important to have people who were willing to spend. For this reason, he ranked second the still-developing New Lake District, "where there are many young people and tourists who like to spend money," third the mall and shopping street near West Gate, and lastly the Central

District, where he and Kelsang had their store. "There are a lot of people here, but they don't all spend money," he told me, motioning to the passersby out the window.

As the city redeveloped, what was a good place one year could become a bad place the next. A former salt-processing worker named Lobsang lived in Yulshul New Village in the West District, but he traveled to Xining's East District every day to work at his caterpillar fungus business. Like many of my interlocutors, he continued to draw a public retirement pension from his work in the salt factory, but he had been making more money through private business opportunities in the city. He and other Tibetan caterpillar fungus businessmen were planning to open a new market near the Small Bridge area of Xining's North District. They were hoping that this new market, which would be an assemblage of independent Tibetan businesses, would generate its own center of gravity. The goal was to create a go-to market that would bypass the older market area in the city's East District where they were currently based. This was to cut profit-taking Muslim middlemen out of the trade as well as to be positioned in a more desirable part of the city.

Xining was not only a good place for these Tibetans to do business; it was also a focal point for schooling and access to health care. Tendzin was a retired cadre from Ping'an, a district of the recently established Haidong City, located just east of Xining. He told me that he came to Xining because it was the center for some of the best things in the province: restaurants, entertainment, parks for his morning walks, and so on. His home in the Central District was also close to the best hospitals. As he had a history of heart trouble, it was important for him to be near the hospitals. Indeed, he had even sold his house in Haidong to help pay for his home in Xining. Despite Haidong's recent urban expansion, Tendzin did not feel that that city was sufficiently developed. The freeway and urban road network connecting Haidong to neighboring Xining took too long to traverse. It was better to simply be in Xining.

My interlocutors similarly viewed schools outside Xining as inferior to those in the city. Xining's Chinese-medium education system was viewed as the best in the province and was frequently cited as an important reason for coming to and staying in the city. Dege Metok, the retired teacher, confirmed this. "Xining has the best schools. The only schools that can compare are those in Tsolho County. Tibetans from all the six [Tibetan ethnic autonomous] prefectures know this and want to come here to buy apartments." Dege Metok was referring to the massive Tibetan-medium boarding school complex in Trika, located in Tsolho (Ch. *Hainan*) County. Although Tibetan-language education was widely viewed as important for maintaining Tibetan culture, a topic further explored in chapter 4, Xining's Chinese-medium education was the best in the province.[28] Kelsang's children went to Xining schools, a decision that was made after he had established his business in the city. The location of the apartment he purchased was influenced both by its being a good investment in a new development and because he and his wife wanted their son and daughter to be able to attend school and play with the children of family members living nearby.

Xining has attracted many Tibetans because it is a center. Within this center there is a hierarchy of commercial and residential areas where Tibetans have tried to establish their homes and businesses. Xining's relative affordability and accessibility compared to Chengdu, as well as its potential for business compared to county towns, have made the city an attractive site that has encouraged further migration of family members to the city. Tibetans explained their reasons for coming to Xining in practical terms such as the pursuit of education and the securing of comfortable housing, all reasonable and responsible objectives in line with national trends that promote conspicuous consumption and the adoption of middle-class values.[29] The material redevelopment of centers shapes the hierarchy of desirable places within and beyond Xining. Moreover, this urbanization process is entangled with discourses of civilization and belonging that influence Tibetans' opinions about Xining's centers and their places within them.

Civilizing the City

The most attractive centers in Xining City are places that have been recently developed on greenfield land, or have been recently redeveloped on the sites of older buildings. Xining's 2017 effort to become a nationally recognized "civilized city" brought into relief the benefits that these "centers" had in the city, insofar as newly developed places became emblematic of *suzhi*, civility, and relative developmental progress. Some of my Tibetan research participants agreed that making Xining a civilized city was overall a good thing, and they praised the most civilized parts of the city for their cleanliness and accessibility. At the same time, they could be skeptical of the logic and urban management of the civilized city, whose governmental practices focused on bodies and behavior to raise the city's overall level of civilization.

Over the summer of 2017, city officials were at pains to demonstrate to the national evaluation team tasked with appraising civilization criterion that Xining was a shining example of civility and orderliness. At this point, the entire country was in the final year of the fifth national competition, and cities, urban districts, and villages were scrambling to earn points necessary to qualify as exceptionally civilized in their categories. Given the city's rank over these other administrative spaces, to win the designation of "National Civilized City" was to obtain the highest such honor in the country. Like earlier communist propaganda campaigns that enshrouded cities in written and printed propaganda, the National Civilized City campaign has used the medium of the visual environment to convey its rhetoric and persuade the population to adopt civilized practices.[30] The Qinghai Xining City Civilization Office stressed the need to turn people into agents of civilized manners by promoting "building a 'civilized city' and educating 'civilized people.'" Public venues were to become places to promote this dual goal, raising the overall civilizational level of the city.[31]

The competition broke civilizational progress into a quantifiable scheme that an evaluation team could easily use to read the urban landscape. This included Communist Party publicity work, which resulted in a multitude of signs, posters, and banners encouraging people to change their behavior. In Xining the propaganda targeted everyday behaviors in shared spaces and emphasized that "the entire body of urban residents should together supervise the care of the city. When uncivilized phenomena occur, work to dissuade and curb them. Contribute your own strength to create a civilized city and build a fine home together."[32] Such uncivilized activities include smoking in prohibited areas, shouting and littering, spitting on sidewalks, dumping trash out of high-rise windows, public defecation, and a variety of pedestrian and vehicular practices that disrupt traffic.

The rush to realize the civilized city during the campaign was an exercise in disciplinary power. Officials deployed a variety of measures to regulate bodies by manipulating public space. Public employees used sidewalk paint to trace out "Civilized Waiting Areas" on the sidewalks of intersections, and volunteers held out "civility ropes" (Ch. *wenming de shengzi*) that prevented people from crossing streets until they received the correct traffic light.[33] Mr. Qi, a Tu ethnicity acquaintance, dismissed these ropes as ineffective, laughing that they were used to "herd people like sheep." More effective traffic control measurements included fences and pedestrian bridges, deployed to stem jaywalking. Many of my friends and interlocutors thought these measures would raise the safety of the city and the manners of their urban neighbors.

Dege Metok smiled when I mentioned road-crossing discipline but also suggested, "Many people say that this is a forceful [Ch. *qiangzhi*] way to passively [Ch. *beidong*] cultivate people. But I think that it works. Without ropes, people run through intersections. Without signs, people smoke in restaurants with pregnant women. I think it starts to work after a while."

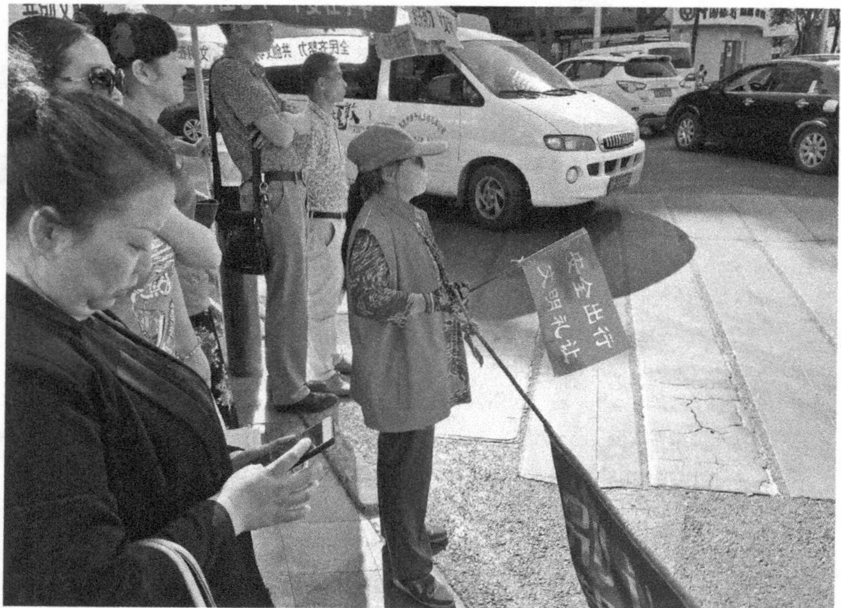

FIGURE 3.1. Preparing for the "civilized city" evaluation, a volunteer holds a rope preventing pedestrians from jaywalking. The flag she holds carries the message "Proceed safely. Treat others with civility and courtesy" (Ch. *anquan chuxing wenming lirang*).
Photo by the author, 2017.

Tendzin, the retired cadre who spoke in a thick Qinghai topolect, insisted that the civilizing campaign was a necessity. Located in a long backward and rural part of the country, Xining, he said, lacked civilization and needed the campaign to help develop the city. He lamented that drivers ran red lights and that pedestrians jaywalked and littered. For him, contemporary Nanning in Guangxi Province was comparable to Xining in the past: relaxed and unrushed, but held back by an undeveloped economy and poor facilities. Once Xining reached a higher level of development like Beijing, the streets, he said, would cease to be confused. Xining was in a difficult midway position in its transition between backwardness and attaining a higher level of development (Ch. *fada*).

Gyeltsen also thought that the campaign was good for the city because of Xining's chaotic patterns of human and vehicular traffic. The civilization campaign only bothered him when it led to traffic police or neighboring businesses harassing him for improperly parking his work truck or motorbike on the sidewalk. Kelsang, on the other hand, was skeptical of the civilizing program because it treated people as passive (Ch. *beidong*) objects rather than active (Ch. *zhudong*) agents. In contrast to Dege Metok, he saw passive measures as ineffective and superficial. He criticized fellow Tibetans who uncritically accepted urban cleanliness as a measure of progress. It was for him just the latest harebrained measure promoted by Xining's inconsistent leadership and contradictory urban initiatives.

Kelsang questioned what it was that civilization was supposed to accomplish. "Is Xining a civilized city?" With a sigh and a laugh, he asked, "For civilization, what do you do? Clean a little bit, make things hygienic? These count as civilization, do they?" He was skeptical of the entire enterprise. "Civilization is an ideology, isn't it? But civilization needs a lot of time and only then can bring about such things. Or is it just carrying out activities?" Kelsang suggested that the campaign was too rapid and superficial to accomplish its goal, a change in ideology (Ch. *yishi xingtai*): "Will a city become civilized after one or two months? In what place in all the heavens would you find such a thing?" Because the changes remained at the level of visual tidiness, the civilizing process (Ch. *wenminghua*) was, as an ideological transformation, destined for failure. "So maybe things are cleaner and people's manners improve slightly. But what is the system [Ch. *zhidu*]? What is the underlying reasoning? This can't be sustained over time." Relying mostly on disciplinary measures, the practices were too superficial to take hold: "Are we just the same as robots? If civilization needs a new city to take form, it is not natural." For Kelsang, new environments, even at a massive scale, wouldn't be enough to change people.

Despite the questionable methods by which authorities hoped to create a civilized city, many of the urban Tibetan homeowners I talked to concurred that the campaign's measures had fostered some desirable improvements in people's activities. They hoped it would make the city, and in particular the places they lived, friendlier, cleaner, and nicer to live in. But civilization and its associations were not distributed evenly across the city. Urban propaganda usually employed images of high-rise buildings, gleaming in steel and glass, to persuade people to desire a civilized city. Planners and publicists had a clear model in mind in their imagery of the civilized city, and it was not that of the remedial ropes and fences constructed ad hoc in older parts of the city. Newer urban subdistricts such as New Lake District were widely accepted as the most civilized parts of the city; they were ready-built for this purpose.

Xining's redevelopment has not only changed the material centers of the city, creating new places largely seen as having good amenities, but it has also created new centers for civilization, places where people's behaviors and speech, and the built environment's modern aesthetics, combine to cultivate high-quality citizens and good living. This urbanizing process has also

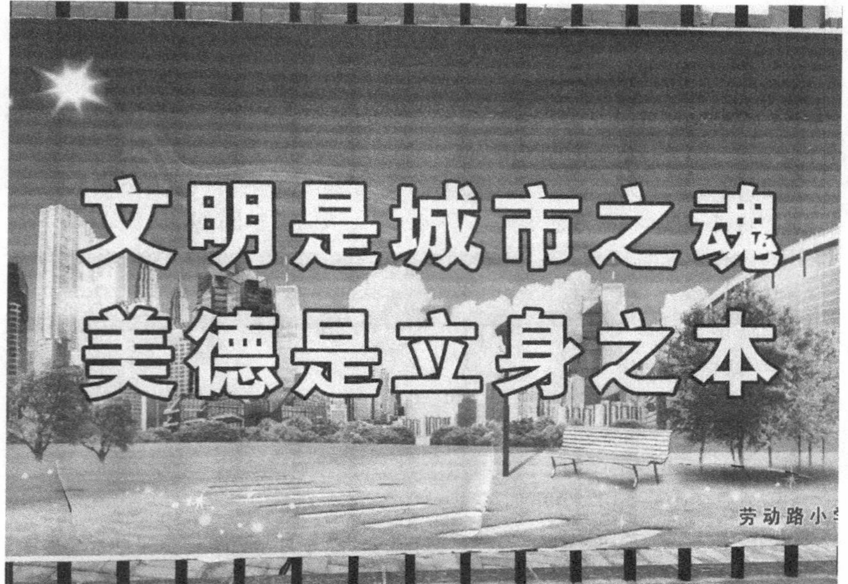

文明是城市之魂
美德是立身之本
劳动路小

FIGURE 3.2. An example of Civilized City propaganda that features modern skyscrapers and eco-aesthetics. It reads "Civilization is the spirit of the city; virtue is the foundation of personal conduct."
Photo by the author, 2018.

worked to imaginatively fix Tibetans, Muslims, and other non-Han ethnic groups into older and less redeveloped parts of the city. Xining residents from all ethnic identities I talked with overwhelmingly considered the East District and the portions of the Central District that bordered it to be associated with *shaoshu minzu*, or ethnic minorities. This owed much to historical continuity, such as the traditional presence of the Muslim quarter and the concentration of Tibetan and Muslim stores in these places. However, the practice of urban redevelopment and the developmental discourses of *suzhi* and *wenming* have contributed to the imaginative delimitation and devaluation of these places.

It speaks to the success of the biopolitical project of the civilizing machine that urbanites have come to desire dwelling in and being associated with the newest parts of the city. In conversations with Han Chinese residents about Xining's development level and the location of the best neighborhoods, I heard many of the same positions that the Tibetans above held: that Xining was less developed and civilized compared to Inner China, that the civilized city campaign could make the streets safer and cleaner, and that, overall, raising civilization levels would be good for the city. They often added an additional detail, however: that Xining, and Qinghai more generally, had many ethnic minorities (Ch. *duo shaoshu minzu*). This was in their view the reason for the backwardness of Qinghai Province as a whole and one of the reasons they wanted to move away from the East and Central Districts of the city.

Through a Tibetan friend, I was put in touch with Luo Xiaoying, a Han woman who had recently purchased a home with her husband in the New Lake District. Although she had lived and gone to college in other cities in China, she had a long history in Qinghai Province. Her grandparents had come to Minhe, a county town east of Xining, from Henan Province during the Third Front campaign, a PRC developmental policy between 1964 and 1971 that promoted heavy investment in China's less developed interior regions for the purpose of protecting China's industries from potential foreign destruction.[34] Xiaoying said she had Tibetan friends, but when we came to the topic of whether Xining was a civilized city, she placed the blame of backwardness squarely on the shoulders of other ethnic groups. In her comparison of the civilizational level of Xining's districts, the New Lake District came out on top both because it was "modern" and "beautiful" and because it had fewer Tibetans and Muslims.

Luo Xiaoying's admission was part of a general understanding of the relative hierarchy of Xining city districts' desirability. She and her husband had purchased a house in the New Lake District after they married in 2009, when few buildings in the new subdistrict had even been completed. She told me why they chose this location: "Very few young people choose to buy in the Central District or the East District. In the New Lake District, there are few *shaoshu minzu* like Tibetans or Muslims [Ch. *huizu*]. They live in Central District, or in East District, which is all Muslims." Given state rhetoric that localizes poverty, lack of *suzhi*, and backwardness in China's ethnic periphery, it made sense that Xiaoying would see the New Lake District, with its spectacular malls and modern boulevards, as being largely devoid of these groups, even though she acknowledged having Tibetan neighbors. Indeed, over a dozen of my Tibetan research participants were proudly living there, sharing hallways and elevators with their Han Chinese neighbors. They were, like Jamtso, fitting into the "urban" and the "modern," their bodily techniques and private property pursuits largely indistinguishable from those of Han middle-class urban citizens.

The fundamental Sinocentricity of the civilizing city was apparent to Kelsang. He asked me rhetorically, "What is the standard of civilization? Is it Chinese civilization?" He contrasted China's civilizational standards with those of the United States, highlighting the tensions among that country's diverse peoples. "Not everything develops in a good direction. Equality of opportunity, equality of participation, do [civilizing policies and practices] consider these? If they don't make any effort to attain such equality, then how can one have happiness? This so-called civilization, does it really help attain the equality of nationalities [Ch. *minzu pingdeng*]?" Kelsang didn't think so. He saw parallels between civilization rhetoric and the urbanization logic that deepened spatially uneven development. Both took away agency from Tibetans, who were compelled to pursue opportunities and submit to urban governmental practices, even though the state fell short of its promise to provide equal access to middle-class comfort.

Ecological Civilization and the Urban Future

As urban development has taken off in China, quality-of-life-related environmental concerns, such as high levels of air pollution and traffic congestion, have drawn increased attention from urban residents and policy makers.[35] As a result of these concerns and related policy interests in "future proofing" cities for environmental change, national planning initiatives have worked to develop cities to be more sustainable, less polluted, greener, and healthier.[36] The resulting green urbanism is part of an urban governmental tool kit that takes inspiration from international methods and practices. Chinese municipal authorities have envisioned eco-cities as cultivating "desirable citizen-subjects" responsive to regulations concerning ecological urban conduct, which can include staying off ornamental grass lawns to maintain their beauty and practicing eco-responsibility through carefully sorting household garbage and recycling into an ever-multiplying number of disposal bins.[37] While maintaining the ambiance, and thereby commodity value, of newly developed neighborhoods, such an "eco-aesthetic strategy," as C. P. Pow has argued, "goes beyond visual codes and aesthetic registers; it is a concerted effort to engender a collective form of eco-aesthetic sensibility that promotes the Chinese state's vision of a harmonious society."[38] Likewise, in Xining, eco-aesthetic urbanization has become part of municipal authorities' governmental vision for a civilized and happy city.[39]

Within Xining, municipal authorities have advanced a number of green projects, including promoting "green transportation" with more fuel-efficient vehicles and designating Xining as a National Forest City and a trial Ecological Civilization City. These projects, as well as related eco-aesthetic greenifying projects throughout Qinghai Province, are intended to promote "eco-cultural self-confidence" among the province's "civilized families" amid a beautiful and pure Plateau natural landscape. To green Xining, authorities have planted thousands of trees, invested in irrigation projects, improved water management and conservation, and paved riverbeds with the goal of reducing water erosion.[40] In Xining's urban districts, these policies are most accessible in the form of the public parks and the greenways that have been constructed along waterways.

Eco-aesthetic normativity, as a biopolitical technique, empowers Xining property consumers to seek out and live in "garden-style" housing communities or near newly developed public greenways marked by open space, flora, and bridges arching over flowing water. Tibetans who could afford to purchase homes in these areas told me that such environments were quiet and peaceful and got them away from the chaos and bustle of other parts of the city. Wangchuk, the young man from the Nangchen pastoral family discussed in chapter 1, told me he had moved to a neighborhood popular with Tibetans and known for its lush greenery, Euro-Western architecture, and Tibet-evoking name (Shangri-La), "not for Tibetan neighbors but because of the environment [Tib. *'khor yug*]. I wanted to live in a spacious and clean environment."

One morning I walked through a greenway in Xining's newly developed New Lake District with my friend Drolma Tso. Like many of the new riverine pedestrian paths in the city, this greenway (Ch. *lüdao*) was a marker of "ecological civilization" (Ch. *shengtai wenming*). From our view on a footbridge suspended above wetlands with remarkably clear water, we watched fishermen throw lines and children splash along a sandy beach. Drolma Tso's parents had recently purchased a New Lake District housing unit for her and her family to live in, so she was very familiar with the housing market in the subdistrict. She pointed out to me the clusters of buildings, both completed and unfinished, at the edges of the waterway. One by one, Drolma Tso fluently compared their affordability and availability. The units in some high-rise buildings were very expensive at the time: over 10,000 yuan per square meter for a ground-level apartment, twice as much as comparable units in less-desirable neighborhoods. This was one of the most desirable parts of the entire city. It was very close to Wanda Mall, a famous national shopping center chain, and although it was a fair distance from the city's bus and train stations, it was not so far from Xining's geographical center to make it feel remote. Drolma Tso and her family were still waiting for their housing unit to be completed, and were now turning their attention to purchasing a car.

The New Lake District's ecological footpaths were attractive for the aspiring middle class, but urban convenience depended on vehicular traffic.[41] A key feature of the subdistrict, in contrast to older parts of the city, was its long urban blocks that, along with new residential compounds that included underground parking, facilitated car ownership. In this sense, the New Lake District was built to mark a clear break with older styles of urbanism and to

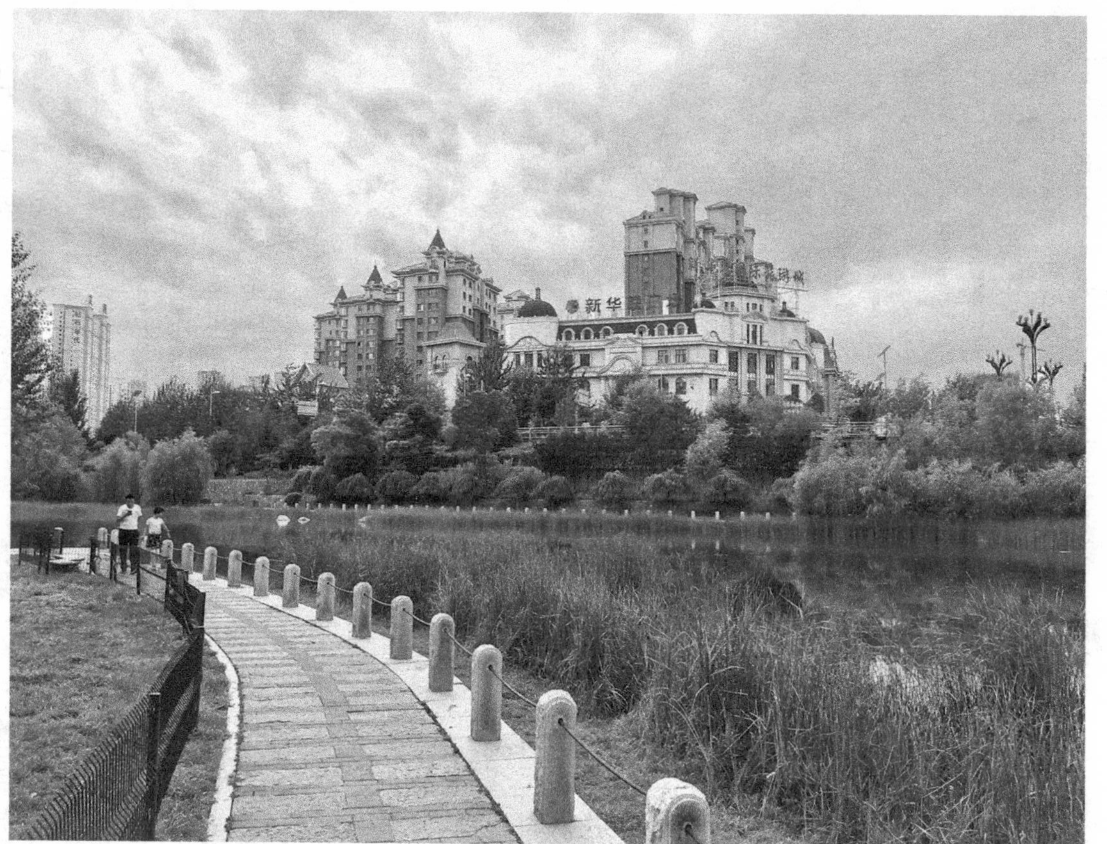

FIGURE 3.3. A greenway with a footpath and wetlands through residential high-rise buildings and shopping malls in the New Lake District.
Photo by the author, 2017.

connect Xining to national urban standards. As one taxi driver told me when we crossed the threshold into the subdistrict, we had finally entered the standard (Ch. *biaozhun*) part of the city, comparable to big cities in Inner China. Not only are "standard" urban areas similar to other redeveloped urban areas, but they are formed from similar policies and practices.[42] The New Lake District was a ready-made environment crafted to propel its residents into a consumer-centered, and civilized, urban future.

For aspiring members of Xining's middle class, the New Lake District was a desirable place in large part because it was built in a clear break from older portions of the city. It materialized the civilized urban ideal of a high-quality property-owning lifestyle and the eco-aesthetic ideal of a clean, spacious, and healthy green environment. These civilized styles work as political techniques that enrolled Tibetans into certain ways of living and behaving in Xining. Popular opinion was largely in step with the understanding, promoted in urban propaganda, that these were good places for living, working, and investing in property.

Bringing the Mountains to the City

Urban redevelopments in Xining are increasingly connected to civilization aesthetics and governmental programs that assemble urbanites into the national urbanization project. As Tim Oakes has shown, however, the aesthetic urban standards that model new urban living and citizenship practices have come under criticism from Chinese urban designers and architectural critics. As these sorts of urban places grow in number and extent, efforts to avoid repetitious styles that lack unique character have become more influential.[43] This is part of a wider practice to brand cities by drawing on what elites posit and promote as a place's unique heritage, a governing practice that seeks not only to attract capital to a place and produce more governable citizens, but that can also help the career advancement of the officials that execute such "face projects."[44] Xining's authorities have been aware of these trends, and over the course of the 2010s they have worked to move beyond visually repetitious urban modeling to create a unique landscape aesthetic that draws from the region's cultural and environmental diversity. The resulting stylistic practices incorporate ethnic groups while also constraining the public representations of ethnic identity.

"There was no concept for a coordinated plan for Xining City," Kelsang told me. "It has no inner spirit [Ch. *linghun*]. Every leader has had a different suggestion and plan." As subsequent mayors of Xining chased the latest trends in urban modeling, Xining had nothing to distinguish it from other redeveloped cities in China. Efforts to bring Xining's past into the present were also too incoherent to give the city a sense of this spirit: "Xining does not have any character, unlike Chengdu, which is a Han place and has the ancient Shudi [culture native to Sichuan Basin] and Wuhouci [neighborhood with famous temple grounds] cultural flavors. Such ancient cities have their own characteristics, their own meanings." He saw this as another misfire of urban developmental policy. A center without a distinctive flavor wouldn't be as valuable as one that did have the unique imprint of a distinctive local or regional character.

The architecture of New Lake District, for instance, had an urban aesthetic grounded in a spectacular modernism that could be found anywhere in China. In the foreword to *The Story of West District*, a 2012 promotional volume, the poet Xiao Dai eulogizes the emerging urban landscape not by turning to history, as did the poets quoted by Jin Yude in chapter 2, but by lyrically describing the effect of wandering car lights reflecting off high-rise windows. Flickering and bewitching, these brightly colored illuminations would draw people's eyes and evoke their dreams and aspirations.[45] While encouraging middle-class dreaming, this aesthetic approach risks drifting into the urban repetitiveness that the rapid construction of standard cities has created across China.

Zhang Xiaorong, who became Xining's mayor in 2015, has written against the stylistic convergence of tall, dense, and stressful urban amalgamations and pointed to a "crisis of distinguishing characteristics" (Ch. *tese weiji*) in urban design.[46] In a 2008 article, he proposed a way out of this predicament: a synthesis for a new urban appearance based on the distilled characteristics of Qinghai Province's natural environment and "bright and colorful" (Ch. *xuanli duocai*) ethnicities. Once distilled (Ch. *tilian*) into essential qualities, environmental and ethnological attributes can be transmuted into designs for urban land use, color schemes for buildings, and unique architectural flourishes.[47] The mineral vocabulary of "excavation" and "distillation" used in this discourse foregrounds a developmental approach in which local resources are to be exploited to help Xining become more attractive for further investment and growth.

Zhang's challenge is to push Xining to develop a style that moves beyond green and "ancient" urbanisms already popular and widely used elsewhere in China. He warns that "if Xining merely adheres to an average version of the 'Garden City' concept, then it will have no unique characteristics. Only if the artistic mood of the plateau character is grasped can the city be built as a 'Plateau Landscape Garden City' and escape the crisis of urban stylistic convergence."[48] His proposal calls for a distinct Plateau landscape style that is both situated within a Chinese civilizational tradition of landscape art and which draws from distinctive regional features. Zhang prescribes "bringing the mountains into the city" by creating large open spaces where people can live without feeling oppressed by tall buildings; they can enjoy the mountains and skies as they are reflected in urban waterways. Rather than a retrogressive imitation of the past, Zhang argues for a focus on exquisite elements whose brightness and color will, when incorporated into simple architecture, create a "rainbow across a blue sky."[49] In this vision, Qinghai becomes a fertile and generative land not only for new urban design, but for all China, as the province's rivers have historically fed the Chinese heartland, and the region's Kunlun mythology has contributed to early Chinese civilization.[50] As discussed in chapter 2, Xining municipal authorities have created parks and monuments related to Kunlun figures, raising the profile of this imaginary.[51]

In June 2016, under the leadership of Mayor Zhang Xiaorong, the municipal government of Xining passed a set of trial guidelines aimed at creating and propagating a new type of urban style, called the "Hehuang Valley style." The guidelines dictate that the urban style be simple, grand, quiet, wise, and, most importantly, created out of distilling and mixing with modern styles the region's unique elements: the Plateau landscape, Hehuang charm, and ethnic lifestyles and customs.[52] The 2016 guidelines outlined three experimental model zones where the Hehuang Valley style would be realized, two in the West District and one in the South District. Indeed, as early as 2008, when construction of the New Lake District was just beginning, *Qinghai News* described the district as being built to have the hallmarks of a Plateau landscape city.[53] The new guidelines deepened the obligation of real estate developers and urban designers operating in the New Lake District and other areas to follow a more particular, regional style in their new projects.

The stylistic requirements of these model zones are also explicitly oriented not only to the natural landscape but also to the Belt and Road Initiative.[54] In the geopolitical and geocultural project of the Belt and Road Initiative, the discursive and material recovery of past connections is used to fuse places together through the idiom of Silk Road civilizations. After Xi Jinping launched the Belt and Road Initiative in 2013, its civilizational aspects have become important both in international diplomacy and in domestic development.[55] In a 2018 interview with the online hub for China's national civilization-themed policy, www.wenming.cn, Mayor Zhang argued that Xining's many ethnicities were diverse yet already assimilated urbanites whose presence stemmed from Xining's history as a node of what he called the Southern Silk Road.[56] Made available as an aesthetic resource in Xining's comprehensive civilizational development, ethnic difference becomes an abstract visual motif based on a mythologized past, rather than a lived urban present.

Sculpting the Civilized City

For years, I watched and waited for the concrete barriers and vinyl banners that concealed a huge construction site in the East District to come down. This was the area where the old Tibetan Market had been and where Xining's new train station was being built. Construction on the new station began in 2010 as the Xining Train Station Comprehensive Transformation Project went into effect.[57] The entire area was re-created to be not only a transportation hub for trains and buses, but also a pleasant environment in step with ecological urban practices; it would contribute to raising the quality (Ch. *pinzhi*) of the urban environment.[58] Right before the closure of the old train station, I was able to snap a photo of a monumental statue set in the station's main square. Located under a massive sculpted arch, the statue celebrated the diversity of Qinghai's main ethnic groups. Once the centerpiece of the heavily trafficked train station square, the monument portrayed Tibetan, Muslim, and Han figures standing together, wearing their respective ethnic attire and thrusting their arms into the air to hold aloft a stylized nuclear atom.

This monument was a product of the socialist era, when nuclear technologies were developed in the province and were cause for national celebration. It was also produced during a period when PRC policies in the province sought accommodation, and then ideological stability, through the "Unity of Nationalities."[59] Placed in the provincial capital at a prominent public site, the statue represented the building of a socialist future. Post-reform Xining's Comprehensive Transformation Project, however, had little need for it. In the summer of 2010, I found the Chinese-language character for "demolition" (*chai*), omnipresent amid China's urban redevelopment, spray-painted in white on the statue's tile-clad base. The statue's imminent destruction was a fitting symbol for the end of Qinghai as a self-consciously ethnically heterogeneous region and for the inauguration, by way of a new high-speed rail station, of a Chinese urban modernity that connected this periphery to an Inner Chinese network of standardized cities.

So when I visited the reopened train station in the summer of 2015, I was surprised to find the statue reinstalled at the edge of the new greenway leisure area that fronted the Huangshui River southwest of the station square. The statue was recognizable, but its relocation had diminished its symbolic effect; the foliage of newly planted trees obscured the statue from even the pathway that ran parallel to it. Park authorities had pasted a sign on the

FIGURE 3.4. Xining's monument to the Unity of Nationalities in Qinghai was marked for demolition but eventually moved to a neighboring site near the new train station.
Photo by the author, 2010.

statue's base pleading with pedestrians to practice "civil dog walking" and prevent their dogs from relieving themselves on the monument.

After the new train station was completed, a new sculpture appeared in the square in front of it. Chen Meng, the director of a Hebei sculpture company and a Qinghai native, had designed a stainless steel monument to the Three Rivers Source region in Qinghai Province.[60] The sculpture consists of three arches, reflecting the three rivers, but whose form is punctuated by jagged edges, sharp changes in profile that represent the peaks of the Kunlun Mountains.[61] In harmony with the vision of the designer-mayor Zhang Xiaorong, the Three Rivers Source sculpture metaphorically brought the rivers and mountains of the plateau into the heart of the city. As Mayor Zhang has argued, the city itself should eventually re-create the waters and mountains of the entire region: "Building a happy and civilized city is good, but we can't just stop in the city's center area. Wishing to clean Xining, to civilize Xining, is good, but we can also reach out into the villages and create a civilized city that encompasses the entire region."[62]

The story of the train station's two statues encapsulates both the changing national urban aesthetic and the greater political shift in the position of ethnic groups in their own homelands. Whereas the harmonious coexistence of,

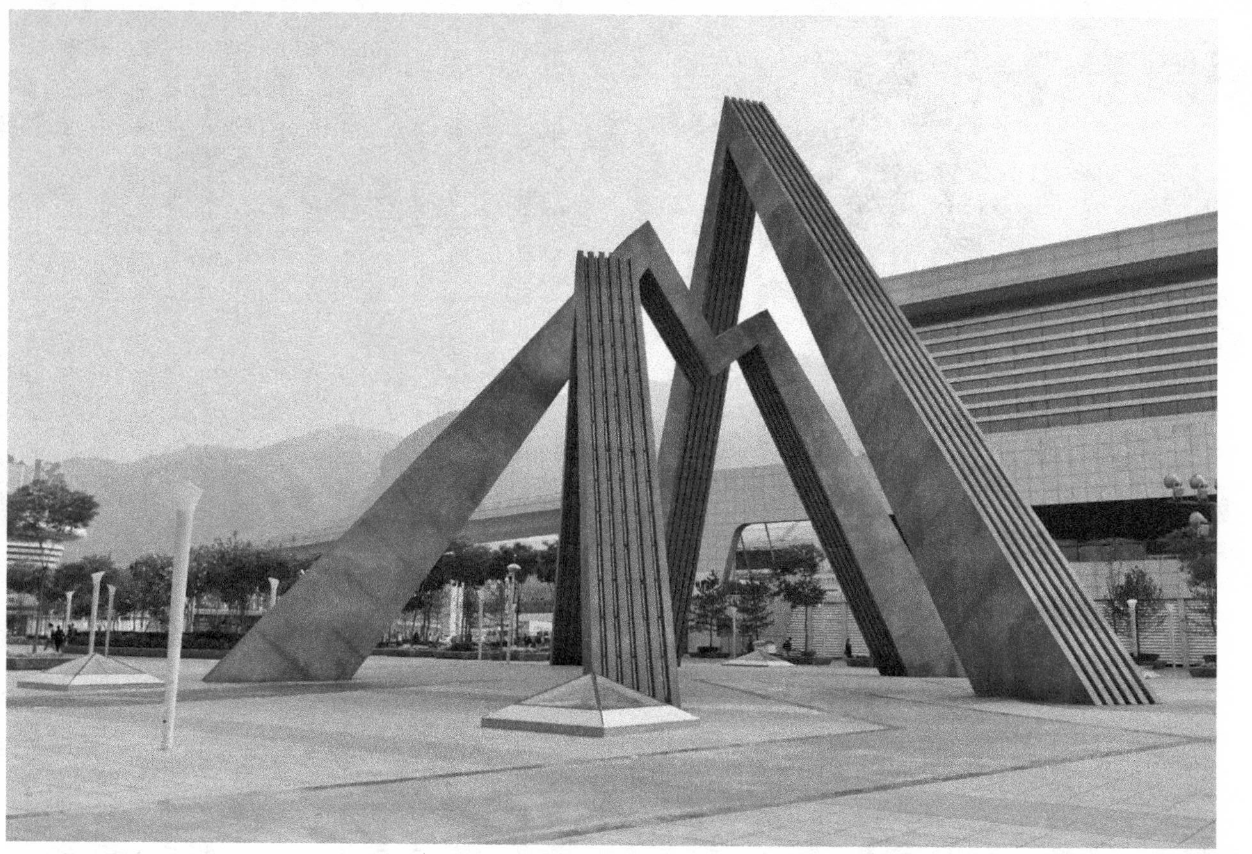

FIGURE 3.5. A new monument designed to convey the natural beauty of Qinghai's water and mountains takes pride of place in front of Xining's new train station. Photo by the author, 2017.

and cooperation between, separate but equal nationalities in China was once celebrated at the key public site of the train station, such calls for ethnic unity (Ch. *minzu tuanjie*) had become confined to propaganda posters in specific neighborhoods. Pride of place at the Xining Train Station was reserved for a monument to the natural environment of Qinghai. This eco-aesthetic appreciation was in step with the contemporary city's appropriation of Tibetans, Muslims, and other regional ethnicities as colorful and sanitized curios. This contrasts with their representation as being equal-yet-autonomous national citizens, the ideology designed into the displaced older monument. Distilled to their most aesthetically and economically lucrative essence, ethnic groups have been assembled into an urban aesthetic whose unique characteristics are ultimately determined by national trends in urban design.

As China's cities have aspired to be world-class urban environments and to be recognized as national exemplars of happiness and civility, their material landscapes have been rebuilt and their citizenry assembled as self-governing participants in a new-type urbanization. Urban redevelopment, coupled with civilization-themed governmental and aesthetic practices, has had differentiated outcomes on urban Tibetans in Xining. These outcomes cannot be understood through a lens of capitalist accumulation and emerging middle-class desires alone.[63] Marginalized by urban redevelopment, subjected to neoliberal governmental techniques, and aesthetically reduced to swatches of color in urban design, Tibetans risk being displaced and homogenized by the civilizing machine and the spaces of uneven development it produces and aesthetically codes. The civilizing machine poses challenges for Tibetans' ability to maintain their urban positionalities and assert a politics of place.

Urban redevelopment has created centers and revalued neighborhoods in correspondence with national understandings of high- and low-quality places. Tibetans' desire to live and work in centers stems from the concentration of relatively better goods and services in larger cities, what Kelsang called the "center problem" in China's developmental policy. Unable to make good incomes or access better health care in their home areas, Tibetans followed centers that urban policies made and remade. Urban redevelopment also changed how Tibetans viewed districts and neighborhoods within Xining. Tibetans, and indeed all urban residents, aspired to be in places associated with higher levels of development and to leave those with lower values. As authorities and residents viewed the New Lake District as in line with national standards for urban and ecological civilization, the old downtown in the Central District lost its relative prestige, and the ethnically diverse neighborhoods of the East District became associated, among many Han and Tibetans, with the lowest levels of desirability and value. While the New Lake District had a civil and high-quality population, older urban areas were associated with rural and ethnic bodies that, in Chinese developmental discourse, localized them as lagging behind newly redeveloped parts of the city.

Aesthetic urbanization has worked to depoliticize ethnic diversity by "distilling" its differences into a nationally appealing urban branding that overcomes the crisis of stylistic convergence in twenty-first-century Chinese urbanism. For Xining, urban redevelopment based on aesthetics of Kunlun mythology, the Southern Silk Road, or Qinghai's position as a hydrological and civilizational source for all of China has given the city a unique character, albeit one indebted to Sinocentric civilizational imaginaries. Such approaches help attract capital and put Xining in conversation with national urban modeling. Moreover, they efface representations of the autonomy of non-Han ethnicities. Authorities have resourced environmental and ethnological difference to accomplish an urban aesthetic of what they want Tibetans, Muslims, and other minoritized groups in the region to be: assimilated, beautiful, and a resource for economic development.

Along with all the changes that the civilizing machine has brought to the Plateau and the redeveloped urban landscape, it has also provided opportunities for Tibetans to connect the city to civilizational supplements beyond those promoted in state policies and practices, a topic further discussed in the next chapter.

Chapter 4

Uncivilized City

One of my acquaintances in Xining was an energetic Inner Chinese student named Xuefei. A practitioner of Tibetan Buddhism who had lived for several months at the Buddhist Larung Gar Academy in Sichuan, Xuefei had come to Xining to improve his Tibetan language. We often met during an informal conversational hour for students. Xuefei frequently offered, at length, his opinions about the Tibetan language, Tibetan cultural practices, and other topics that came to his mind. One day, when we were discussing the extensive vocabulary related to *tsampa*, the roasted barley staple, the simmering tension between Xuefei and a Tibetan graduate student who often attended the conversation hour boiled over. "I don't like *tsampa* with Tibetan butter. The taste . . ." Xuefei trailed off, contorting his face in disgust. This wasn't the first Tibetan food item at that meeting for which he had expressed distaste. The Tibetan graduate student, still smiling but clearly irked, told Xuefei that he seemed to have a low opinion of all things that Tibetans ate. Over Xuefei's protestations, the graduate student then listed all the foods that Xuefei had said he didn't like: *tsampa*, butter tea, mutton, cheese, and so on. Xuefei defended himself. It wasn't because they were Tibetan that he disliked them, it was that they had objectively bad qualities—too sour, too rich, too smelly, not cleanly prepared—they were simply not good. The Tibetan graduate student then grew visibly upset, and, using Chinese, scolded him: "You Han always act like this, and not just about

Tibetan things, about everything. 'This is good and that is good. This is bad and that is bad.' Everything has to be good or bad. There is no in between. People can't just enjoy something for what it is."

While Xuefei had expressed his disgust with *tsampa* in a stark appeal to commonsense notions of what was good or bad, his concern was not specific to Tibetan food. It was part of a more generalized disposition toward taste and hygiene that coded certain things and places as good and clean and others as bad and dirty. He carried with him his own pair of chopsticks, which he kept in a dedicated pouch that he extracted from his school bag when we ate at restaurants. He didn't trust the hygiene of our neighborhood restaurants, which were mostly Muslim noodle shops. He approached the food in them cautiously, dismantling his meals into edible and inedible piles and discarding the latter. He spoke of the lack of hygiene in Larung Gar and the fear he had felt around the wild (Ch. *yeman*) men that inhabited Kham areas of Sichuan. Given his genuine interest in Buddhism and in the Tibetan language, Xuefei was likely unaware that he was promoting a connection between dirt, wildness, and the customs of China's ethnic periphery that worked to stigmatize Tibetans in the city. By criticizing these aspects of Tibetan ethnic distinctiveness, he implicitly suggested certain Tibetan practices did not belong in the civilized city.

Distinction making has rested at the heart of the urbanizing process and the politics of urban place. Sorting places and bodies into the good and the bad, the civilizing machine has raised its model urban spaces over others, encoding them as exemplars of civilized behavior, cleanliness, and high quality. It has also worked to devalue urban spaces where Tibetans and Muslims lived, associating them with dirt and crime. With their presumed connection to a rural and ethnic past, these were places that were not included in the time-space of urban modernity. This chapter explores how Tibetans have negotiated and criticized urban stigmatization, contrasting the importance of interiority and Tibetan dispositions against the superficiality of Sinocentric urbanization.

Following an overview of theories of dirt and the politics of aesthetics, and how these relate to social order and the spatialization of groups and values in the urban context, the chapter examines how unclean neighborhoods and bodies have become stigmatized in Xining City. While the civilizing machine has devalued ethnic places in the city, urban Tibetans differentiate dirt and cleanliness not only through the aesthetic of the civilized city, but also through contextual notions of pollution. Tibetans have also criticized Xining's lack of "tolerance," which civilized urbanization has discursively promoted yet failed to realize. By pointing out intolerance, Tibetans mount a critique of morality in the spectacular city. The following section then discusses intellectuals' and artists' misgivings in regard to the threat that the "Great Concrete Plain" has posed to the Tibetan social body. In utilizing, and also distorting, the dominant urban aesthetic, these critical intellectual and artistic works have influenced Tibetans' attitudes toward the city. The final section discusses how the countryside has been reconfigured as a place where Tibetanness can be maintained through the unconscious acquisition of bodily techniques and moral dispositions.

Progress, Pollution, and the Aesthetic Spatial Imagination

Geopolitical spatial imaginings, political geographers have argued, fuse together time and space. In political rhetoric, the essentializing and exoticizing of certain regions and the peoples that inhabit them naturalize relative barbarity and backwardness in some spaces, and locate civilization and advancement in others. This can lead to social totalizations that, as John Agnew has written, can "turn relative differences into absolute ones."[1] Looking at the regional political effects of spectacular urbanization, Natalie Koch has argued that cities' developmental levels, relative to an othered rural periphery, are key to the way that the urban comes to assume its imaginative primacy.[2] In order to rise in value, the urban distinguishes itself by not being what its periphery is. Such distinguishing of value can also stigmatize bodies that move from "backward" time-spaces into "advanced" ones. As discussed in earlier chapters, in the geopolitical imaginary of China's contemporary developmentalist state, ethnic autonomous regions and prefectures are viewed as peripheral spaces that have needed Chinese assistance to modernize and develop.[3] This geographic imaginary is also part of urban development insofar as the redeveloped urban has become linked to the future and the unreconstructed rural to the past. Indeed, these imaginaries have become so pervasive as to be hegemonic. Images of shiny skyscrapers and urban greenways have become emblems of progress.

Ethnographers of urban development in Asia have endeavored to make sense of subaltern participation in such dominating urban sensibilities without, as Sherry Ortner has forcefully argued, resorting to simplistic explanations of resistance or subordinate false consciousness.[4] In her study of peri-urban Lhasa, Emily Yeh has found that Tibetans there exhibited an acceptance of a Gramscian hegemonic commonsense when they received state gifts including spectacular housing, but that they also retained a fear of state coercion that could result from the refusal of the "image engineering" projects officials bestowed on them.[5] In his study of urban redevelopment in Delhi, Asher Ghertner has argued that a rule by aesthetics had become the dominant form of governmentality in the city. There, the sensibilities of a world-class urbanism (aesthetically similar to China's new standard urban areas) were deployed as a system of rule that permitted the clearance of neighborhoods that authorities, middle-class Delhiites, and ultimately the dispossessed poor came to deem as dirty and disorderly. The aesthetic of the clean and beautiful world-class city became powerful because it was "internally appropriated by the population it would govern." For this to occur, Ghertner has argued, the "vision of social order must be imprinted on [the population's] sensibilities, inscribed in their senses."[6]

Yet Ghertner has rejected assumptions of false consciousness, arguing that so-called slum dwellers may indeed partake in the aesthetic that excludes them from the city, but that they have also appropriated the aesthetic in order to participate, as coequal urban citizens, in imagining having their own modern and middle-class urban houses as a form of a future-oriented "infrastructure of hope."[7] In a similar register, Emily Yeh has argued that Chinese development "shapes the cultural idioms through which development is understood, and these in turn constrain and shape the possibilities for future maneuver."[8] Furthermore, she has argued that local histories and understandings are important in the politics of spectacular development. Commonsense desires for new developments like housing and good-sense critiques of these developments' construction quality and the spatial arrangements they produce are not mutually exclusive.[9] In both Delhi and Lhasa, populations with little ability to directly challenge state policies have therefore found aesthetics to be an avenue for exercising a degree of agency.

China's civilized urban spaces have become sensible as such in contrast to everything that they are not. Neighborhoods where residents are not speaking standard Mandarin, where passersby spit on the sidewalk, and where buildings are decades old appear as spaces not fully incorporated into or transformed by the civilizing machine. The marginalization of such negative spaces has been of concern to theorists of social pollution, who have accounted for how social order can be read in cultural notions of repulsion toward grime. Mary Douglas has called dirt "matter out of place" and linked it to a fundamental need to and for order. For her, concerns over actual hygiene are often not what they seem to be: "In chasing order, in papering, decorating, tidying, we are not governed by anxiety to escape disease, but are positively re-ordering our environment, making it conform to an idea."[10] An ordering notion of dirt and waste is also important for Julia Kristeva, who argued that by expelling filth—part of what she calls the abject—individuals and communities act to preserve the integrity of their boundaries and prevent their psychological dissolution as subjects.[11] The philosopher Olli Lagerspetz has critiqued this paradigm, however, arguing that theories of symbolic pollution have emerged in Western scholarship largely as part of a project to illustrate the distance the civilizing process has put between Euro-Western modernity and its premodern past, as well as the self-discipline that this has entailed.[12] Even when seeking to redeem the abject, to retrieve it from the margins, the paradigm risks reiterating peoples and places as the dirt of progress.[13] Nonetheless, contemporary Chinese urban development has embraced an aesthetic of the civilized city, and urban authorities have encouraged citizens to use appearances to distinguish urban order from ethnic and rural disorder. The civilizing project has used such a notion of progress to justify its transforming of places and subjectivities.

Appearances of dirt matter in contemporary Xining. In the assemblage of the civilizing machine, stubborn reminders of a disordered rural past reveal the incompleteness of urban civilization. Neighborhoods dominated by non-Han sensibilities have become conflated with grime and crime. For example, Han Chinese acquaintances, ostensibly looking out for my safety, often told me to avoid shops and restaurants in Muslim neighborhoods of Xining's East District—they were dirty and dangerous places. In turn, Tibetans and Muslims would assign similar negative associations to one another and to their respective urban neighborhoods. But it would be a mistake to interpret these understandings only through the civilizing machine's production of uneven spaces of relative progress and abjection, much less through an uncritical commonsense acceptance of the dominant urban aesthetic. In Amdo, dirt could not only come to represent a lack of teleological progress; it could also take on connotations of defilement and immorality within the ethnic and religious context of the region. As Andrew Fischer has argued, while twenty-first-century Tibetan-Muslim conflict is "rooted in political economy," it is also "more importantly rooted in a sense of cultural and social dignity that is inherited from an indigenous conception of local hierarchy and power."[14] Fischer has argued that Tibetan boycotts against successful urban Muslim restaurants were reactions stemming from the relative devaluation of Tibetan agricultural products. Rumors of defiled foods reinforced perceptions of Muslims as untrustworthy and dangerous and symbolically put economically ascendant Muslims socially and morally below Tibetans.[15] As this example illustrates, aesthetic and hygienic interpretations of dirt in contemporary Amdo have not been formed in a vacuum, but are in dialogue with other values and prejudices.

Discourses of pollution also matter for understanding Tibetans' criticisms of the civilizing machine. China's civilized cities purport to be places of cleanliness, *politesse*, and high quality, characteristics that ought to be realized in the redeveloped urban landscape. However, Tibetans have worried about the effects of urbanization on bodily health and moral disposition. These concerns have been expressed in terms of the condition of the *sem* (Tib. *sems*), a term that is roughly translatable as "mind" or "heart," but which also has significance in a karmic register.[16] As Jane Caple has demonstrated, some Tibetans have linked practices including the aestheticization of monasteries to promote tourism to the potential decline of monastic communities. Monasteries such as Kumbum and Rongwo are today closely integrated with secular and urbanized spaces; too much contact with urban distractions can lead to interpretations that monks' *sem* have lost focus to the point they are unable to concentrate on religious activities. A resulting "narrative of moral decline" has discursively established certain places as degraded, indexes of which can be read through embodied practices.[17] As I will show below, Tibetans also have also offered a narrative of moral threat that implicates urban environments more generally. For while all Chinese citizens face stresses while living and working in the city, Buddhist notions of *sem* and karma have unique implications for understanding urban environments as immoral. Furthermore, these notions have been used by urban Tibetans to criticize the commonsense urban aesthetic.

Dirt in the City

In contemporary China, dirt belongs in the countryside, the location of old earthen housing, scarce modern amenities, the odor of livestock, and farmers' skin darkened through manual labor under the midday sun. Asher Ghertner has argued that the language of the abject gains effective force in urban environments as it moves from an aesthetic image to a widely held sensibility to a form of governmental practice.[18] The resulting aesthetic-guided governance orders by locating and naming abject spaces, and then expelling them through redevelopment.[19] In Xining, the differentiation between desirable, clean, and wealthy neighborhoods, on the one hand, and urban areas of dirt and crime on the other, could be found in nearly all my research interlocutors' spatial imaginaries. This aesthetic was not merely that of "civilized city" propaganda; it also interacted with contextual notions of dirt and its relation to interiority.

In a shared urban geographic imaginary that was not reducible to any single ethnic group, portions of Xining where non-Han groups including

Tibetans and Muslims lived were associated with dirt. This reflects developmental discourse that locates China's minoritized ethnicities and poverty in the same places; these urban areas were seen as material and symbolic links to nearby rural hinterlands.[20] In my research, Han Chinese often viewed the city's East District as a dirty and dangerous place. These views could also be found among urban Tibetans, many of whom also lived in the East District, including both the recently redeveloped Economic Development Zone and the Muslim-dominated areas near the Tibetan Market visited in chapter 1. Muslims, in turn, associated these negative qualities with places in the East and Central Districts where Tibetans lived in concentration.

My Tibetan interlocutors almost universally described the East District as a dirty (Tib. *mi gtsang gi*) place with dusty streets and unhygienic food. The main reason Tibetans gave for the urban district's grime was that it was full of Muslims (Tib. *kha khyi*) and thieves (Tib. *rku ma*), often conflating the two. Tibetans told stories of deceitful Muslims who would overcharge for their products, take large cuts when they worked as middlemen selling animal products and caterpillar fungus, and were generally seen as focused on gaining profit to the detriment of making fair deals.[21] This deceit was linked to their hearts, which were not good (Tib. *snying rje med gi*). As one participant told me, "Almost all Muslims are the same. While there are some good Muslims, most Muslims would do anything for profit, even kill their own family members." In my discussions with Tibetans, as well as on social media posts, Muslims were frequently invoked in stories of neighborhood kidnappings, with halal noodle restaurants occasionally doubling as kidnapping sites for Tibetan women and children. In one particularly graphic Weixin post, a Muslim noodle shop was even portrayed as selling human flesh.[22]

The air could also be filled with defiling pollution, such as that linked to the butchering of animals. Though necessary for the pastoralist economy, butchers in Tibetan areas have been conventionally linked to being unclean.[23] Furthermore, many Tibetan Buddhists in post-reform China continue to view the practice of slaughtering as defiling, and the act remains stigmatized today.[24] During Eid al-Adha (Ch. *zaishengjie*), Muslims brought livestock into the city to slaughter them fresh and distribute meat to family, friends, and the needy. My Tibetan friends who lived in the East District started complaining about the smell of death coming from the dismemberment of sheep and cows on city streets. I myself recall being overwhelmed by the smell of burnt flesh and hair from the torches used to cauterize slaughtered animals. While walking through this atmosphere to lunch, as the odor pervaded the air and filled our nostrils, my friend Lhari wrinkled her nose and summed up the situation: "dirty" (Tib. *mi gtsang gi*).

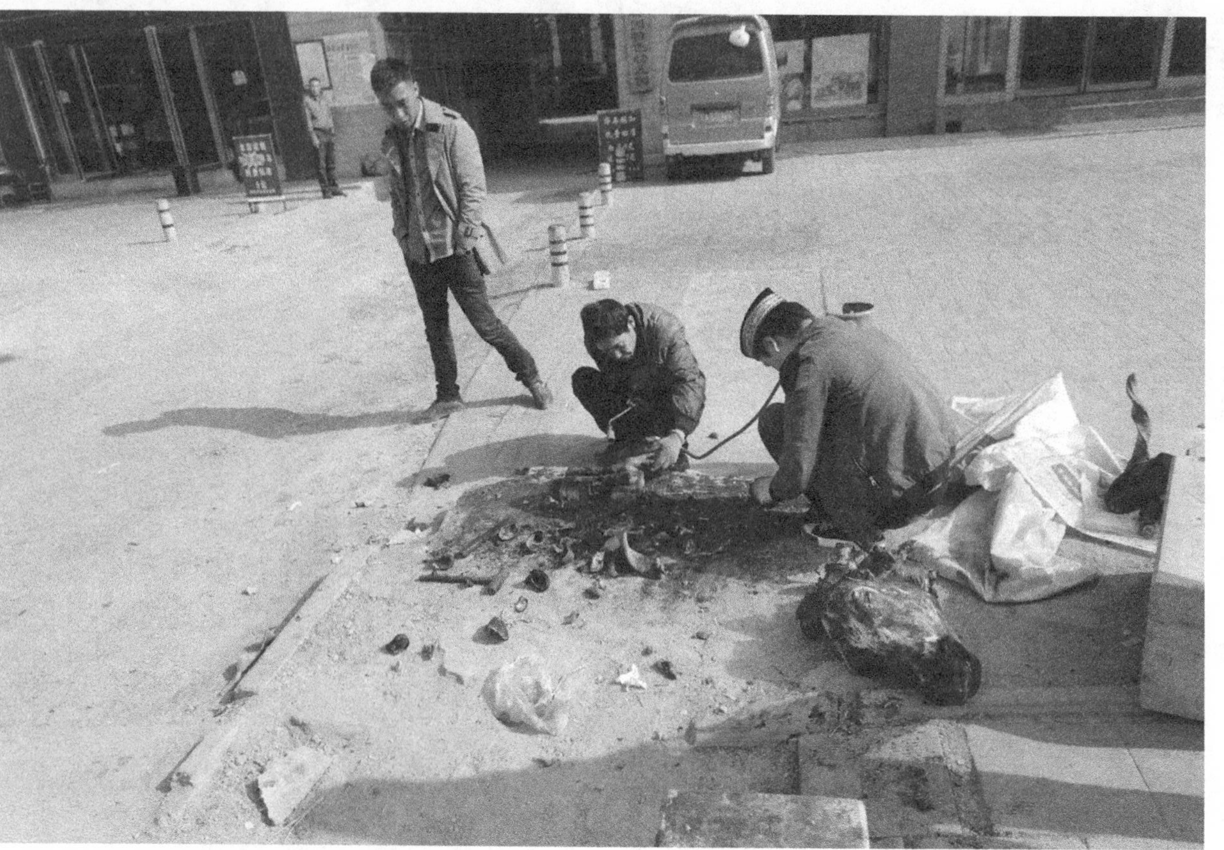

FIGURE 4.1. Cauterizing animal parts during Eid al-Adha in the East District.
Photo by the author, 2013.

Fear of uncleanliness and moral decay has also been turned onto fellow Tibetans, as Jarmila Ptáčková has noted in her discussion about pastoralists moving into towns, where they may be looked down upon as "dirty and criminal."[25] Such perspectives reveal the disruption of traditional notions of social position that placed pastoralism above sedentism; this revaluation has accompanied the devaluation of agricultural products and the displacement of pastoralists from the grasslands.[26] I was startled that pastoralists were aware of and even willing to engage with their own relative devaluation. For instance, Sherap sold unadulterated, grassland-fresh dairy products in a strip of stores near Xining's Tibetan Hospital. His yogurt and cheese were created by a Tsekhok herding collective that included his family. One evening as we sat in a small room in the back of his store, its walls sooty from the coal stove in the center of the room, Sherap confronted me with a question. He motioned for me to look down at his leg, where he scratched his dark pants. "Do you think we are dirty?" he asked. His wife, who had been making tea and bustling about, took a sudden interest in the question. "Do you think we are dirty?" he asked again. Even with an urban business, modern processing machines, and a very clean storefront, Sherap was still anxious about being perceived as dirty. My outside opinion only lightly assuaged the concerns of the couple, who looked at each other gingerly when I assured them that they were not dirty.

Muslims' identification of Tibetans as dirty could be reinforced by interpretations of Muslim notions of cleanliness in food and ritual practice. During my summer visits to Xining between 2015 and 2018, I spent months in a hostel in Xining, where I befriended a spirited Hui woman named Ma Li. She warned me to avoid the Great Crossing downtown area, which she stressed was full of Tibetans, whom she described as dirty and thieving. She emphasized to me the dirt and grime of the area. Non-halal restaurants there, she explained, used recycled cooking oil, didn't sanitize dishes and chopsticks, and allowed their food to be contaminated with writhing maggots. Muslim restaurants, on the other hand, were exemplars of cleanliness, as they must be because of the strict rules of halal food preparation. She then mimicked Muslim bodily practices of hygiene for my benefit by acting out the cleaning and clipping of her fingernails with the small personal hygiene kits typically sold in front of mosques.

One morning when while waiting for the hostel water, which frequently cut out, to be turned back on, Ma Li stressed to me the cleanliness of Muslims, contrasting this characteristic to the dirtiness of Tibetans, who she said avoided showering or bathing in any way. As a consequence, they stank like mutton. She offered a hypothetical: "If a Muslim couple go to bed together and have sex, in the morning Muslims will clean themselves; you have to do this to be clean. But Tibetans are dirty, they won't wash themselves." While acknowledging that younger Tibetans were cleaner in urban areas because of showers, she stressed that most Tibetans remained dirty, which she viewed as normal in their culture. Even without a shower, Muslims could clean themselves by using a pot of water and a bit of soap. The economy of this method was impressive, and Ma Li acted it out for me: wash around the mouth three times, clean out the nose three times, wash the hand and the arms up to the elbow, wash the face, a little water for the feet, the rear, and private parts.

Given their relatively small numbers in the city, Tibetans were especially at risk of being associated with rurality, and anxieties about this could surface in everyday conversation. One evening while getting dinner, Dege Metok waived away a member of the waitstaff offering a cup of black tea (Tib. *ja nak*), a drink interchangeable with boiled water as a standard beverage in Xining. She leaned in to give me an explanation. "Sometimes we women don't want to drink black tea." I was puzzled, so she explained. "Really you should only drink it three or four times a week or even less because it can accumulate (Ch. *chenzhuo*) in your skin and make you black. Tibetans are not as light as Han, so we have to be careful with drinking tea." Indeed, Dege Metok often joked about being black (Ch. *hei*) and how this was undesirable because it gave her a farmer's skin tone.

Though tea pigments that mark bodies as rural can be avoided by skipping the beverage, when Tibetan bodies are perceived as backward simply for being identified as Tibetan, the sense of discrimination becomes more personal. Drolma Tso said that she could overhear Han discussing the dirtiness and wildness (Ch. *yeman*) of Tibetans when she sat in Xining's restaurants. This upset her greatly. Likewise, a Tibetan office worker from Trika working in Xining criticized Han discrimination against Tibetans: "Here many Han think Tibetans are dirty, but actually [the Han] are more dirty. They say we have dirty clothes, but really they only see superficial things. They don't know Tibetans' inside qualities." Jamsto, the daughter of Nangchen pastoralists, pushed back at stereotypes that Tibetans were dirty, asserting that while they might appear dirty on the outside, they remained clean on the inside (Ch. *neixin*). Dirt was only skin deep.

Tibetans imagined dirt and crime to be located largely in Muslim areas of Xining. Although this reinforced dominant imaginaries of Xining's ethnically diverse East District as the location of backwardness and a lack of quality and civilized behavior, it also interacted with Tibetans' and Muslims' mutual assignment of dirt and impurity to the other. In the sensory environment of urban modernity and amid concerns over the need to be clean (or to be seen as clean by others), the body and the neighborhood have become sites where dirt accumulates. Locating and pointing out dirt could also be a sign of intolerance, however, and therefore bring accusations that Xining City lacks the civility of which it aspired to be an exemplar.

Intolerance

The term *baorong*, translatable as "tolerance" or "inclusivity," is widely used in contemporary Chinese state discourse in contexts ranging from ethnic policy reform to Belt and Road Initiative development to the crafting of a "municipal spirit" (Ch. *chengshi jingshen*) for China's individual cities.[27] In Xining, the term has been employed to promote the harmonizing of religious and ethnic difference. For instance, Xining mayor Zhang Xiaorong advocated for a "tolerant spirit" (Ch. *baorong de linian*) to be crafted from such local difference to create Xining's urban aesthetic.[28] In 2007, Xining adopted "Tolerance, Honesty, and Pragmatic Innovation" as an urban motto, and the city has used it since then to promote goals including the maintenance of *minzu tuanjie* (ethnic unity) and the development of a civilized city.[29] The term was also used in street-level propaganda concerning both these themes during my fieldwork. From the perspective of policy makers, *baorong* is an ideal for social order and development. Yet for Tibetans, whether the city was *baorong* depended on whether fellow urbanites treated them with tolerance and acceptance or as people out of place.

Despite the city's lofty rhetoric of an urban spirit of openness and inclusivity, Xining could be a rather intolerant place. Tsebhé, a pastoralist from Golok who lived in Xining's New Lake District with her mother, explained to me her uncle's negative experience in the city. He was a herder who helped produce dairy products that Tsebhé and her family sold to urban restaurants. On a particularly hot summer day, he took a car to Xining to see a doctor. When he arrived in Xining he smelled strongly of the fresh milk and meat he had been carrying in his robe. These were gifts for Tsebhé's family. Soon afterward, she traveled with him to the hospital on a public bus. The bus was very busy, and two Muslim riders started to complain about her uncle's smell and appearance: "Ah, you are too dirty," one of them exclaimed. "Don't touch me!" Tsebhé explained that this discrimination (Ch. *qishi*) continued at the Chinese hospital: "In the eyes of the staff, there is only clean and dirty. Although they might be able to see what's on the inside, all they think about is cleaning the body or washing clothes. That is all they tell us to do." Tsebhé went on to explain, "Afterward I felt that [the people criticizing her uncle] didn't have a tolerant way of thinking [Ch. *baorong de xintai*]. Civility should mean that people can be respectful of these sorts of things."

Xining was rarely described as having a tolerant population. Kelsang felt that Han Chinese in Xining were less tolerant than they were in other major cities, such as Chengdu. As he told me, "If you ask someone on the street there for directions, they are willing to help you. But here in Qinghai, if I ask, they won't help at all." By way of explanation, he said that Chengdu was more developed than Xining and had a population with "a little higher quality." Yet even Han from more developed cities could act as agents of intolerance. One afternoon my friend Somtso Jyid recounted to me an incident when Inner Chinese travelers had stopped her on the street near a downtown shopping mall to ask for directions. She helped them, and after chatting for a bit, they requested her name and phone number to potentially meet later. After realizing she was Tibetan, she said, the tone of the conversation grew awkward. She concluded they would not contact her, and they never did. She was sure it was discrimination. A Tibetan restaurateur named Tsewang was pained by the admission that although many of her customers became drunk and boisterous, she found it hardest to forgive the Han customers. She told me that she was trying to be welcoming toward them on the same terms as the Tibetans, but she felt they were ultimately less respectful. Despite urban policy makers' aspiration to make Xining a city of "openness and inclusivity," Tibetans often felt mistreated.

Occasionally, it was Tibetans who argued that Tibetans had low quality. Dege Metok, who had spent most of her adult life in either Xining or county towns, admitted that she thought some urban Tibetans lacked *suzhi*. She described to me an ongoing problem concerning a lawn in a public park in the East District's Economic Development Zone. On weekends, pastoralist Tibetan migrants were leaving garbage and broken glass bottles for park employees to tidy up. They had ignored repeated requests to keep off the grass and clean up after themselves. For Dege Metok, this was low *suzhi* because the Tibetans repeatedly ignored the rules. This was an uncommon application of urban values to criticize fellow Tibetans. My interlocutor Lobsang even laughed at the double standard that Tibetans used to exonerate themselves from bad behavior: "Among Xining Tibetans there are also some bad Tibetans. Probably because we are Tibetan, we don't think Tibetan people are as bad as Han or Muslims." Tibetans were more tolerant of themselves.

As the civilizing machine has redeveloped Xining, dirt has become matter out of place. In the imaginary of Chinese urban development, new urban spaces are clean and crime free. Grime and vice were proper to unredeveloped parts of the city that had connections to rural and ethnic and bodies.

Adopting the language of urban quality and tolerance, however, Tibetans offered their own urban imaginaries about what peoples and places were dirty or tolerant. Still, their understandings went beyond the hegemonic commonsense promoted through the civilizing machine, as Tibetans plugged their own religious and cultural notions of pollution, deceit, and dignity into the urban assemblage.

Empty on the Inside

Although commonsense understandings of urban progress have been important for popular spatializations of dirt and crime in Xining, I found Tibetans were also concerned about the negative effects of urbanization on individual Tibetans and the Tibetan collective body. As discussed above, Tibetans refused commonsense notions, perpetuated through the civilized urban aesthetic, that they were dirty. Instead, they appealed to Tibetans' internal goodness, which was grounded in Buddhist morality. Although Tibetans could embrace the cosmopolitan comforts of the city, they also appealed to an imaginary of the urban that held it to be an environment conducive to immoral behavior. Tibetans' discussions of the social and psychological effects of the city contrasted the superficiality of the urban landscape with Buddhist interiority. This both highlighted Tibetans' personal dilemmas with urban life and allowed an avenue for a counter-civilizational critique of China's civilizing machine.

In reform and post-reform Tibet, disturbances of the *sem*, the sentient mind that incorporates physical, emotional, and karmic aspects, have been linked to a variety of afflictions, including bodily illness, emotional disturbance, and moral decline.[30] Emily Yeh has explained that Tibetans in peri-urban Lhasa frequently invoked the importance of maintaining a happy *sem* rather than embracing morally compromising profit seeking. These Tibetans held urban areas to be linked to moral decline, as epitomized by alcohol consumption and an associative link between prostitution and growing instances of divorce.[31] Jane Caple has described a discourse among Amdo Tibetans in which urban access is changing monks' *sem* for the worse by providing them with environments where immoral activity is more likely to occur: "The notion that minds are changing is essentially a notion that morality is . . . declining."[32] In these accounts, urban environments are places that have negative influence on Tibetans' *sem*, which can be susceptible to attachments to material things, to greed and desire.[33]

As places seen to foster such attachments, the new urban developments with their glassy, high-rise aesthetic provided an image that was frequently criticized.[34] My participants often used the notion of the outside or surface (Ch. *waimian*, Tib. *phyi gi*) to criticize urban redevelopment and to draw attention to the ways that cities were actually bad for Tibetan minds and bodies. "You see that?" a male shopkeeper asked me, pointing out the window to a row of new high-rise buildings. "Many say that they cause afflictive emotions [Tib. *nyon mongs*]." As he explained, an influx of Chinese migrants had spurred a demand for taller buildings. "It makes people greedy," he continued. "The old people say that it is bad for their *sem*. They hate it here and want to go home." In this example, the new building development served as a synecdoche for the city itself. Urbanization drove a demand for new things, and Tibetans were joining the rush to purchase new housing. With new housing came a growing desire among Tibetans to spend money on interior decoration. Self-conscious about the high costs necessary to outfit their apartments, several interlocutors blamed an urban culture that required such expenditures to create a pleasing environment. For example, Tashi, the NGO worker from Tsolho Prefecture, drew a connection between contrasting Han Chinese judgments on new buildings (as good) and on Tibetans (as dirty and dangerous): "It is only about the surface with them. Just like with apartments. They do not know the quality of an apartment or a house, a body or a mind." Overlooking the inner, innate qualities in objects and in persons betrayed the civilizing machine's misplaced focus on external material development to the neglect of inner substance and quality.

Despite the real pleasures, comforts, and even joy that urban life brought, my participants had misgivings about the emotions that these comforts stirred. Were the pleasures of urban life as superficial as the glassy spectacle of new buildings and the colorful sheen of consumer shops? One of my interlocutors worried about the urban lifestyle, with its focus on shopping and its frayed social connections. She shared with me the phrase "Empty on the inside, but fancy on the outside" (Tib. *nang stod ba, phyi rdzig po*), using it to describe this problem of urban life. One day while I was shopping with my friend Drolma Tso, we visited the hypermodern Wanda Mall and another new shopping center nearby, which was elaborately ornamented with rococo-style moldings and gilded statues that vaguely recalled imagery from Western mythology. Containing the latest trends in shopping and immaculately clean, both malls swelled with customers window-shopping and visiting its restaurants. "These malls are so new—this is the most fun place in the city to be," I said to Drolma Tso, seeking confirmation. "Do you like it?" She replied in the affirmative, but then she paused and looked around to appraise the mall we were still inside. "My friend told me that these new shopping centers are superficial," she added as a qualification. New urban

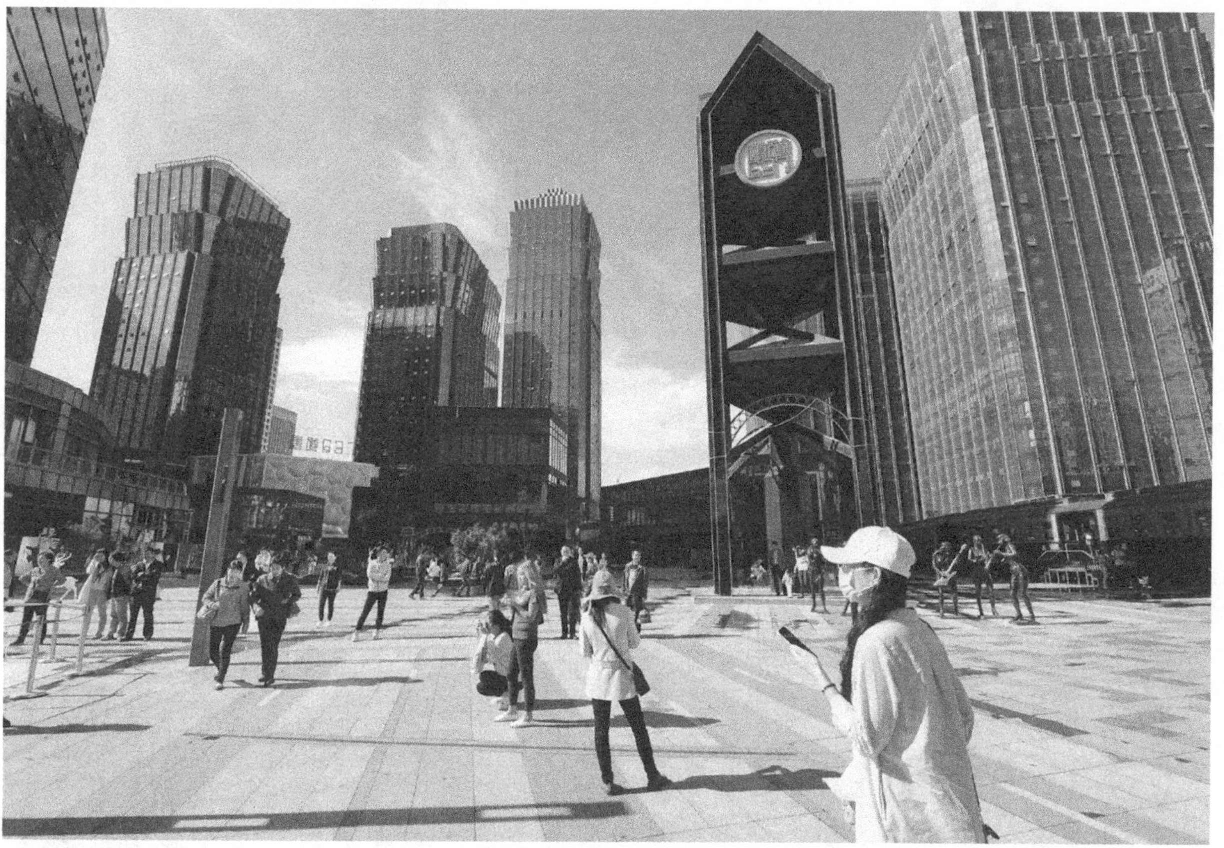

FIGURE 4.2. In Xining's New Lake District, sunlight reflects off the glass surfaces of new buildings in a shopping area.
Photo by the author, 2018.

developments were again cast as wholly exterior. China's new urbanism had no depth.

Slaves to the City

Although Drolma Tso and other Tibetans adopted and even enjoyed the consumer aspects of urban culture, suspicions about the negative effects of spectral superficiality were widespread.

Considering that my interlocuters referred to afflictive emotions and what their friends and families had reported about monks' thoughts on these subjects, I sought out a source that articulated these negative ideas about the urban. One morning I texted my friend Sengé, asking him, "Are there Tibetan lamas teaching that cities are bad? Who are they?" He sent me back an English-language video with clips from the founder of Shambala Buddhism, Chögyam Trungpa. Sengé was a multilingual intellectual, so I wasn't surprised that he had shared the videos of Chögyam Trungpa, who had been based in the United States. Still, I found it hard to believe that the criticisms of materialism in his teachings were key for Buddhists on the eastern Tibetan Plateau. I wanted to know what other Tibetans, and especially urban Tibetans, were seeing and reading about the city. So, I asked Sengé more specifically: "Are Tibetans within Tibet reading or listening to teachings that identify urbanization as bad for Tibetans?" In response, I received a number of Weixin screenshots not of religious sermons, but of the writings of the poet Kyabchen Dedrol.

Kyabchen Dedrol was a founding member of the now disbanded group of young Tibetan writers who called themselves the Third Generation of Tibetan Poets. After gathering at a forum for writers in Xining in 2003, the movement was officially founded two years later.[35] Breaking with the themes and ornaments of past generations of Tibetan writers, the Third Generation has used, among other contemporary motifs, the image of the corrupted city to show how Tibetan sacred places and traditional ways of life have been debased through Chinese urbanization. As Lama Jabb has written of the Third Generation, "Their immediate concern is to give expression to the experience of traversing the 'great concrete plain': That is, the contemporary existence of Tibetans under the industrialized, urban conditions of China's developmental project. This current lived experience in the new towns and rapidly transforming countryside is perceived to be 'distant' from the timeless 'snow-mountains and black yak-hair tents' of Tibet's past."[36] In their poetry, Lhasa in particular is portrayed as polluted by alcohol, prostitution, drugs, and other immoral activities, conveyed through a sensorial panoply of putrid odors and discomfiting sights. In this poetry, Lhasa is symbolic of the negative influence of Chinese development on the Tibetan Plateau. In the words of Lama Jabb, the whole of Tibet is "symbolized by Lhasa disappearing in 'concrete.'"[37] The poets of the Third Generation, including Kyabchen Dedrol, have been very critical of the great concrete plain (Tib. *ar 'dam gyi thang chen*), which poses an existential threat to Tibetan ways of life and also comes to stand for the deceptions of the phenomenal world.

Kyabchen Dedrol has been a provocative figure whose poems and commentaries on contemporary Tibetan dilemmas have been shared over social media and hosted on popular literary websites. For instance, in the writings that Sengé shared with me, Kyabchen Dedrol takes to task the teachings of *khenpos* Jigme Phuntsok and Tsultrim Lodrö, famed scholars from the Larung Gar Buddhist Academy in Sichuan Province. The Larung Gar *khenpos* have sought to proscribe vices such as gambling, lying, and drinking. As Holly Gayley has noted, these "Buddhist leaders are shifting the purport of moral choices from individual self-cultivation and the soteriological goal of a favorable rebirth to a concern for Tibetans *as a collective in this life*."[38] At the heart of Kyabchen Dedrol's criticisms of the Buddhist leaders is their qualified embrace of the urbanizing developmental logic of the contemporary Chinese state.

Religious revival in post-reform China has allowed modernizing religious leaders to promote recalibrated Buddhist ethics and bodily practices and, as Gayley has argued, challenge the Chinese civilizing project by promoting a Tibetan Buddhist project that both draws from the living standards and propriety of contemporary Chinese urban life and is distinct from it.[39] Gayley has contended that the *khenpos'* writings have worked to promote a Tibetan version of development that encourages Buddhist ethics while discouraging the negative influences brought through modernization. This has also included attempts to reverse Chinese perceptions of Tibetans as backward and dirty. Tsultrim Lodrö has argued that urban Tibetans should embrace modern standards of hygiene, such as regular washing and wearing clean clothing.[40] He has even recommended that pastoral Tibetans move to urban areas and do business. Distant from the vices he locates in rural areas, such as drinking and slaughtering animals, Tibetans can accumulate merit as well as catch up to other ethnic groups' levels of economic development.[41]

The phenomenon of prominent Buddhist figures encouraging Tibetans to change their behaviors, take up new livelihoods, and move to urban areas has been controversial and resulted in Tibetan intellectuals criticizing the clerics' positions, as well as heavy-handed enforcement of ethical guidelines in villages that have sworn oaths to follow them.[42] For example, in a Weixin note that Sengé shared with me, Kyabchen Dedrol argues against "monks and lamas" who tell Tibetans that they are backward and should abandon their traditional rural ways of life. He argues that this advice encourages Tibetans to quickly leave behind the crafts (Tib. *lag rtsal*) that sustain Tibetan livelihoods, such as picking caterpillar fungus and raising livestock. Rapid attempts to urbanize can only result in Tibetans becoming guests in their own lands, reduced to urban wage labor in which they are "slaves to the city" (Tib. *grong khyer gyi bran g.yog*).[43] In a related note, Kyabchen Dedrol also criticized the teleological developmental logic that presumes Tibetans must end up in urbanized towns and cities. Given the historical record of capitalist economics producing inequality and conflict in Western societies, he questioned whether these are really "advanced ideas" if they lead to impoverishment and the destruction of Tibetans' way of life.[44]

Kyabchen Dedrol brings to mind through these notes an image of urbanization that is not dissimilar to the impressions of the great concrete plain found in Third Generation poetry. In those writings, descriptions of the corrupted city are juxtaposed against those of the countryside: expansive grasslands, yaks, and clear blue skies. Unbounded nature is being darkly disrupted by the emergence of urbanization. In his analysis of the Third Generation poet Dongdrug, Lama Jabb writes that "a fallen Tibet is portrayed along with its silenced mountains, lakes, and poets, and images of Tibetan modernity cast in rapid urban and industrial development assail the wild grasslands."[45] The city is posited as antithetical to Tibet itself, which is represented through its natural landscape.

The imagery of the defiled city, a pure Tibetan natural environment, and the corruption of Tibetan ways of life has also appeared in contemporary popular music lyrics and music videos. The apotheosis of this is perhaps the 2017 video for the song "City" by the musician Lobsang Nyima. The lyrics to the song were penned by the famous Xining-based author and performer Menlha Kyab.[46] The video, with cinematography by Lhudrub Dorje, begins with Lobsang Nyima playing the stringed Tibetan instrument called a *dramyin*. This footage is followed by a bird's-eye-view panning shot of the valleys and snow mountains of the Tibetan Plateau. Suddenly, the "turquoise sky" that Lobsang Nyima will momentarily sing about turns into an urban landscape hued in yellow smog. In a scene reminiscent of the closing sequence of Stanley Kubrick's film *2001: A Space Odyssey*, the viewer is propelled between the two planes of these opposing landscapes. In the video, Lobsang eventually ends up drinking in an urban bar and getting into a dispute on the streets, singing that "people's *sem* are driven to anxiety and constant toil" in the city, where one's inner feelings must be protected from deceitful people.

These urban images are intercut with Lobsang Nyima and his fellow musicians standing on rugged peaks looking out over the sublime snowlands landscape. In the lyrics of Menlha Kyab, the city cuts off "the bridge for the mind" (Tib. *mi sems zam ba*) by which people can follow the rainbow path to escape from samsara and its six realms of reincarnation. This powerful image of the countryside contrasts deeply with that of the urban. Aesthetically, the city and the country are portrayed as complete opposites in their relations to Tibetan minds and lived experience.

In the works of Kyabchen Dedrol, other Third Generation poets, and popular musicians such as Lobsang Nyima, urbanization is a stain on the Tibetan Plateau, which is otherwise defined by its aesthetic and symbolic purity. For them, the urban is not a place where immoral behaviors can be avoided, as *khenpo* Tsultrim Lodrö has suggested. Instead, the great concrete plain eliminates the very environments that have sustained the Tibetan way of life and been conducive to Buddhist morality. In a reflection of the image of the corrupted city found in these art forms, I found that many of my Tibetan interlocutors held an imaginary of the Tibetan countryside as a place less influenced by Chinese culture and urban development. In order to sustain Tibetan customs and morality, they sought to resource their rural homelands, strategically using them to maintain the Tibetanness of their families and the greater Tibetan community.

Assembling Tibetans and Tibetanness

A common refrain I heard during my fieldwork was that urbanization threatens Tibetanness. Considered abstractly, the greatest threat to Tibetan culture in urban places was posed by the everyday activities of Han Chinese. Urban Tibetans worried about assimilation in urban places, where they could lose their mother tongues and distinctive bodily and moral dispositions. In correspondence with the negative images of urbanization discussed above, urban Tibetans envisioned the countryside as a site where certain aspects of Tibetan distinctiveness lay in reserve. Rural communities where Tibetans retained a distinct majority were sites where young Tibetans could gain an education in the characteristics that gave shape to their group identity.

The countryside was viewed as generative of a repertoire of secular and religious practices that made for what could be described as a Tibetan habitus. Marcel Mauss argued that bodily techniques, also called *habitus*, are socially assembled in bodies through the training that begins with children's imitation of parental figures and continues through other forms of authoritative education.[47] Likewise, for Pierre Bourdieu, ingrained "structuring, structured dispositions" become the practical modus operandi for particular social groups.[48] For these theorists, the "education" that produces habitus is primarily unconscious, imitative, and unwritten, most effective at young ages, and, crucially, embodies the values of a prevailing social authority.[49]

The desire to periodically send children back to grasslands and villages from Xining City shares Kyabchen Dedrol's vision that in rural places, Tibetans learn the distinctive techniques (Tib. *lag rtsal*) that set them apart from others. Most salient in my research was the conviction that visits back home allowed children to participate in village festivals and to be exposed to the wisdom and authority of elders and religious figures. Participants continually discussed the inadequacy of learning moral dispositions through artificial means. In echoes of Mauss and Bourdieu, urban Tibetans felt that ad hoc efforts to teach language and respect for elders wouldn't be enough to check the negative influences of urbanization.

As discussed above, Tibetans frequently described Xining as a place where the population lacked or had low *suzhi*. This lack could be contrasted with better conditions in the countryside. Lobsang, the Yulshul entrepreneur and retired salt factor worker, explained to me,

> People in Xining are reckless in their pursuit of even the smallest gain. For example, if you give a Xining person an envelope to carry, they will tear it open. But people from my home would certainly not try to open the envelope on the street; they would take it directly to you. Xining is not a civilized [Ch. *wenming*] city. The Muslims and Han in particular are very uncivilized and unscrupulous. Many people have selfish hearts. No one in our hometown would do you wrong, so we think Xining is very uncivilized!

Criticizing the deceit and immorality common to urban life, Tibetan parents considered their hometowns as places where a better form of morality could be inculcated in their children. In the early 2000s, Dege Metok sent her son to her hometown for an entire year to study Tibetan at a middle school. Her main goal was not her child's Tibetan language acquisition, but to teach her son Tibetan manners. She felt that the people in Xining, including Tibetans who had "turned Han" (Ch. *hanhua*), lacked strong morals. Dege Metok stressed that Han students exhibited disrespect toward their teachers, and felt that this disrespectfulness was imparted to Tibetan students in urbanized places. She contrasted this with how students in Tibetan areas made way for teachers in hallways and rose in unison to greet instructors upon their entry into the classroom. She also appreciated the disciplinary approach of Tibetan teachers, whose application of corporal punishment made students respectful. In comparison, Han teachers allowed youth to become disobedient and impudent.

A young mother named Lhumo Tso, who was living on the twentieth floor of a just-completed high-rise building in the New Lake District, stressed the importance of the hometown (Tib. *pha yul*) for learning good behaviors. For this reason, she was planning to send her young child back to the *pha yul*: "Though my husband's family cannot speak Tibetan, the way they respect [Tib. *brtsi bkur*] elders is very good. I want her to learn that." In comparison to her dwelling in the city, her native home was a place where her children could visit family and participate in seasonal farming labor and local festivities. The contrast between a rural hometown and urban apartment is one I heard frequently. While Tibetans could potentially feel a strong connection to Xining, housing there was typically discussed as a house (Tib. *khang ba*) or a place to stay (Tib. *'dug sa*). Urbanized Tibetan towns like Rebgong could be discussed as hometowns, as I saw in one Weixin image of the town's redeveloped urban core with *pha yul* printed over it. In my research, however, Xining was never given this distinction.[50]

Parents were also anxious about losing the ability to unconsciously perform and visually read regional styles through bodily techniques. In rural areas, sartorial markers like jewelry and boots as well as bodily techniques such as gait and dancing style alert Tibetans to the presence of co-ethnics from different home areas. As urban migrants begin to wear mass-produced clothing and disengage from these place-based fashions, they risk losing the ability to make sartorial and embodied distinctions. For instance, Tsewang told me, "I am afraid that if my daughter goes to school in the city, she will not even know how to wear a Tibetan robe." She meant not only the robe and its style, but also how and where to tie the sash to hold it in place. Not wearing a Tibetan robe was a loss both of an embodied way of belonging to a home place and of a uniquely Tibetan method of identification that combined style and technique.

In Xining, there were many Tibetans who couldn't speak Tibetan. This was a frequent topic of discussion. Those who did speak Tibetan would portray those who didn't speak the language as very aware of this lack and desirous of learning Tibetan. If they weren't making an effort to learn, that was cause for concern. As I myself was a student of Amdo Tibetan, my friends sometimes joked that I should start teaching Tibetan to their Chinese speaking co-ethnics. Moreover, Tibetan speakers often viewed the Chinese-speaking Tibetans of Huangzhong and Ping'an as tragically "turned Han," telling victims of earlier assimilatory pressures. Other Tibetans who had migrated to Xining in their youth bemoaned how the city had deprived them of their mother tongue. A Chabcha Tibetan who lived in Xining since his early teens and felt he spoke poor and declining Tibetan told me, "When I was young I didn't have the environment to study Tibetan, so I am now thinking whether I should send my son to the village to study Tibetan."

Fearing that this language problem would be worse with their own children, he and others like him hoped to stave off linguistic decline by immersing their children in a Tibetan-language environment. Norbu, the Xining policeman discussed in chapter 1, despite planning to live long-term in Xining, was very attached to his hometown; he wanted his children to grow up there. As he explained, "I have seen many of my colleagues' children losing their Tibetan as they study in the city, and I don't want to let my children go down the same path. If a child grows up [Tib. *skye*] in a Tibetan home, they will have knowledge of Tibetan writing and speech."

Yet these parents still wanted their children to learn Chinese. They were very aware of the importance of a Chinese education in an increasingly competitive economy. At the same time, having their children learn Tibetan was essential in order to retain their cultural heritage and social distinction. So they strategized to take advantage of the double language (Ch. *shuangyu*) public education tracks that were available in Qinghai Province: the Tibetan-plus medium, in which students studied all subjects in Chinese excepting Tibetan and English language, and the Tibetan-only medium, in which courses were taught in Tibetan with the exception of Chinese and English languages.[51] Parents also considered Chinese-only instruction, found in Xining and throughout China, in which Tibetan is not taught at all. By manipulating where children were living at certain stages in their development, parents sought to maximize their children's potential to excel in Chinese while also learning their own language. As Tsewang explained, "I am planning to send my daughter to primary school in Xining, but then afterward send her to junior high and high school in the county town [of my home area]. If my financial situation allows it, I would like to send her to Lhasa after she turns ten." In this case, Lhasa served as an environment steeped in Tibetan culture and history, even if its bilingual schools did not offer Tibetan as the primary medium of education.[52] Whatever a family's strategy was, a shared goal was to guarantee that children, in their youth, would be exposed to Tibetan environments and the dispositions that could be learned in them.

Religious practices were also learned skills that could be acquired in the countryside. Dorjé Gyal, a clerk at the Tibetan Hospital in Xining, was rarely able to make it to his hometown because of his busy work schedule. But he went out of his way to make sure his children would be able to acquire Tibetan. He followed the pattern that his father had employed with him when he was a student in Xining in the late 1990s. At that time, his father made sure he spent his school vacations in Trika. When he was there, his father made him do farmwork and talk to elders. He also made Dorjé Gyal participate in local religious practices and festivities: "I participated in every religious festival, giving offerings and throwing wind horses [prayer flags]." And indeed, it was during these summer festivals that many of my urban Tibetan friends would disappear from Xining for weeks. Tsebhé also told me another way that urban behaviors impeded religious life. In Xining, it was difficult to find good monks to carry out funerary activities, which included staying at homes and reading scripture for days on end. When her relative died in the city, her family looked into securing the services of local practitioners. But they determined that the monks had been compromised by the urban setting, their ritual practices unreliable. Because it was too difficult to arrange for a lama from her home area to come to the city, they instead conveyed the body to Golok so that scriptures could be read by more suitable monks.

But home areas also risked being compromised by explosive urbanization. Dorjé Gyal drew a link between the decay of religious traditions in his home village and the arrival of the Han Chinese. He told me, "Once we had a masked dance called *Lhatse*, but now that has disappeared, so people get together and sing songs. Now because many Han people have come to the area, the place has been 'turned Han.' Today, much of the area belongs to the Han." I asked him where these Han came from, and he offered a long history of migration, beginning in the Tang dynasty and punctuated by an influx of Inner Chinese "educated youth" (Ch. *zhishi qingnian*) migrants in the late 1950s and early 1960s. While in this narrative Han Chinese had clearly lived for a long time in the area around his hometown, they were still narrated as outsiders. Furthermore, contemporary infrastructural development had brought their influence to a crisis point; he worried that his home area would end up just like Xining: "I don't like the new highways. As traffic becomes easier, this means that more Han will come here and stay. All they care about is making transportation convenient, but they are also mining natural resources and destroying the environment."

Finally, urban and rural places could be seen to have different effects on Tibetans' *sem* and emotional state. As Lhari told me, her urban work frequently caused her stress (Tib. *sems khur che gi*) and discomfort (Tib. *sems mi bdi gi*). When she was at home with her family, she felt relief. Furthermore, because of the different environment (Tib. *khor yug*) there, people treated others better. They lacked the guile of urbanites and had better personalities (Tib. *sems khams*). One day I discussed with my friend Dondrup, a writer and former monk from Tsolho, how the city affected people's psychology. With economic growth, he argued, come desire (Tib. *'dod sems*) and competitiveness (Tib. *'gran sems*). Though it appeared to Tibetans that economic growth and its changes were primarily located in the city, Dondrup thought that this was more myth than reality: "People in the city view the countryside as not having any competition or envy [Tib. *phrag dog*]. Rural peoples' moods are seen as being happier than the moods of urban peoples." For him, many of the negative personality traits assigned to urban people could also be found in the countryside.

The preservation and strategic use of rural home areas as reservoirs of Tibetanness have been dependent on an imaginary that links Tibetanness to particular places. Back home, Tibetans could unconsciously learn to respect elders, participate in festivals, and speak Tibetan, among other culturally distinctive behaviors. Urban-dwelling Tibetans felt that they could preserve their social distinctiveness by circulating their children to their home areas, which would mitigate the "turning Han" that made Xining a difficult place to learn Tibetan dispositions. At the same time, urban expansion was seen as threatening to erode the Tibetanness of the countryside, risking its disappearance as a place to acquire Tibetanness and find respite from the city's negative effects on *sem*. Nonetheless, it was difficult to match the reality of rural life with perceptions of it. As Dondrup suggested, and the *khenpos* certainly held, rural places were not immune to vice.

As the Chinese civilizing machine advances on the Plateau, it creates spaces of uneven development beyond and within cities and urban towns. Xining's urban spaces are inscribed with differential values: the old with the new, the backward and the advanced, the dirty and the clean. Peripheralized within the redeveloping city, non-Tibetans frequently stigmatized Tibetans as dirty and backward, rural "matter out of place" in urban Xining. Rather than accept this developmental abjection, Tibetans, working from understandings of Buddhist morality and pollution, as well as interethnic antipathies that pre-dated contemporary urbanization, tailored these frameworks to fit into urban geographies. They associated Muslim bodies and neighborhoods with dirt and crime. Tibetans also pointed out hypocrisy in claims that Xining was a tolerant and inclusive city, accusing Muslims and Han Chinese denizens of acting intolerantly and discriminatorily.

Tibetans did not merely reject the commonsense spatial valuations promoted by the civilizing machine or displace them to others. They engaged with new aesthetic standards that accompanied urbanization. As Tibetans joined the "community of sense" increasingly familiar to them in urban settings, they engaged in criticisms of it. The civilized city and the greed and consumption it promoted could be viewed as superficial, lacking the sort of interiority and morality that Tibetans possessed. Aesthetics in imagery, poetry, and music also influenced Tibetans' sensorial disposition toward the city. Tibetans' artistic productions could, in the words of Jacques Rancière, "intervene in the general distribution of ways of doing and making."[53] By creating works about the urban in which Tibetans could demonstrate their fluency with the urban environment and the social orders it created, they disrupted the utopian aesthetic of contemporary Chinese urbanism. They revealed that the realization of Chinese urbanization and its community is contingent on a hierarchy in which the works and voices of minoritized groups like Tibetans are rendered invisible within the city. Imaginatively fixed to the rural and the backward, Tibetans nonetheless appropriate hegemonic ideas about the urban to reveal its inconsistencies and dangers.[54] While the urban could be fun and bring stability, its glassy high-rise buildings could also represent an urban condition bad for Tibetans' *sem* and threatening to their traditional ways of life. In these cases, Tibetans' rejection of urban places as intolerant, uncivilized, and bad for their hearts and minds is premised on the notion that urbanization has created environments that have negative effects on both individual Tibetans and the Tibetan collective body.

Urban dwellers anxious about losing Tibetan language and identity in their children have imagined the countryside as a cultural reservoir where a Tibetan habitus can be inculcated more effectively than within the urban environment. The countryside became a place where the Tibetan bodily assemblage could be completed; a site where moral action, bodily comportment, and the techniques of Tibetan Plateau lifestyles came together. In terms of the assemblage of the civilizing machine, this guaranteed that these bodies would retain their capacity as Tibetan bodies, which could then be plugged into the civilizing machine to maintain Tibetanness amid urbanization.

Tibetans in Xining did share, to a degree, what Emily Yeh has called "a reversal of the contemporary valorization of the urban."[55] Yet Tibetans were also actively manipulating the dominant aesthetic that has been produced by this valorization, that is, the image of China's standard, world-class urbanism. Tibetans displayed a critical good sense toward China's urban aesthetic, and they used it to critique Chinese urbanization's pretensions of developmental advancement and heightened civilization. While reformers like *khenpo* Tsultrim Lodrö argued that urban places could be positive for the future of the Tibetan people, artists like Kyabchen Dedrol saw them as corrupted and corrupting environments. Scholars have discussed disagreement over whether urban modernity threatens Tibetanness as an intellectual debate between elites divided into various camps of traditionalists and modernizers.[56] I argue, however, that it is important to acknowledge that urban Tibetans participate in both sides of this debate over the urban. As they do so, the politics of aesthetics, centered on a shared urban image, if not content, is important. Tibetans' contemporary imaginaries of the urban and the rural have provided an avenue through which a lack of consensus within the Tibetan community about the overall effects of urbanization still unites them within a shared community of sense.[57] Moreover, they partook in a shared sensibility with other citizens in contemporary China insofar as they recognized the image of China's twenty-first-century "standard" urban form. As they did so, they attempted to stage themselves as coequal members of the urban community, capable of being seen and heard in their appropriations and criticisms of the urban environment and the inequalities it maintains.[58] The critique that Tibetans leveled against this urban form suggests the ways they would like to participate in the assemblage of the civilizing machine to make it better meet their goals and concerns, even if this means plugging rural areas into it.

While the civilizing machine has transformed Tibetans, Tibetans are also bringing their own capacities to the urban assemblage, making it productive of new forms of urban Tibetanness. The city has been imagined as a place of cultural destruction and also as a place of cultural and political possibility. All across Xining, Tibetans are creating environments where Tibetanness can thrive in the urban landscape. The next chapter will explore how Tibetans make places within a city that is fearful of uncontrolled expressions of ethnic and religious identity, and how such places contribute to Tibet's urban future.

Chapter 5

Building a Tibetan Xining

Early one summer evening, at the intersection of New Construction Road and South Mountain Road, Tibetans were gathered on a wide extent of sidewalk that frequently served as both parking lot and informal public square. Around twenty people were dancing, and passersby circled around them, enjoying the entertainment. A fellow onlooker started to chat me up using Amdo Tibetan. Suddenly, a small group of curious people gathered around us, listening intently to my fumbling speech. Over the blasting of the music, one man asked me if I had personally met the Dalai Lama. I said that I hadn't. Then, another man started to ask another question about the Dalai Lama. Quickly, a third man stepped between us, brushing the second man's shoulder to stop him midsentence. The intervening man looked me in the eye and then whispered to everyone *chapsi, chapsi*, the Tibetan word for "politics." I felt a rush of adrenaline, having inadvertently entered into a sensitive, even dangerous, discussion in a crowded public space. Then the course of questions shifted to blander topics: my age, where I studied, if I had children. Just as suddenly as everyone's attention had turned toward me, it shifted back to the dancers.

The intersection where this dancing square had emerged was a location that Tibetans heavily trafficked. Located in the Central District, it included the Qinghai Tibetan Hospital, a number of Tibetan restaurants, stores, and food stalls. It was also where one went to catch a bus or rent a car to visit

Kumbum Monastery. Tibetans came to the area from out of town to see doctors at the hospital or to attend to relatives who were patients there. While in the city, they bought circular Tibetan breads from sidewalk vendors and purchased video CDs of popular musicians from Tibetan-run stores. These sights, sounds, and tastes helped contribute to the widely shared notion among Xining urbanites that this was a Tibetan part of the city. But these sensations coexisted with others that impinged on this place.

Just south of the intersection, where New Construction Road tapered off into a smaller alley, a very different sensory experience could be found, one that brought to mind the politics that the man in the dancing square had warned about. Shouts and training-drill whistles emanated from within the compound of the Qinghai Police Vocational School. Much louder was the combination of club music and drill drumming that came from a large military complex located southeast of the Tibetan Hospital. From a vantage point just off the alley, I could see soldiers inside pulling themselves up climbing walls, driving trucks across the training field, and marching in formation. Seeing and hearing this, I pulled my digital audio recorder from my camera bag and strolled from that vantage point back to the alley, passing between the south side of the Tibetan Hospital and the northern edge of a housing complex purchased by a Tibetan cadre retirement organization. My recorder picked up shouts and drumbeats from the police and military training grounds, as well as the squeaking shafts of spinning prayer wheels called *mani khorlo* and the looped playback of scripture-reciting electronics. As I moved across this urban landscape, I was moving between different articulations of Xining, made accessible through the prehension of different sensory experiences.

In Xining, urban redevelopment has facilitated a new wave of sensibilities tied not only to the aesthetics of China's twenty-first-century urban forms, as discussed in chapters 3 and 4, but also to restrictions over what could be built in municipal territories. These restrictions were both informed and policed by the sensorium of a state-regulated Hanness that worked to normativize the urban landscape. While municipal reterritorialization in Xining implicitly promoted the *hanhua*, or "turning Han," of urban places, Tibetans were not simply being assimilated through their experiences of living in the city. This chapter shows how Tibetans have generated an alternative urbanism that works within and draws from dominant sensibilities by channeling these sensibilities to create places with material and rhythmic intensities that make such places sensorially and socially available to Tibetan co-ethnics. Through practices both coordinated and uncoordinated, Tibetans and their more-than-human companions have built a rhizomatic urban form that sustains Tibetanness amid the civilizing machine.

The chapter begins with a discussion of how and why Tibetans channel their places within Xining City, a municipal territory in which practices of place are restricted by virtue of being located within territories that carry explicit and implicit normative dimensions. This is followed by two sections that explore, respectively, Tibetans' place-making practices in private interiors and in the shared corridors and yards of housing communities, and Tibetans' efforts to build religious structures in closely regulated urban territories. The final section draws from ethnography and the works of the writer and filmmaker Pema Tseden to explore the role of animals and animal products in the city and Tibetans' negotiation of which animals and diets belong in what places.

Agencies within Urban Territory

Recognizing that no single geographic concept can fully account for the specific ensembles of territory, place, scale, networks, and other geographies that transform urban landscapes, Bob Jessop and his colleagues have argued for considering these geographical dimensions in their mutual imbrication, analyzed as cases of particular "dynamic articulations."[1] From a related perspective, Helga Leitner and her colleagues have argued for the co-presence of these dimensions, arguing that they shape the possibilities of contentious politics, which they define as "concerted, counter-hegemonic social and political action, in which differently positioned participants come together to challenge dominant systems of authority to promote and enact alternative geographies."[2] By clarifying how territory, place, and other geographies influence and interact with one another, scholars, as well as activists, can better understand how geographies can be manipulated to resist the inequalities imposed by existing power structures.

Several territorial scales have operated in Xining City and influence Tibetans' efforts to dwell in the city. By building places within Xining, Tibetans have staked out their claim to belonging in the city. At the same time, however, the lens of "contentious politics" is of limited use when applied to the situation in western China. First, the notion emphasizes outright resistance, which, because of the sensitive nature of Tibetans' protests, limits Tibetans' ability to engage in this form of politics. Second, it neglects how consent contributes to hegemonic power. As discussed in earlier chapters, Tibetans were active participants in the civilizing machine; they were not external to it or the "commonsense" notions of developmental progress and middle-class aspirations that it promoted. A subtler politics is needed to grasp how Tibetans channel dominant sensibilities and territorial encodings as they articulate an alternative subaltern urbanism.

The contemporary Chinese city is legally structured through municipal territories that proscribe what people can and can't do in specific parts of the city.[3] From the perspective of ethnicity, this means that many of the legal rights and privileges extended to *minzu* autonomous territorial administrations under the 1984 Law of Regional Ethnic Autonomy, such as preferential hiring for *minzu* groups, are not extended to urban areas.[4] Located outside these territorial administrations, Xining is an ideal site for the Chinese state's contemporary project of promoting "ethnic intermingling" and assimilation into *Zhonghua minzu*, the overarching national identity comprising all of China's fifty-six recognized ethnic groups.[5] This identity has a territorial quality insofar as it is dominated by nonethnic autonomous territorial administrations that are effectively Han. Thomas Mullaney has argued that the category of Han could be considered as a sort of "collective identity" different from ethnicity, one that is hierarchically dominant to it. Because of its position as an often taken-for-granted identity within China, he has argued that Han therefore possesses a "powerful and hegemonic neutrality."[6] This is not an impartial neutrality, but an unreflective one that has the power to shape institutions and their relation to other group identities, akin to whiteness and its institutional and legal power in the United States.[7] Hanness thus dominates the *Zhonghua minzu* identity and informs urban political institutions, making its norms the norms of the urban environment.

Rather than being a primordial essence, however, Hanness is reinforced by the very national projects it informs. In the post-reform period, urbanization has privileged the Han identity at the expense of minoritized ethnic identities.[8] Relatedly, Oren Yiftachel and Haim Yacobi have argued that in Israel's "mixed cities," state policy has promoted an ethno-national Judaization that functions to exclude Palestinians from urban space.[9] The seemingly neutral assertions of professional planners and urban aesthetic schemes have concealed the normative and demographic promotion of the dominant ethnic group. For example, "the problem of planners and architects" participating in neighborhood development in occupied Jerusalem, as Eyal Weizman has written, was in part "how to naturalize the new construction projects, make them appear as organic parts of the Israeli capital and the holy city."[10] Through mandating the widespread use of architectural styles inspired by biblical archaeology, such as cladding structures in pale rough-hewn limestone, and by restricting where and in what manner Palestinians could build houses in the city, the Israeli state attempted "to sustain national narratives of belonging while short-circuiting and even blocking other narratives."[11] Chinese urban territorial rule is also informed by aesthetic design and normative regulations that shape urban landscapes. This includes not only the restrictions and expectations imposed by the urban territories of community districts (Ch. *shequ*) and housing communities (Ch. *xiaoqu*), but also national state organs like the Religious Affairs Bureau. These institutions have worked to promote an ideal national urban citizenry that is ultimately based around an ideal Hanness and the subordination of religious practices the state views as potential threats.[12]

Without resorting to contentious politics, Tibetans have subtly channeled territorial norms and restrictions through their acts of urban place-making. Both with and without intention, people and things create places that deepen their capacity to belong in the urban environment. This can occur through material acts of building and dwelling, or through acts of speech, such as sharing information about restaurants or shops. Networks of rumor can elevate places in a social imagination, for, as Yi-Fu Tuan has put it, "a place is its reputation."[13] And reputation mattered in Xining, where Tibetans were continuously orienting one another to the places that made up an expanding Tibetan city: where new businesses were located, where certain products could be purchased, where buses to particular outlying towns and monasteries could be boarded, and other such knowledges. Places could only take on reputations as Tibetan places, however, if they could be recognized as such.

The sensorial environment has played a key role in the assembling of a Tibetan Xining. As Tibetans have migrated to the city, they have made places by creating or manipulating buildings and things or through bringing affective materials and sounds into the urban environment. These places further contributed to others' sensible place experiences. According to Tuan, the experience of place is synthetic and linked to all the senses, including not only sight and sound but also smell, which makes places "distinctive, easier to identify and remember."[14] Strong sensorial inputs contribute to intense affects, what Sarah Whatmore has called "the force of intensive relationality—intensities that are felt but not personal; visceral but not confined to an individuated body."[15] This perspective on affect also accounts for the agency of nonhuman materialities. As Jane Bennett has argued, objects in assemblages can be "vivid entities not entirely reducible to the contexts in which (human) subjects set them, never entirely exhausted by their semiotics."[16] So while Tibetans may have brought to the city many sensible materialities that served as co-agents in place creation, these materials could affect other urban residents'—and even state organs'—sensoriums in different ways, leading to other interpretations and to potential negative reaction if they violated territorial norms.

Tibetans created places across urban territories that were of varying sensory intensities. These places were often topographically discontinuous, rather than wholly concentrated in one or two urban quarters. Nonetheless, they remained rhizomatically connected. According to Deleuze and Guattari, "the root-tree and canal-rhizome are not two opposed models: . . . the second operates as an immanent process that overturns the model and outlines a map, even if it constitutes its own hierarchies."[17] Tibetans' rhizomatic geographies *channel* the dominant hierarchical forms of the civilizing machine, drawing from them even while establishing hierarchies related to the identity of Tibetanness. Rhizomatic place-making tactics have both avoided potentially violent repressive action from the Chinese authorities and have allowed Tibetans to create an urbanism that relieves the assimilatory pressure of "turning Han." By plugging their own capacities and projects into the civilizing machine, Tibetans have been assembling an alternate urbanism without continuously engaging in contentious politics.

A rhizomatic and assemblage understanding of place-making accounts for and draws our attention to a Tibetan urbanism that might otherwise be overlooked. In the territories of Xining, a constellation of Tibetan urban places has emerged: the recorded voices of monks reciting scriptures echoing through back streets, inscriptions on the walls of building corridors, Buddhist prayer wheels in housing communities, grasslands animals brought to the city, and many others. These places create an affective environment that interpenetrates with municipal territories and the sensible practices of other ethnic groups.[18] Attuned as they are to apprehend these places through their bodily dispositions, Tibetans' perception of and further discussion about them can shift them from individual to community consciousness.[19] The result is the place of a Tibetan Xining, or Ziling.

Building in the Housing Community

The redevelopment of Xining has occurred simultaneously with the transformation of China's urban territorial system. Since the 1990s, the central government has promoted private house ownership. As this has happened, urban governments and property developers have come to control more land at the expense of socialist institutions and their *danwei*, spatially self-contained communities of work and residency.[20] In their place, territorially based *shequ*, or community districts, have grown in importance and taken on a range of responsibilities in different urban contexts.[21] In China's west, *shequ* political organizations have replaced village governments as farming areas have been annexed by an expanding Rebgong town, and they have also served as facilitators of the state security apparatus in Ürümqi.[22] As I have argued elsewhere, Tibetans in Xining professed little interaction with their community districts outside the occasional health checkup that young volunteers offered elderly members of households.[23] Nonetheless, the participatory ethos promoted through private property ownership was still prominent, and community districts did have a formal legal role in the hierarchy of urban territory.

Rather than *shequ*, Tibetans frequently discussed the importance of their *rakor*, or housing community (Ch. *xiaoqu*). Containing multiple buildings ranging from four-to-six-story structures to towering high rises, housing communities were private walled and gated compounds where people lived and shared a common yard, which typically included some combination of shrubs, exercise equipment, parking spaces, a square, and a fountain. Every urban homeowner or renter I met could name what housing community he or she lived in. Through their efforts to make changes to their *rakor*, Tibetans learned what sorts of places could be created and activities could be practiced in them without drawing the unwanted negative attention, or even intervention, of housing community neighbors and managers. In Xining, Tibetans often made their homes in housing communities that were neutrally Han, even if they also incorporated a degree of vernacular and Euro-Western elements.[24]

The normative influence of the housing community could be found in the hallways of housing corridors. In these hallways, urban inhabitants regularly encountered advertisements, graffiti, and door decoration in the stairwell landings. These privately owned but shared inner passages had walls that residents, locksmiths, and various businesspeople filled with messages differentially available to urban residents, depending on their capacity to perceive them.[25] Walls and doors had become places where Tibetans channeled the civilizing machine, altering their implicit Hanness to assemble them for Tibetan dwelling. In every housing community I visited, nearly every residential door had decorations that signified the ethnicity of its residents. Such décor is common throughout Han regions of China, where paper strips called *duilian* are placed around doorframes to invite prosperity and good fortune. Tibetan household décor used a written language and symbology different from Han Chinese designs but, upon first impression, very similar to them. For instance, the inverted Chinese character for fortune (Ch. *fu*) was often substituted for a shimmering gold foil sticker of the *Nam chu wang den*, or "Tenfold Powerful One," an auspicious Kalachakra monogram.

Featuring images and written messages different from those on their Han neighbors' homes, Tibetans' door decorations still maintained the basic form of the *duilian* and fit in easily with the dominant visual order. In our discussions of neighborly relations, Tibetans often told me that they were able to identify new Tibetan neighbors through these door treatments. In some instances, the décor was the only such cue they had encountered. During the Lunar New Year, Han Chinese imagery could also exhibit a sensory creep beyond individual residences, entering the more public, ostensibly unmarked spaces of the housing community. In one of the apartments in an ethnically mixed housing community where I lived, a Han resident eager to welcome the New Year covered our housing unit (Ch. *danyuan*) entryway with images of the incoming zodiac animal, the horse, as well as *duilian* inviting clouds of auspicious fortune to enshroud us.

A common site for the establishment of Tibetan place is within homes, beyond the visual order of shared spaces. In Tibetan rural areas across Amdo, distinctly Tibetan Buddhist structures like prayer wheels, temples, and stupas had pride of place in publicly accessible spaces. In Xining, however, these places were further spaced out and less visible. While such places were important to urban religious practice, Tibetans also channeled religious architectures into interior spaces. Nearly every Tibetan home I visited had a *chö khang*, or shrine room, typically located in its own room or tucked into a corner of a windowed balcony. These shrines contained images and statues of deities and lamas associated with their family's home areas, as well as ferocious images of protective deities. In front of these images, residents often placed offerings of fruit and fresh water, and the images of deities were also treated to ceremonial offering scarves and their own sensorial experiences of incense and prayers. The *chö khang* is a multisensory place that satisfies what Charlene Makley calls the "physical compulsions of sensory desire" in Tibetan Buddhist ritual.[26]

I visited the home of Chöying, who had been living in the North District for twelve years when we met in 2014. She had come to the city from Rebgong to care for the children of her brother, who was then working for a state enterprise in Xining. Now she lived there with her own son and participated in the *rakor* by cleaning it for supplementary income to support her family. The flat she owned was in a building whose apartments had been purchased by Golok retirees, one of whom was hanging a lambskin robe to dry on a laundry line when I entered the housing community. "No matter if I am in the city or the village," Chöying told me, "I prostrate and do *kora* every morning." While she did *kora*, the Tibetan term for circumambulation, around a stupa when she was back home in her *dewa*, in Xining she and her Tibetan friends did *kora* around the Great Thangka that was being housed in the nearby Tibetan Medicine and Cultural Museum of China, where it was invisible from the street.[27] Her apartment was decorated with Tibetan imagery, including a wall hanging of the Potala Palace, a knit Tenfold Powerful

One, and a shrine with a large statue of the Green Tara behind a multicolored plastic lotus. Another woman who worked in the Qinghai Tibetan Hospital also traveled several blocks from home to practice Buddhism. She entered the Tridu County Housing Community, discussed further below, to circumambulate its *mani khorlo*, while her parents stayed home and prostrated at their *chö khang*. The mother of Dekyi, the cosmetics entrepreneur introduced in chapter 1, did one thousand prostrations every morning in front of the Green Tara in their *chö khang*. Her daughter confirmed that the sounds of her prayer recitation, starting at five in the morning, permeated the entire apartment for hours.

Like household shrines, privately owned apartments featured customizations and delicately molded woodwork throughout: cabinets for *tsampa* and teacups, ornate door frames, and raised, heated beds. These selections were not cultural residuals, but were actively refashioned and reimagined for modern home interiors, made to fit into the layout and architectural space of the modern high-rise housing unit.[28] A web designer and homeowner in his mid-thirties from the nearby farming county of Xunhua was in the process of renovating the woodwork in his kitchen: "We are Tibetans, so when guests come we want it to be apparent [Tib. *snang*] that this is a Tibetan home." Likewise, several of Xining's popular Tibetan apartment restaurants were decorated with knit Tibetan designs and traditional Tibetan implements. Wangmo, the owner of one small chain of such establishments, told me bluntly that they decorated it in such a style "because it is a Tibetan restaurant." The walls of the booths were adorned with poles modeled on those used to prop up black yak-hair tents and with photos of jewelry and Tibetan singers from the owner's hometown in Tsolho Prefecture.

Such design aesthetics weren't necessarily reducible to the realization of the traditional rural within the modern urban; cosmopolitan tastes fostered new syntheses. I interviewed another restaurant owner, named Tselo, who had worked for fifteen years editing video footage at Qinghai's main public Tibetan-language television service. Tselo and his wife had converted their apartment into a restaurant. By day, the wife and her cousin ran the restaurant, and by night, they converted its bench seating into their beds. They had decided to design their restaurant around an environmental theme. After personally experiencing the desertification of his home area, Tselo became interested in environmental protection. He was particularly concerned that his urban-dwelling children wouldn't value Tibet's unique ecosystem. The restaurant could help instill some environmental consciousness through its design. As he explained to me, "I use old wood for the tables so that I don't need to cut down a living tree. Additionally, the color of the tables is aged and worn, which the Chinese think makes them look antique. Foreigners also consider this the color of environmental protection. For the window decoration, we use the styles of those from old [Tib. *sngon chad*] Gyelrong [a region in Kham]." While the restaurant's décor and seating remained unmistakably Tibetan, Tselo was channeling his and other Tibetans' concern with contemporary environmental degradation into a cosmopolitan eco-aesthetic.

The locations of these restaurants contributed to a rhizomatic Tibetan urbanism. While tourist-oriented regions of the city, such as Culture Street, hosted a concentration of well-marked Tibetan restaurants, apartment restaurants were invisible from the street. They could be located on the fifth or tenth floor of a high-rise building within a residential housing community, and except for Tibetan door decoration, no external signs or advertising marked their presence. My Tibetan friends learned about the restaurants through word of mouth, increasingly turning to them as venues for social gatherings as the establishments became more numerous and well-known. By channeling the form and amenities of the modern housing unit, such as converting family kitchens into restaurant kitchens and small bedrooms into private gathering rooms, Tibetan restaurateurs were creating new places for Tibetans to interact within ethnically mixed housing communities.

In his study of urban rhythmanalysis, Henri Lefebvre remarked that city life can be tied to social rhythms including "calendars, fêtes, ceremonies and celebrations" that shape the tempo and public expression of urban life.[29] In Xining the Chinese lunar calendar shaped the rhythm of urban life. The Lunar New Year consumed the entire city, affecting public transit times, closing stores, and generating the loud and lively bustle (Ch. *renao*) of firecracker reports that dominated the urban soundscape and clouded housing communities with smoke for the duration of the weeks-long festival. Funeral practices were another urban community activity that ethnicity rhythmically shaped. Han funerals last several days and were frequently held in the shared public space of housing communities. Their tents and mourners occupied a considerable amount of shared space and produced noises such as trumpeting and wailing that could be heard across the complex.

In distinction to this practice, Tibetans I interviewed didn't even consider carrying out large funerary rites in housing communities. Some Tibetan health- and death-related practices could, however, be seen in less conspicuous places. When my neighbor, a Tibetan man in his thirties, died unexpectedly, his grieving family made offerings to encourage a better rebirth for him. Every morning for nearly a month they went to a small area of concrete pavement just outside our unit door and burned a small pile of *sang*, a scented offering. Makeshift *sang* altars also smoldered at roadside margins near the Tibetan hospital, and I occasionally saw boxes or plates of *torma*, offerings hand-molded into the forms of animals and deities, placed along sidewalks. Like the everyday rhythmic practices and sounds of *mani khorlo* spinning and the electronic scripture recitations near the Tibetan Hospital discussed above, these Tibetan rhythms were sensible despite the overwhelming Hanness of Xining's ethnically neutral territories. They contributed to Tibetans' rhizomatic urbanism.

Many housing communities and public squares hosted Tibetan circle dances that were organized either informally or through community district organizations. At the center of these dances were mobile music units—dollies with a battery pack, speakers, and a video CD player or a hook-up cable for a smart phone. These dances produced a rhythm not only through audio, but also through the bodily techniques of performers. One man in a housing community joked with me how he could distinguish Amdo Tibetans and Kham Tibetans from their dancing styles; the Kham people, he showed me with an overexaggerated gesture, danced with their arms flailing up into the air, and Amdowa danced with their arms down. While these dances could sustain Tibetan regional diversity by displaying and contrasting different bodily styles from across the Plateau, they were also open to passersby and attracted other ethnic groups, in particular Han dancers.

Writing in the Qinghai Provincial Party School publication *New Heights* in 2016, school member Zhang Luning argued that as the number of Tibetan homeowners had increased in Xining, the popularity of Tibetan-style dancing (Ch. *guozhuang*) in housing community spaces across the city had also grown. For him, this was a sign of Tibetans' successful integration (Ch. *rongru*) into city culture. Writing about an ethnically mixed community in Xining's high-cost Shangri-La housing community, he explained that Tibetans there are "already well adapted to urban life and their ethnic identity is not clearly evident [Ch. *bingbu mingxian*]. They are difficult to distinguish from Han residents in terms of values and behaviors. Some property management [Ch. *wuye*] personnel said that only by going deep into their homes could they then clearly perceive these residents' Tibetan ethnic identity and cultural characteristics."[30] For this representative of the party-state, dancing in shared space signified assimilation; ethnic difference was being successfully banished from shared housing community spaces. However, as I encountered time and again when I visited dance circles in public squares, within housing communities, and near Qinghai Tibetan Hospital, Tibetans were still finding rhythms, sensibilities, and even moments to talk politics during dances. To all appearances, the community meanings in these activities

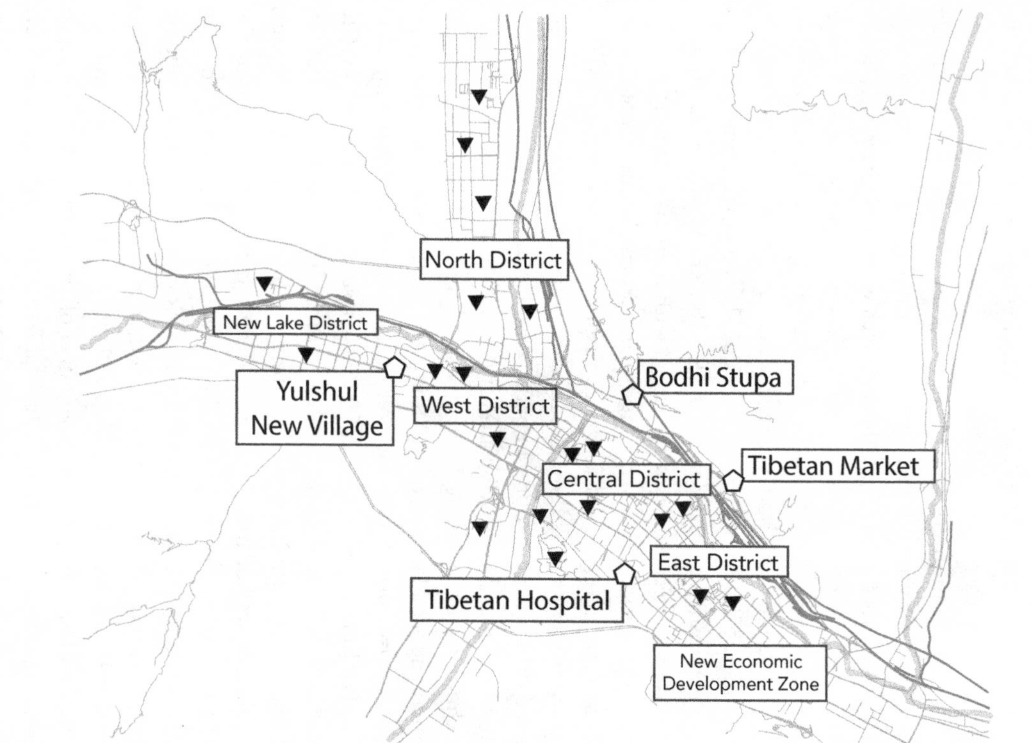

FIGURE 5.1. Using differently sized shapes, this map depicts the varying affective intensities and social reputations of Tibetan places in Xining. The pentagons demarcate places mentioned in the text, and the triangles suggest sites such as restaurants, stores, and homes. Even if topographically disconnected, these places remain topologically connected. Map by the author.
Courtesy of OpenStreetMap contributors.

remained inscrutable to outsiders, who saw the dances as already assimilated into the general fabric of urban leisure.

Xining Tibetans have channeled their place-making to coexist within the acceptable visual orders and rhythms of Xining's ethnically neutral, but implicitly Han, urban landscape. This has not meant, however, that their place-making activities were all acts of resistance against state territoriality. Tibetans pragmatically worked to make places that were effective interventions in the city's affective environment. These places and interventions let their co-ethnics know where they lived, satisfied needs for religious practice, and created milieus for interaction with other Tibetans. Spatially discontinuous and created without coordination, these places were rhizomes in Tibetans' alternative urbanism.

Building Religious Venues in Mixed Communities

In the post-reform period, Tibetans have persisted in religious practice, constructing and remodeling temples in villages and towns and pursuing new avenues for monastic financing.[31] They have also built places in urban environments. During my fieldwork, religious sites in Xining were important places for Tibetans, not only for the accumulation of merit and other religious practices, but also for socialization with friends and family and the sharing of information about urban places and opportunities.[32] Nonetheless, large concentrations of ethnic bodies engaged in religious activities could draw the attention of urban authorities. If these activities weren't sufficiently "integrated" into an ethnically neutral hegemonic urbanism, they risked being read as socially insular and politically threatening. As a result, Tibetans channeled territorial rule, seeking out what religious places could be made, where they could be built, and how they could be adjusted to make them politically acceptable.

Social science researchers providing policy recommendations for Xining's municipal authorities have discussed areas where Muslims, Tibetans, and other marginalized ethnic groups concentrate in Xining City as sites of potential political instability. They have argued that in these places, the formation and perpetuation of "ethnic subcultures" may lead to these groups' social exclusion from the Han population and eventual unrest.[33] According to public management professor Ma Shaodong, Xining's mixed communities (Ch. *hunhe shequ*) exhibit less ethnic division than the concentrated communities (Ch. *jiju shequ*) of the East District, where most of the city's Hui Muslims dwell. Ma has recommended further promoting mixed communities, as they are patterned on the intermingled dwelling of ethnic groups (Ch. *zaju*) and are thereby conducive to group interactions. In this view, increased interaction and intermingling of the general urban population, which is overwhelmingly Han Chinese, would "gradually eliminate ethnic differences" and bring about social harmony.[34]

Lacking large officially sanctioned religious sites like mosques, mixed communities have the potential to dilute the intensity and rhythmic regularity of religious practice and therefore ethnic difference. During the majority of my fieldwork, the 2014 Xining Municipality Measures for Religious Affairs Management was the latest set of rules to restrict the construction of venues for religious activity (Ch. *zongjiao huodong changsuo*) in Xining City. In coordination with similar national and provincial guidelines put into place in the post-reform period, these measures compelled those intending to construct religious structures to apply for permission from the Religious Affairs Bureau branch of their urban district, which would then consult the relevant community district.[35] According to these guidelines, "Without approval and registration, organizations or individuals must not illegally establish venues for religious activities."[36] As Robbie Barnett has argued, such venue-specific regulations indicate "the importance of location in Chinese legal thinking about religion—a presumption in post-liberalization China, and perhaps earlier, that religion belongs in certain places."[37] In Xining City religion belonged in particular places, and housing communities with mixed ethnic makeups were not such places. Indeed, community districts (Ch. *shequ*) that included mixed communities were more likely, given the community's overall ethnic composition and their Han-dominated (and thereby "neutral") elected grassroots governments, to see these venues as out of place. Moreover, the municipal government had tasked cadres to "resist superstition" and "oppose cults" in community district territories. Their targets included not only heterodox groups with small followings, but also self-immolators, who were seen as participating in a cultish deviation of Tibetan Buddhism.[38] Illegal venues for religious activity risked creating conditions in which bad religious elements could take root in the city.

Nonetheless, Tibetans still attempted to build religious places. The most conspicuous religious structures could be found in Tibetan retirement communities, spread across Xining and in other cities such as Chengdu.[39] These communities were created when cadres in Tibetan autonomous administrations coordinated with linked government offices stationed in urban areas to purchase, at below market cost, a cluster of urban housing units. In my research, I found that these purchases could range from a half dozen units across a few floors in a building, to a whole housing unit (Ch. *danyuan*) with a dozen apartments, to an entire building. In rare cases, a deal was reached to develop a distinct walled housing community. In one such housing community, named after Tridu County (Ch. *Chengduo xian*) in Qinghai's Yulshul Prefecture, residents had built an entire circuit of *mani khorlo* prayer wheels. Housing community inhabitants and visitors to the nearby Tibetan Hospital frequently circumambulated and spun the *mani khorlo* and lit *chömé* yak-butter lamps in an adjacent hall.

In another housing community, Yulshul New Village, residents had built several Tibetan Buddhist religious structures in a similar fashion. I interviewed several inhabitants of Yulshul New Village, including Lobsang, who had lived there since 2007, moving in shortly after it was completed. He explained to me the negotiations over creating the *mani khorlo*: "Originally, in consultation with our Yulshul government office, we planned to construct a stupa and Tibetan-style housing, but the Xining government would not permit it. Still, the Yulshul people living here purchased the *mani khorlo* because they felt it was important to have them in their *rakor*. When my wife and I have time, we go to circumambulate and turn them, and often meet neighbors and friends there." Though their vision for a full Tibetan-style housing community couldn't be realized, the completion of the prayer wheels was an important goal for this community and contributed to the rhizomatic network of Tibetan places in Xining. I often met Tibetans in the West District who traveled to Yulshul New Village to do *kora* around its *mani khorlo* circuit.

While these retirement communities had some limited success in channeling territorial control over religious place-making, Tibetan residents in mixed communities lacked the necessary population concentration and coordinated planning to be as successful. According to an official from the Religious Affairs Bureau, their office was having to refuse more building permits because of a rising number of requests to build nonstandard or irregular (Ch. *buguifan*) structures in housing communities. One September morning in 2014, I visited the Luxurious Garden Community, an ethnically mixed housing community, to interview Pema, a man involved in a dispute over the construction of *mani khorlo* within the walls of this housing community. Tibetan residents living in several buildings there, including clusters of units purchased through retirement organizations as well as active work units, had contributed money to build a circuit of wheels next to one of the buildings. Walking the length of Luxurious Garden Community searching for the disputed site, I passed many concrete manifestations of Chinese culture: statues of sages, bas-relief landscapes resembling traditional paintings, concrete sculptures of calligraphy scrolls, and so on, but no instances of anything evidently Tibetan. When I finally located the prayer wheels, tilers

Figure 5.2. Prayer wheels and butter lamps in Yulshul New Village.
Photo by the author, 2017.

were just finishing the roof that would protect them and their turners from the Plateau sun and rain.

In the shade created by this roof, Pema and his wife Sonam explained to me how the Tibetan community's attempts at place-making had led to conflict with the housing community authorities. After raising funds, the residents began to build a structure to house the prayer wheels without obtaining prior approval from the district Religious Affairs Bureau, the housing community, or the community district. They didn't know where to request permission to build such a place, and were hoping that it would qualify as an "elderly activity center," which Pema thought would have made sense, as most community districts had such a center, and *mani khorlo* were heavily used by older Tibetans. Pema gave an account of the process: "Before the residents bought these two building units, they made a request to the construction boss to build a small platform for *mani khorlo*, and the boss set aside a place for us to build them. We made many requests to the government to get permission, but nobody took us seriously. Then we started to build the *mani khorlo*, and the local government immediately came and said we were not allowed to build it." On the first day of construction, the complex's private management firm notified the local community district government, which subsequently ordered bulldozers to demolish the site. Resident Tibetan women then used their bodies to obstruct the bulldozers, calling their operators Japanese devils (Ch. *Riben guizi*), a degoratory term that rhetorically positioned this destructive act as an unjust assault on the Chinese nation. After much wrangling, the structure was destroyed. The authorities demanded the residents reapply through what they outlined as the proper avenues for seeking permission. Sonam then said that residents gathered signatures and started to formally request construction permission. Authorities finally accepted the residents' seventh request, and they were able to restart construction. The structure would never qualify for public support as an activity center, however, and residents struggled to raise funds to finish the project as they had envisioned it.[40]

Housing communities like Luxurious Garden Community are, as Yiftachel and Yacobi described, "classified and represented as 'mixed,' but dominated by one ethnonational group."[41] Pema estimated three hundred households were Tibetan, and that the rest of the just over fifteen hundred households were mostly Han Chinese. With Tibetans amounting to nearly 20 percent of the total Luxury Garden Community population, such a balance of Tibetans to Han residents reflects the population mixture that policy-makers have sought to realize across the city—that is, environments where non-Han ethnicity and religion are for the most part hidden from view.[42] Tibetans that attempted place-making in such mixed communities risked an unsuccessful channeling, a misreading of the possibilities of creating ethno-religious places in the city. Though the residents of Luxurious Garden Community were eventually able to build their *mani khorlo*, they had to adjust their project to make it less out of place, both legally and sensibly.

Restrictions on religious activities were imposed not only on places, but also on professions. Tibetans who were civil servants were not supposed to practice religion and had to find alternative places to make merit and give offerings. This meant that they couldn't visit the two most visible temples located in the heart of Xining's Central District: Golden Pagoda Temple (Ch. *Jinta si*) and Great Buddha Temple (Ch. *Dafo si*). These old and officially registered religious venues were popular, but they were out of the way compared to the more conveniently located irregular religious structures found in housing communities. Nonetheless, the visibility of urban *mani khorlo* in *rakor* made them risky places for government employees to visit. Ralo was a young man who worked as a police officer in Xining. He told me that he rarely visited Buddhist sites like the Great Buddha Temple or Kumbum Monastery because if he was seen at them, it would create trouble for him and his employer. When he left the city for holidays, however, he lit yak-butter lamps at the monastery near his home. Another government office worker also avoided the temples in Xining, but every week he climbed a hill above his housing community to throw the prayer flags called wind horses, or *lung ta*.

The majority of Xining's publicly accessible Tibetan Buddhist places have been built in compliance with the state. Rindzin met me in a stylish modern office with fish tanks, leather couches, and a long glass-topped coffee table. A director for the Qinghai Tibetan Research Association, she presented me with a large postcard of one of the association's proudest achievements, the Bodhi Stupa located along the mountain ridge north of the city. Her group worked closely with the government to get the structure approved and constructed on a high peak observable from city streets. She motioned out the window of the tenth-floor office toward the north of the city, where I could see the stupa glistening in the sun. Many of Xining's Tibetans were visiting this stupa in their itineraries of the city's Tibetan Buddhist sites. The Bodhi Stupa, clearly visible and prominent above Xining, even served as an icon of twenty-first-century Tibetan urbanism. In the music video for the popular song "Fly" (Tib. *'phur*) by the Tibetan pop group ANU, the camera's view soars over the top of the Bodhi Stupa to show Xining City spread out below, illustrating the vital intensity of a subaltern Tibetan urbanism amid the sprawling city.[43]

FIGURE 5.3. Postcard of the Bodhi Stupa, which was created with the support of the Qinghai Tibetan Research Association.
Photo by Li Guodong.

No matter what sort of housing communities they lived in, Xining's Tibetans faced restrictions when they attempted to build religious places outside the interiors of their private homes. Tibetans in Tridu County Housing Community and Yulshul New Village were able to build religious structures in their housing communities, but only in coordination and negotiation with the municipal government. Tibetans in the mixed housing community of Luxurious Garden Community, however, were less aware of the legal restrictions that shaped what sorts of religious venues could be built. Only after facing obstacles did they learn how to channel their place-making to fit the normative urban environment. Outside of housing communities, Tibetans have remained resourceful, finding ways to practice religion and even build a new, highly visible Tibetan urban stupa.

Placing Animals in the City

As discussed in chapter 4, Tibetans with whom I spoke, young and old, often claimed that urban life was eroding Tibetan culture. These discussions centered on the contrast between the urban and the rural, the latter of which was populated by both Tibetans and the wild and domesticated animals that have given Tibetan livelihoods their unique stamp. As scholars including

Karine Gagné and Emily Yeh have shown, the material presense of animals and animal products in the Himalayas has been both socially and politically important.[44] Disputes over animals have not only brought to the forefront ethical questions about how particular ethnic or religious groups treat or ought to treat animals, but animal issues can interact with anxieties over sovereignty and the transgression of territorial boundaries. Animals, in their material, semiotic, and agentic capacities, also have a role in the politics of place in urban territories.

Over tea and oil cakes in his small Xining apartment, Rinchen Lobsang, an older Tibetan former party cadre and cultural activity organizer, explained to me the crucial link between the pastoralist way of life and its flora and fauna. During our sprawling interview, Rinchen Lobsang repeatedly reminded me that Xining City was a place antithetical to Tibetans' home environments: "Tibetans usually don't like to live in the city because they are born in places with mountains, water, wild animals, and birds. Tibetans and Mongolians are born on the grasslands and are accustomed to its lifestyle, to herding and taking care of its animals. It is in our very nature to see the grasslands' green plants and to take in their scent." He then explained how urbanization disrupted this way of life and how sheep and birds near his home area had turned black from nearby coal mining. Urbanization and mineral resource extraction, which he accused the Chinese state of promoting, were for Rinchen Lobsang incompatible with the Tibetan multispecies *domus*, a term James C. Scott uses to refer to the ecological complex that constitutes agricultural dwellings and livelihoods.[45]

This domus, assembled through Plateau places, plants, and animals, has been difficult to bring into urban areas. Tibetan writer and director Pema Tseden, in his award-winning 2015 film Tharlo, poignantly illustrated the apparent misplacement of livestock in the urban. In the film, a pastoralist named Tharlo carries his weaning lamb into a township photo studio. A Tibetan husband and wife, in traditional Tibetan gowns, are already posing inside for a family portrait against a changing backdrop that shows, in turn, Lhasa's Potala Palace, Beijing's Tian'anmen Square, and the New York skyline. The photographer and photo sitters realize that something isn't right; their costumes don't fit in with the New York urban backdrop. The couple decides to change into modern Western clothes for their American photo. But the photo still isn't right. The herder Tharlo then provides his lamb for the wife, who eagerly holds it. The double prop change feels absurd, but the husband smooths out the contradiction: "It's OK, we used to be herders." Their pastoral past is not neatly divided from the modern, urban present.

Livestock practices can also make Tibetans feel out of place in the urban environment. In *Tharlo* the police eventually investigate the pastoralist clutching his lamb; the protagonist's unrushed actions and wandering eye appear suspicious among the purposeful rhythms of town life. Pema Tseden's short story "Life in Town" also explores the friction between Tibetan religious tradition and urban place using wild animals.[46] In the story, a Tibetan man, acting on the counsel of a lama and tantric practitioner, carries out the practice of a "life release," or *tsétar*, of fish in a city pond. In this urban setting, the action draws not approval but derisive laughter. Disdainful onlookers know that someone else is destined to scoop out the fish. Embarrassed, the Tibetan man and his family rush away from the fountain.

Tsétar is a powerful place-making tool. It is a meritorious activity (animals are often dedicated to a sick person) in which animals are freed from captivity or impending slaughter to live out their remaining days unharassed by humans. It can occur as a mass phenomenon, rhythmically set to recurring holy days; and *tsétar* status can also be passed from old animals to young ones, therefore spanning temporalities of multiple lifetimes.[47] The freed animals can't be slaughtered by anyone without incurring karmic retribution. Yet such animals are, in the eyes of non-Tibetan urban neighbors and housing authorities, misplaced livestock. One afternoon I found a *tsétar* sheep in Xining's Tibetan-dominated Tridu County Housing Community, where it was tied to a tree and fed from a bucket. In later conversations, my friends told me it would bring merit to the entire community. Lobsang from Yulshul New Village also saved money to purchase animals for life releases. Still, Tibetans I interviewed who lived in mixed housing communities rarely saw these animals or any other Tibetan livestock in their neighborhoods.

In private housing communities, the rules governing what sorts of animals can be present (and for what purpose) juxtapose territorial regulations against the desires of different ethnic groups. While it was common during the Maoist period for urban dwellers across the country to keep small numbers of livestock such as chickens and pigs within communal spaces, in contemporary commodity housing, dogs and other pets (Ch. *chongwu*) have replaced these animals, as residents are concerned less with supplementary sustenance than with maintaining a clean, civilized urban environment.[48] Pets have a place in the city, while livestock and wild animals are relegated to a rural outside. During late spring, friends from pastoral areas would share images over Weixin of horses in anticipation of the summer horse festivals. Yet in practice and in imagination, these horses remained tethered to the countryside. Horses were out of place in modern urban living; one memorable image shared at this time humorously showed a horse filling out an apartment couch while its owner sat next to it reading a newspaper in a chair.

Sometimes animals couldn't make it into cities for other reasons. Jamsto told me that her family's protective deity (Tib. *srung ma*) was the wild yak. Her mother's clan would hang the skull of a wild yak inside her home, but in her urban home this animal head was viewed as out of place. As Jamsto told me, "You can't take the wild yak into the city." Yet her mother was still visited by the wild yak in her dreams, where it warned her of bad things that might befall her family.

More controversially, my fieldwork coincided with the collapse of the Inner Chinese market for Tibetan mastiffs, large dogs with bushy manes known for loyally guarding Plateau houses and tents. Affluent Chinese urbanites had been purchasing these dogs at increasingly exhorbiant prices until the market collapsed in the early 2010s. Discovering that the dogs sufferred in the confines of urban apartments or in shared urban places, their owners began to abandon them.[49] Among my friends, this phenomenon, as well as the poaching of bears for medicine, was seen as another instance of the Chinese destruction of the Tibetan environment and way of life. Pema Tseden's 2011 film *Old Dog* explicitly deals with this theme. In the film a Tibetan man sells his family's dog to a Han Chinese middleman in the nearby town. The man's elderly father is upset by the loss of the dog and recovers it from the middleman. "I'd sell myself before I sold the dog," the old man tells his son. As the story proceeds, the father has to continuously work to protect the dog from would-be thieves who are trying to put it back on the market. In the film, this experience, as well as the dog's eventual demise, becomes an allegory for the changes that Tibetans are experiencing in an urbanizing world where Tibetan animals are valued as commodities rather than important companions in the Tibetan domus.

Finally, Xining's cosmopolitan urban environment drove animal juxtapositions that retained both ethno-religious division and led to sensible encounters in which urban resources were channeled into new styles of consumption. As discussed in chapter 4, some Tibetans expressed disgust at, and actively avoided, parts of the East District where the sights and smells of Muslim butchery were overwhelming. In urban markets, Han butchers sold cuts of pork in stalls set afar part from where Muslim butchers offered halal beef and chicken. The urban restaurant industry, however, has worked to break down ethnic culinary divisions. It has introduced new contexts of gastronomic consumption that led my Tibetan friends to eat foods they said they would not have eaten at home, such as poultry and fish. For example, sandwiches from Kentucky Fried Chicken or shellfish from a southern Chinese seafood restaurant gave mobile Tibetans the chance to revisit their travels to cities like Beijing or Guangzhou, where they had first tasted this food. Tibetans could also take advantage of the wide variety of available foods and vegetarian culinary options in the city to participate in the rhythms of the Buddhist calendar, such as the annual *Saka Dawa*, a holiday dedicated to the life and enlightenment of the Shakyamuni Buddha. I met several Tibetans who had given up meat during the month of *Saka Dawa*. As one woman who was "eating white" (Tib. *dkar za*), or going vegetarian, explained to me, giving up meat was an important meritorious act all the more necessary in Xining because the city was a place where people did bad things.

Animals have been important companions in Tibetan place-making processes on the Plateau. Their placement within urban areas has become a moral and social dilemma that speaks to overarching political issues. The difficulties of moving livestock and mastiffs to urban housing communities suggest the limits of animals' capacities to assist Tibetans in place-making in their urban homes. At the same time, animals and animal products have an affective potential that Tibetans have channeled into their own urban cosmopolitanism. They have taken advantage of urban resources to adapt their diets and engage with Buddhist rhythms; and in *rakor*, where Tibetans' presence is relatively concentrated, the occasional sacred sheep can spread merit.

Subaltern urbanism in Xining, within the hierarchies of Chinese urban territory, has occurred in part through rhizomatic place-making. While the city's continuously changing territorial norms and rules shape the materiality of these places and the means through which they are established and maintained, these norms and rules haven't fully contained or controlled the ability of such places to contribute to an alternative urban Tibetanness. This alternative urbanism sprouts up in private homes and in shared spaces such as *rakor* hallways, courtyards, and in streets and alleyways. As AbdouMaliq Simone has written about the peripheralized urban places he calls the streets, "People claim the use of specific places in the city in order to secure projects . . . through making things, connecting different things, tearing things down, as well as shaping actions, attitudes, and affects. As a result of concretizing these claims, particular ways of doing things become possible, while others remain off the radar." While certain acts, such as Tibetans' desire to build more religious structures in the city, remain difficult to accomplish, "something else can always be done, and, as such, the street embodies this articulation of potential and restraint."[50]

While Tibetans create places in order to assemble and maintain a Tibetan city, they are not the only agents. Agency is also found in an affective landscape that Tibetans both contribute to and experience as they build places to practice religion and to signal their presence to their co-ethnics. An alternative urbanism is assembled through the affective intensity of human and nonhuman place-makers and through Tibetans' perception of them. Furthermore, as Colin McFarlane has argued, approaching "urbanism as a process of ongoing dwelling as assembly" can provide "a ground for thinking how the city might be assembled differently."[51] The sociality of affective assemblages helps reveal how Tibetans come to feel in place and help other Tibetans belong in a city that implicitly privileges a "neutral" Hanness. Reputation also matters for assembling the imaginary of the Tibetan city. The site where a new restaurant has opened, the size of the *mani khorlo* in Yulshul New Village versus those in Luxurious Garden Community, the places where Tibetans from different regions are dancing and how they do it, and other topics of conversation can lead Tibetans to new sensible encounters and topologically unite place-making practices, contributing to a greater urban Tibetan consciousness.

The places that Tibetans have made are only partially visible to urban authorities or to other ethnic or religious groups. This is because their place-making doesn't necessarily entail a contentious break with the norms and reterritorializations of the civilizing machine. Tibetans channel the tools provided to them by the civilizing urban assemblage in order to create rhizomatic places within it. Channeling is therefore a careful manipulation of dominant rules and sensibilities that makes it possible to pursue alternatives in an urban landscape that privileges and promotes, territorially and sensibly, an ideal neutral Hanness. The majority of Tibetan places have been made in compliance with, rather than in resistance to, territorial rules, and are created with a fluency in the hegemonic sensibilities of national middle-class urbanism. Despite occasional slipups, incremental place-making has slowly created a rhizomatic Tibetan Ziling, a co-present subaltern urbanism only partially visible to other groups.

This coexistence is not the same as segregation or separation. Ziling shares Xining's territory, materiality, and many of its aspirations, but it also deviates from the project of the civilizing machine. While municipal officials and some social scientists promote ethnic interaction and mixed communities as the solution to "ethnic subcultures" and their alternative urbanisms, their technocratic vision doesn't grasp the subtle politics of place-making. As marginalized groups made places, they were continuously working around and through urban spatial and social engineering projects, affecting, perceiving, and perpetuating their own urban worlds.

Conclusion

Urbanization as Civilizing Machine

Over the course of 2015, the wedding photos of a young Tibetan couple went viral on social media across China and eventually garnered international news coverage.[1] A Tibetan advertising agency based in Chengdu produced the photos, which presented contrasting images of modern Tibetan life: The young couple was featured drinking coffee at a Starbucks café, roaming urban streets in modern business attire, and posing with the gravitas of influential businesspeople next to a helicopter. The other photos in the set showed the same couple wearing traditional Tibetan clothing, climbing the steps of the Potala Palace, and peeking out of a grasslands tent. These images became a sensation because they showed Tibetans living two seemingly contradictory lifestyles in two very different settings. But unlike the film character Tharlo, who was out of place in a relatively small town, this couple appeared confident in the big city. They belonged equally to both the urban and the rural. In an email exchange, Phuntsok, the boss of the advertising company and the groom in the photos, explained to me the reasoning behind these photo-shoot settings: "The city and the grasslands are two scenes that are representative of young Tibetans' lives." He argued that the blending of the traditional and the modern was a practical necessity: "We want to protect our cultural essence. Certainly, it will change along with technological development, just as the earliest Tibetan works were printed on paper leaf, and today they are digitized and available online. Are these writings and scriptures the real essence of Tibetan culture? Only the medium has changed, but the cultural contents will never change as long as we have awareness [of our identity]. In that case our ethnic culture can never be lost." Phuntsok's optimism about the potential of urbanization to change, but not eliminate, Tibetanness is exhilarating for a new generation of young Tibetans who seek a sense of belonging in both urban places and in the Tibetan Plateau villages and grasslands their families come from. As this book has shown, however, Tibetans' efforts to find their place in the city have not been made easy by China's civilizing machine.

The Civilizing Machine and the Concrete Plateau

I have called China's model of state-led urbanization the civilizing machine. At China's western margins, this machine has manifested as a teleological developmental process that claims to simultaneously improve material economic conditions, so-called material civilization, and to raise the cultural and social developmental level of China's ethnic peripheries through a "spiritual civilization" that supplements material development. On the eastern Tibetan Plateau, the civilizing machine has gathered peoples, places, and ideas into a national urban assemblage calibrated to improve and stabilize China's ideal twenty-first-century citizenry.

To inform and guide its policies as a civilizing project, China's urbanization has relied on structuring dichotomies including center/periphery, urban/rural, and advanced/backward. The pursuit of centering, urban development, and social and economic advancement has affected the geopolitics and micropolitics of urban places. For example, the center/periphery dichotomy plays a significant role in the chronotope of pacification that situates Xining and the eastern Tibetan Plateau within a history of Sinocentric political order and a mythology of Sinocentric Kunlun civilization. Municipal authorities, writers, and developers have assembled urban monuments, gnarled old trees, toponyms, and tourist attractions to materialize and enunciate this connection, muting alternative histories and stories while stressing the technological and economic advancement introduced by historic Chinese rule from urban settlements. These commemorative places have emphasized the eastern Plateau's integral yet peripheral status to Inner China's economic core and civilizational center.

All three of these dichotomies come together in the civilizing machine's biopolitical project of creating responsible, aspiring middle-class citizens who happily participate in urban society as private property consumers. To that end urban planners and developers have redeveloped Xining's municipal landscape in line with national and world-class urban models, adding spectacular skyscrapers, roadways, green corridors, and shopping malls. Such urban redevelopment has remade Xining in the image of the center. Nonetheless, these practices are inseparable from the pretensions of a civilizing process that ultimately devalues China's peripheral borderland ethnic groups as backward, rural, and in need of development. Furthermore, Xining's expansion and reconstruction have produced intra-urban peripheries that urbanites associate with high concentrations of Tibetans and Muslims. In comparison to the city's new housing communities and urban subdistricts, these areas of ethnic concentration have gained the stigma of being insufficiently urban, unable to foster the high-quality urban population that "civilized cities" promise to deliver.

While the civilizing machine produces such peripheries, it also continuously works to transform them. Within urban territories such as housing communities, municipal authorities have enforced religious regulations and promoted community practices, such as mixed ethnic dances, that privilege what is essentially a neutral Hanness. Mixed communities, where Tibetans dwell as demographic minorities, have been a key tool in urban social engineering efforts to eliminate the "ethnic subcultures" that are seen as posing a security risk to social harmony and political order. Toward the same goal, the municipal government has distilled and amalgamated ethnological and environmental "essences" as part of a political aesthetics that uses urban design to deemphasize ethnic difference. The politics of aesthetics, as both the policing of place-based expression and the promotion of dominant imaginaries, is key to the workings of the civilizing machine.

But has the civilizing machine been successful in assimilating the places and peoples of the Tibetan Plateau into its project of material and spiritual civilization? Based on my research in Xining City in the mid-2010s, the answer is a cautious no. This is because urban Tibetans participated in the civilizing machine by plugging their own capacities into it. They have been continuously inventive, using urban resources to facilitate economic projects and to create material, imaginative, and affective places that have enriched Tibetanness in the city. They have acted as subalterns who, as Dan Smyer Yü has suggested, both draw from a dominant Chinese technical modernity and supplement it through continuously reformulated notions of Tibetan identity.[2] They have embraced the possibilities and opportunities of urban life while also remaining skeptical about its effects on Tibetan culture (Tib. *rig gnas*) and civilization (Tib. *rig gzhung*). As a result, their subaltern urbanism utilized the civilizing machine but turned it toward different ends, those of their families and a greater Tibetan community.

Despite their position at Xining City's topographical and economic margin, Tibetans have taken advantage of the city's position as Qinghai Province's capital and economic center. In Xining, they have topologically assembled a Tibetan city that extends beyond formal urban boundaries. For instance, the Tibetan Market acted as a hub for the flow of bodies and goods between rural and urban areas, becoming a social and economic center for a mobile Tibetan community. Tibetan entrepreneurs increasingly moved out across the city as well, opening shops wherever Tibetans lived, and business was good. This rhizomatic extension of entrepreneurialism to a series of urban centers and subcenters had a parallel in Tibetans' pursuit of residential housing. The urban housing market assembled Tibetans into a national market of homeownership and consumption grounded in aspirations toward a world-class urban lifestyle. Nonetheless, Tibetans plugged their own projects into urban venues: they customized their homes, created affective places within their housing communities, and engaged in entrepreneurialism that satisfied not only their personal dreams, but also contributed to a wider Tibetan community. These practices were carefully channeled from dominant normative rules, calibrated to remain sensible to their co-ethnics but not to attract the negative attention of the local state or potentially discriminatory neighbors. This was not always successful, however, and Tibetans weren't completely satisfied by the restrictions and assimilatory pressures they faced.

Tibetans also actively challenged the "spiritual" pretensions of China's civilizing machine, showing it to produce intolerance, discrimination, and a moral decline that was threatening to "turn Han" Tibetans' hometowns. Rather than being incompatible with embracing urban possibilities, Tibetans' critiques of the urban are tactical engagements with a massive urban developmental project that Tibetans cannot openly resist without facing potential repression. The state has always retained recourse to coercion to attain its goals of social stability in its national and urban peripheries; Tibetans' capacities to modify the civilizing machine were constrained. Although Tibetans wanted more control over where economic opportunities were located and who could access them, more agency to practice religion where and how they wanted, and more state support for the sorts of education they desired, their horizons were ultimately shaped by what authorities might permit or overlook. By being cautious of urban elements that threatened their identity and by feeling out the elements they could make work to their advantage, Tibetans were able to sustain, at least provisionally, a subaltern urbanism amid a civilizing machine calibrated to transform them on its own terms.

The Urban Geopolitics of Place

John Agnew's statement in *Place and Politics* that "states in which coercion rather than consent is the rule do not allow place-based political expression" deserves to be revisited.[3] This book has sought to demonstrate that a lively and expressive politics of place can exist within the hegemonic horizons imposed by a potentially coercive illiberal state. Although the Tibetans discussed in this book lived continuously under the threat of state violence, their enrollment into the civilizing machine created possibilities for place-based political expression that combined the use of urban resources and creation of locales for Tibetan interaction with a sense of ethnic community. Because the civilizing machine's redevelopment contradictorily produced uneven and hierarchized spaces of development while also attempting to homogenize difference, the civilizing machine nurtured peripheries that were conducive to alternative social projects. Tibetans found ways to engage in place-making practices that expressed their individual and community goals. AbdouMaliq Simone has examined such "under the radar" actions as the "invisibilities [that] constitute the city as a place of play, as something always in play, immune to any overarching image or plan of what it is to be."[4] While the civilizing machine assembled the material environment to conform to particular future-oriented aesthetics, Tibetans both appropriated and challenged the aesthetics that guided urban redevelopment. In this sense, they partook in what D. Asher Ghertner has called "the domain of subaltern aesthetic politics" in which "partaking in the normative workings of dominant aesthetic codes" allows everyday acts of consumption, cosmopolitan dreaming, and critique to be part of urban politics.[5] Despite their disempowerment and the continuous threat of state coercion, Tibetans were contributing to a vision of a shared Tibetan urban future.

The urban geopolitics of place that this book has discussed proposes an approach different from other recent interventions in urban geopolitics. First of all, scholars of urban geopolitics have shown how political conflict can take the form of urbicide, which visibly and viscerally reshapes urban landscapes through destruction.[6] They have also demonstrated how urban planning has contributed to durable patterns of exclusion and conflict in both the Global North and the Global South. But in cities where conflict and exclusionary planning have occurred, the link between politics and the urban is typically one of violence and contestation.[7] Planning can also have generative effects. In cities across the Global South, urban growth is not only remaking livelihoods and locales, but also providing new kinds of resources—material, informational, and social—around which marginalized or segregated groups can pursue their aspirations. A focus on *generative* urban geopolitics is important for uncovering how marginalized and indigenous groups at the peripheries of states such as China and India, whose governments have led urbanizing campaigns that draw from national modelings, find political expression not only through contestation, but also through modification of the urban places that are increasingly part of daily life.

Likewise, as Natalie Koch has argued, developmentalist states that invest heavily in spectacular urbanism may circulate images of their world-class cities to promote patriotism across national space, including centers and peripheries.[8] Indeed, urban sensibilities and imaginaries are important in the geopolitics of relative national and regional status. Urban geopolitics can also function at a micropolitical scale and work through not only topographical imaginaries, such as that of the nation or a capital city, but also through topological connections between affective places. As this book has demonstrated, Tibetans' sense of an urban Ziling has resulted from an assembly of memories, materialities, and religious and social investments in place amid an urban fabric that appears to be dominated by spectacular urban developments. Through their own reworkings of the civilizing machine, this subset of the national urban population created their own sensible urban forms, which remain relatively invisible to outsiders. Rather than citizens overlooking state injustices "when they are taught to focus on the spectacles at the center," urban Tibetans were very aware of planners' machinations and the continued threat of center-driven assimilation.[9] And while they could be proud of the Tibetan subaltern urbanism they were fashioning, they were also invested in what could be called a counter-civilizational geopolitical project that largely rejected nation-building conceits and remained critical of urbanization and its potentially negative influences.

Understanding the politics of place in a rapidly urbanizing world requires new approaches that can integrate macro-scale geopolitics with the micropolitics of everyday life, as well as recognize subtler forms of politics expressed through the built environment, social values, and relations with nonhumans. The concept of the civilizing machine also has the potential to be used in other contexts of rapid urban development around the world—for instance, specially zoned urban developments that have depended on Chinese investment and private developers. Such urban projects have promised to bring modern amenities and high standards of living to their inhabitants. Nonetheless, the construction of urban projects like the That Luang Lake Special Economic Zone (SEZ) near Vientiane, Laos, and Kilamba New City near Luanda, Angola, have displaced local populations and subsequently marginalized those who could not afford to buy into them.[10] Studies of the urban politics of place in these cities can highlight the ways that marginalized populations negotiate and challenge new urban valuations and developmental unevenness in the reassembling city.

While Chinese urban projects can be marshaled for nation building, they can also have wider geopolitical dimensions, such as when projects are financially or rhetorically linked to the Belt and Road Initiative. For example, the Chinese-funded urban development of Forest City, located in the Iskandar Malaysia SEZ on the Straits of Johor across from Singapore and marketed as linked to the Belt and Road Initiative, has led to accusations from Malaysian critics that an influx of Chinese nationals into the privately policed Forest City could erode Malaysian sovereignty.[11] Regarding the Forest City as a deployment of the civilizing machine, we can also ask how Sinocentric material and spiritual civilization can influence, or be challenged by, Malaysian populations living and moving within the Forest City. Finally, China isn't the only country that produces civilizing machines; other states have also promoted urbanization projects grounded in self-consciously sui generis cultural and political projects and deployed them across national space, as can be seen in India's Smart Cities Mission.[12] As India's peripheral Himalayan frontier is increasingly urbanized and drawn into a national urban network, investigating how marginalized and indigenous groups express an urban politics of place can further reveal the politically generative potential of urbanization.[13]

Despite civilizing machines' colonial pretensions to dominate and transform their peripheries, their production of uneven development and social hierarchies creates possibilities for different capacities and projects to be plugged into the machines. By creating and connecting places, marginalized populations have redirected and will continue to redirect these machines toward different ends. They refuse to be bystanders in an urbanization process that they desire and have the capacity to leave their stamp upon.

Afterword

China's peripheries are constantly changing. During the last few years of the 2010s, PRC policies toward borderland territories, including Hong Kong and the ethnic autonomous regions of Tibet, Xinjiang, Inner Mongolia, and Ningxia, have undergone dramatic shifts. Breaking with the policies of Hu Jintao and earlier reform leaders, Xi Jinping has pushed for more rapid legal integration and cultural assimilation.[1] While my research period coincided with the early years of Xi's presidency, during the period when I was writing this manuscript, between 2017 and 2020, the governmental practices I observed and studied with regard to borderland assimilation have either accelerated or taken on new valences. At the heart of this change has been a commitment to transforming places through urban and infrastructural development and through control of the sensible and communicative environment.

The Xi administration has sought to draw national peripheries closer to the center by eliminating what it views as threats to national security and social harmony, which are often described as manifesting themselves in connections to outside places and political influences. In state rhetoric, calls for ethnic and political rights at the periphery have been increasingly viewed as forms of antistate activity and therefore a security concern.[2] By drawing borderland peripheries closer to the center through increased connectivity, authorities have reduced the political possibilities of China's peripheries, making them places where political expression beyond patriotic support of the state becomes increasingly difficult. For instance, the Hong Kong National Security Law has set up a legal framework for criminalizing criticism of the PRC and the Communist Party. New institutions with direct ties to the mainland can bypass the existing Hong Kong territorial legal system as they pursue alleged collusion with foreign or separatist forces.[3] One of the most obvious outcomes has been a chilling effect on the creative place-making that has marked democracy demonstrators' street activities and become emblematic of their ongoing movement for political rights.[4] Moreover, mainland authorities have leveraged transportation infrastructures, such as the Guangshengang XRL high-speed rail, to draw the city further into mainland circulations. The in-filling of eastern Lantau Island as an alternative central district for Hong Kong indicates the disruptive potential of new urban infrastructure for economically and symbolically re-centering borderland urban sites and devaluing older infrastructures of power.[5] The spectacular power of urban construction signals the PRC's commitment to urban transformation as a key tool to accomplish both its economic and political objectives.

Such transformations are occurring in China's northwestern Islamic borderlands as well. Over the past several years, governments across China have sought to remove "Saudi" and "Arab" influence from religious structures, closing and even demolishing mosques that exhibit such features, as well as removing Arabic lettering from storefronts.[6] The crackdown has symbolically encouraged Muslim communities to re-center themselves on China, rather than on foreign religious or linguistic influences that originate from beyond the country's national boundaries. In Xinjiang, tomb sites have been shuttered, destroyed, or converted into museums; mosques have been demolished; graveyards have been razed for urban development; and the material culture of home life has been turned into tourist spectacle. These actions disrupt Xinjiang Muslims' capacities to build and maintain their own places, sacred and mundane, and thereby maintain their own cultural and political identity.[7] In the summer of 2021, a year after the circulation of a plan to de-Arabicize nineteen urban mosques in Xining, cranes began removing the domes and minarets of Xining's mosques, flattening and sinicizing them.[8] It remains unclear to what degree these architectural restrictions will affect smaller-scale place-making agency and its possibilities of social and political expression.

Authorities have also engaged in a personal geopolitics focused on changing hearts and minds that targets both present and future generations. Under Xinjiang party secretary Chen Quanguo, authorities have detained hundreds of thousands of Uighurs and Kazakhs for reeducation and labor. Moreover, campaigns to promote interethnic marriage and dispatch patriotic Han Chinese to live with, surveil, and "gather the hearts" of Xinjiang Muslims have introduced totalitarian elements to everyday domestic life.[9] With the penetration of the intimate place of the home and with few opportunities for unsurveilled expression left for the region's Muslims, possibilities for agency are further reduced. Education has also been important to these micropolitics. In mid-2020, in a shift that signified the influence of second-generation ethnic policy reform in China's peripheral lands, national and provincial education authorities suddenly announced that the Inner Mongolia Autonomous Region would abandon bilingual education that used Mongolian as the primary language, leading to public protests that were rapidly criminalized.[10] Coupled with its urbanization of rural spaces that minoritized groups strategically use to retain their ethnic identities, state policy is working to linguistically consolidate and homogenize the *Zhonghua minzu*.

Finally, an important practice for bringing Tibetanness into the urban environment and the modern consumer economy has been entrepreneurialism. Charlene Makley has written that the end of the first decade of the twenty-first century was a time of increased restriction on outside money, in particular from foreign donors and nonprofit organizations that were central to development projects in many Tibetan areas in Qinghai.[11] From this perspective, my book has covered a period of efflorescence for Tibetan businesses that occurred after this restriction of outside money, as many Tibetans were trying to make the best of rapid urbanization and the consumer economy that grew with it. Nevertheless, in recent years government support for Tibetan entrepreneurism has become unevenly distributed, linked to interpersonal networks, and predicated on working in step with prevailing policy trends.[12] Whether Tibetan businesspeople will have economic success in the long term, with continued dependency on the state both for financial assistance and for the maintenance of urban geographies where lucrative trade is possible, remains to be seen.

The civilizing machine continues to act in China's peripheries. Whether people in these places will continue to be able to leverage the resources that urban development has made available to them to create their own places amid the civilizing machine, or whether more restrictive territorial codings will diminish possibilities is a pressing question. While it has become increasingly common to debate whether China-centered development activities in Hong Kong and along the Belt and Road Initiative are forms of colonialism, we should also recall that the peoples of Chinese Inner Asia have lived under such conditions for decades. Their experiences and practices have much to teach students of a geopolitically active Global China.

Boston
October 2021

Notes

Introduction

1. The Demonstration City of Progress in Ethnic Unity (Ch. *minzu tuanjie jinbu shifanqu*) designation is connected to and supplements other harmony-oriented programs for minoritized ethnicities, including unity-themed education and constructing a happy city. It also connects to aspirations to share institutional information between nine New Silk Road cities to ensure ethnic and religious cooperation between them. (*Qinghai Daily* 2017a).

2. Police demands for registration, and their subsequent apology, occurred during a rise in police security after Uighur stabbings of civilians in Kunming (Grant 2017).

3. Lattimore 1980; Cliff 2016.

4. Historical writings on Tibet employ many different regional distinctions to refer to, variously, the biogeographical regions surveyed by the bodhisattva Avalokiteśvara, zones of administrative rule under the Tibetan empire, the mountain ranges of eastern Tibet, and more (Lama Jabb 2015, 41–42; Kapstein 2004, 4–5). The three regions known as Chol Kha Sum conventionally refer to administrative divisions of Tibet under the Yuan dynasty. While the accuracy and dating of this terminology have been questioned, the term today chiefly refers to the three regions of Tibet: Ü Tsang, Kham, and Amdo (E. Yang 2016). Referring to this macro-region understanding, Lama Jabb (2015, 43) has written that "there is absolutely no doubt that Tibet, constituted of *Cholka-sum*, was etched into the Tibetan imagination and part of common parlance well before the establishment of Communist Chinese rule. This Tibet roughly corresponds to the Tibetan Plateau and is what Tibetans mean by *bod* even today."

5. Rohlf 2016.

6. Rohlf (2016, 167–78, 232–37) argues that the anti-PRC rebellions in eastern Tibet at this time were likely not caused by these agricultural settlers, who mostly arrived after the rebellions had ended or in areas that were relatively depopulated, like the Tsedam basin. The rebellions in Amdo and Kham between 1955 and 1958 were largely a rejection of communist social reforms, including collectivization and the disruption of the traditional roles of political leaders and religious institutions (Shakya 1999, 136–44; Weiner 2020, 161–80).

7. Party members in these permanent sites of rule, connected to party operations in Xining City, ordered and oversaw the collectivization of Amdo land. Tuttle 2013; Weiner 2020.

8. The historian Tsering Shakya (1999) described the bombing of monasteries in eastern Tibet. Destruction during Tibetan resistance to communist liberation and

during the Cultural Revolution claimed thousands of monasteries. Those that remained intact were reduced in size (Blondeau 2008, 160; Goldstein and Kapstein 1998). Makley (2007) demonstrates how road construction in Labrang was used to disrupt monastic space and authority.

9. Caple 2019; Makley 2018; Goldstein and Kapstein 1998.

10. Yeh 2013a; Makley 2018; Bauer and Huatse Gyal 2015; Zhaxi 2018; Ptáčková 2011; Robin 2009.

11. Yeh and Makley 2019; Hillman 2014.

12. Kolås and Thowsen 2005; Zenz 2014.

13. Sułek and Ptáčková 2017.

14. Caple 2019; Makley 2018; Gyal 2019.

15. Makley 2018.

16. Yeh 2013a. Fischer (2013) has emphasized the hand of the state in guiding and promoting the market on the Plateau while also drawing from Polyani's (2001) theory of double movement to argue that the social disembeddedness caused by capitalism also produces social resistance and reaction. The disempowerment arising from the PRC's monopoly on decision making and resource control leads to his argument that Tibetan entrepreneurial activity is so dependent on subsidy and state-led policy that it can hardly be called agentic (Fischer 2013, 23). Tsering Bum (2018) has also argued that Tibetans' choices are the only ones available to them as the state urbanizes health care and education access.

17. Zenz (2014, 280–81) has also found agency among Tibetans in their own civilizing project, finding and seeking to civilize their own co-ethnics' "backwardness."

18. Hillman and Tuttle's (2016) volume *Ethnic Conflict and Protest in Tibet and Xinjiang* takes this approach, its chapters looking at how structural inequalities and policy decisions can contribute to mass events. Andrew Fischer (2013) also interprets ethnic conflict, including the March 2008 unrest and ongoing incidents of self-immolation as a social reaction to the uneven and disempowering spread of capitalist modernity on the Tibetan Plateau.

19. Yeh 2013a; Makley 2018. Both books explore the self-censorship and fear around committing "political problems."

20. Grant 2018b.

21. Just as Tibetans can be turned Han, so can other groups be turned Tibetan. Both groups are identity formations that societies and states have assembled together from heterogeneous individuals through reiterative practice. Scholars including Sara Shneiderman (2013) and Nancy Levine (1987) have shown that groups in Tibetan borderlands have, over time, changed ethnic identifications in a multi-directional fashion in response to various economic and political opportunities and pressures, often in conformance with official taxonomic systems. For a related argument in an Amdo area see Wallenböck 2016.

22. Whether a nationality, an ethnicity, or any other group identity, Tibetan is not an essentialist category that animates Tibetans' identities and actions at all times. As Rogers Brubaker (2004) has argued, cognitive awareness of groupness in one moment does not mean that the group exists as a real category "out there" in less attentive moments. Vasantkumar (2012) has argued for the importance of looking beyond ethnic categories in explanations of social interactions in the context of Labrang in Amdo.

23. Mullaney 2011.

24. Ma Rong 2007; Leibold 2013; Leibold 2015.

25. Jinba Tenzin 2014; Roche and Yudru Tsomo 2018.

26. Lama Jabb (2015, 39–43) argues that "Tibetan" (Tib. *bod*) has become a dominant imaginary over the last century as nomads and farmers from all of Tibet's regions have participated in an imagined community.

27. As Stevan Harrell (1994, 27) has suggested, ethnic consciousness can be "sharpened, focused, perhaps intensified by the interaction with the center."

28. Grant 2018a.

29. Fairbank 1968.

30. Needham 1959; Henderson 2010.

31. Fiskesjö 1999.

32. Duara 2001, 103. As Geremie Barmé (2013) and Wang Gungwu (1984; 2013) have shown, the recent retrieval and deployment of the term "civilization" in China echoes usages of the term that were transmitted from Japan in the late nineteenth century. The intellectuals of modern China gave the concept renewed significance as they deployed the term as part of a new conceptual vocabulary primed for the modernization of the Chinese state and its citizenry.

33. Duara 2001.

34. Tong Lam (2010, 888, 902) describes the "internal civilizing mission" in which the Qing Ministry of Civil Affairs drew from Euro-American and Japanese policing models and also worked to create a governable national citizenry and to police a territory that foreign empires would recognize as "civilized" under international law, thus warding off further territorial seizures. During the Republican period, the state used a hybrid notion of Western external civilization and Chinese internal civilization in the New Life Movement, which combined outward proscriptions on impolite and backward activities such as spitting in public places and blocking traffic with the rejuvenation (Ch. *fuxing*) of Confucian morality. The movement sought to create a national community that synthesized this morality with Western standards of clothing, hygienic foods, housing, and behaviors (Dirlik 1975; Duara 2001).

35. Anagnost 1997.

36. Cartier 2013; Oakes 2017.

37. Barabantseva 2009, 235; Goodman 2004.

38. Cliff 2016, 39. Cliff's field site of Korla was the first city in Xinjiang to be designated a "Civilized City." This title and the program of which it is a part will be further explored in chapter 3.

39. See Shneiderman (2006) and Samuel (1993) on Tibet's own civilizing project.

40. Elias 2000. The English word "civilizing" is formed from "civilization," a concept with important, and shifting, political and cultural connotations in European languages. Over the past thousand years, across Europe "civilization" came to index the process whereby a people become increasingly refined and separated from coarseness of behavior, as well as an attained state with an ultimate contrast in civilization's Other—barbarity (Williams 1976; Mazlish 2001). Part and parcel of Western colonialism has been the *mission civilisatrice*, in which the discourse of "civilization" has structured policies and practices that have been used to colonize, dispossess, and displace those the colonizer deems uncivilized.

41. Elias (2000) saw the French middle classes and Europe's Francofied nobility as the main drivers of this civilizing project, which would become associated with France.

42. Cliff 2016; Yeh 2013a. For Fischer (2013) exclusionary urbanization in Tibet has parallels with twentieth-century efforts to bring "industrial civilization" to Latin America.

43. Simone 2010, 288.

44. DeLanda 2006.

45. Gidwani 2008, 79. Gidwani (135) writes that development as a machine creates "composite bodies" "whose workings bear the trace of the aleatory: an irreducible indeterminacy. Things simply happen despite the best of designs." Also see Deleuze and Guattari 1987.

46. DeLanda 2006, 34. Geographers have focused on socio-material assemblages to show how people and building materials are brought together to produce specific forms of urban dwelling, as well as to bring attention to how political agency is distributed not only among people, but also with materials (McFarlane 2011; Anderson et al. 2012; Dittmer 2017).

47. Guattari 2009, 111.

48. Also see Deleuze and Guattari 1983.

49. For examples see Agnew and Shin 2017; Cramer 2016.

50. Rose-Redwood 2008; Till 2005.

51. Koch 2018.

52. Graham 2008; Rokem et al. 2017.

53. Weizman 2007; Rokem et al. 2017.

54. Graham 2008; Fregonese 2020. From a different perspective, Rinzin Dorjee (2017) has looked at the urban not as the object but as the means of violence. He has used the term "urbanicide" to describe the assimilatory combination of land expropriation, resettlement, and urban expansion that threatens Tibetan livelihoods and culture.

55. Agnew 1987.

56. Solinger 2018; L. Zhang 2010.

57. Hsing 2010.

58. Hillman 2013.

59. Discussing the multiplicity of the global city, Sassen (2005, 40) writes, "Recovering places means recovering the multiplicity of presences in [the urban] landscape."

60. Bogaert 2018; Roy and Ong 2011.

61. Hsing 2010; Chu 2014.

62. These prefectures are called in Chinese, respectively, Huangnan, Hainan, Haibei, Guoluo, and Yushu.

1. Circulations and Dreams on the Urbanizing Plateau

1. Chinese statistics have used twelve- or sixth-month periods to qualify populations as urban or rural, and Fischer (2013, 33) has used economic embeddedness—where livelihoods are located—to differentiate between urban and rural populations.

2. Lefebvre 2003, 17.

3. Brenner and Schmid 2015; Brenner 2014.

4. Gros 2019, 70; Allen 2016.

5. Chan 2014, 4.

6. Chan 2014, 4.

7. Zhou and Ma 2003; Chan and Hu (2003) explain that over the course of the 1982, 1990, and 2000 censuses, urban administrative boundaries and actual urban processes diverged. Concrete urban processes ultimately changed faster than the statistical definitions that measured them.

8. Ho 2001; Lin and Ho 2005.

9. Chan and Wei 2019.

10. The second census of 1964 excluded those with agricultural *hukou* from the urban population. By 1982 (the year of the third census), cities and towns had grown to the point at which there were so few holders of agricultural *hukou* that, much as in the first census, all residents within these administrative units could be counted as urban (Zhou and Ma 2003, 180–82).

11. Ho 2001. Zhou and Ma 2003, 181.

12. Chan and Hu 2003; Wu and He 2015.

13. Zhou and Ma 2003, 178–79; State Council 2008.

14. State Council 2008.

15. Scholars have noted that the more objective and visual (Ch. *jingguan*) approach to enumerating the urban population in the census is more in line with international standards. Wu and He 2015, 201; Cai and Zhang 2015, 35.

16. Liu et al. 2019.

17. Compared to earlier censuses, the 2010 census had a more complex way to determine where populations were de facto living. It simultaneously counted de jure registered residents—urban *hukou* holders—and also added nonregistered residents who had lived at the site for at least six months. In addition, it excluded de jure residents who had been gone for more than sixth months. This contrasts with the 1990 and 2000 censuses, which did not exclude urban *hukou* holders who had left the administrative unit (Wu and He 2015, 186–89). Moreover, the time span for calculating de facto presence or absence was reduced from one year to six months between the 1990 and 2000 census collections, reflecting more fine-grained efforts to count the population (Zhou and Ma 2003, 187).

18. Chan 2014.

19. The language of housing reconstruction often treats older housing stock as disorderly or dilapidated (Robin 2009; Gyal 2015). In pastoral areas, the implementation of "ecological construction" programs with the purported aim of protecting forests and grasslands has been used to displace pastoralists from their pastures and resettle them in concentrated housing blocks (Yeh 2005, 2009b; Ptáčková 2011). See Bauer and Nyima 2010 for a comprehensive description of related policies and programs.

20. Ptáčková 2020.

21. Ptáčková 2020; Cencetti 2015; Levine 2021.

22. Ptáčková 2015; Bessho 2015.

23. Duojie Zhaxi (2019) argues that Tibetans are encouraged to engage in supplementary nonfarm labor (Tib. *zhor las*) to pay the difference to complete state-subsidized housing construction. When disbursing housing subsidies, state inspectors look for concrete and brick, which they view as the standards of modern housing.

Tibetans' favored material is, however, timber, typically purchased from Xining markets and trucked to the countryside. In a study of two Amdo farming villages, Wang Shiyong (2014, 1119) found that "the majority of Tibetans are engaged in various types of unskilled manual labor such as construction work—carrying heavy loads, mixing cement, and so forth." He notes that while farmers were increasingly also doing skilled labor, they were reliant on state expenditure and were marginalized in competition with non-Tibetans.

24. Zhaxi 2020, 121–26.

25. Hillman (2014) and Makley (2018) have discussed the movement and consolidation of villages in Tibetan areas with regard to construction projects and environmental protection measures. In her discussion of "rural voids," Driessen (2018, 71) argues that processes of rural emptying out (Ch. *kongxinhua*) can go beyond consolidation to complete abandonment by both the developmental state and eventually the villagers themselves, who leave behind the stigma of rural dirt and state-designated poverty in rural regions and move to urban areas.

26. Levine 1999; Sułek 2011; Fischer 2013; Wang 2014; Goldstein, Childs, and Wangdui 2008; Zhaxi 2020.

27. Makley 2013; Hillman 2013.

28. Cartier 2015; Chan 2010; Yeh and Henderson 2008, 15.

29. Qinghai People's Congress 2014. As of the time of writing of this book, accomplishing the 60 percent rate in or shortly after 2020 was a likely possibility, as urbanization increased rapidly from 33.90 percent in 1995 to 50.30 percent by 2015 (Qinghai Provincial Bureau of Statistics 2017, table 2–3).

30. Qinghai People's Congress 2014. See also Roche, Hillman, and Leibold (2017), who discuss national plans to encourage ethnic "mingling" through administrative urbanization.

31. The city's sixth formal urban plan, created in 1981, was a product of the new, more market-oriented approach to city planning that accompanied Deng Xiaoping's reforms. It moved the city away from socialist planning for industry and housing. The 1995 modification of the sixth urban plan had a more expansive urban footprint that used special developmental zoning to promote development at the city's periphery (Gaubatz 2008, 194). See also Grant (2018c) for a discussion of recent modifications to these plans.

32. Xining Statistical Bureau 2021b.

33. For example, 2019 annual statistical samples showed Xining's four core municipal districts as having urbanization rates ranging between 94 percent and nearly 100 percent (Xining Statistical Bureau 2020).

34. This accounted for a Tibetan population rate of 5.5 percent of Xining's overall population in 2012 (Xining Statistical Bureau 2013, table 1–11, 45). Xining's administered counties have lower urbanization rates, but they are also increasingly urban both in terms of built-up area and population; Xining's Huangzhong County was even upgraded to a municipal district (Ch. *shiqu*) in 2019 in line with plans to attain a high level of "new-style" urbanization. More generally, Xining has gained counties following national trends encouraging cities to "lead counties" in their development (L. Ma 2005). Neighboring Huangyuan and Huangzhong Counties, located, respectively, to the south and west of Xining's municipal district core, were added to Xining City's administration in 1999 and 2000. In 2019, Huangzhong was scaled up to a

municipal district (Qinghai People's Congress 2019). Xining City began administering Datong County, to its north, at the much earlier date of 1966.

35. As of time of publication, detailed statistics from the seventh census on the Tibetan population in Xining were not yet available (Xining Statistical Bureau 2021a).

36. Gidwani and Sivaramakrishnan (2003, 190–91) also argue that this circular migration, which statisticians have a hard time accounting for, fosters a regional modernity in which the "culture of work is one of liminality and fluidity: migrants are part of a traveling culture that exposes them to diverse worlds of association and signification that sow the seeds of discontent. Such are the modest origins of counterhegemony."

37. According to Ekvall (1939, 53–58), some Muslim traders would stay for long periods on the grasslands, living with Tibetan hosts for months while conducting trade with them and securing access to the whole community through their host. Tibetans would also travel in the winter to markets in Muslims villages far from their homes to sell their grassland goods. Also see Horlemann (2012c, 163).

38. These hostels were called *xiejie*, or "houses of repose," and had, according to Bianca Horlemann (2012b, 132–33), mostly disappeared by the 1930s when the Ma family warlords monopolized trade and the cash economy became dominant in the region.

39. Zhong 2001.

40. From a notice posted on site (People's Government of Xining City Chengdong District 2013).

41. From a notice posted on site (Qinghai Ramadan Industrial Trading Company 2013).

42. Trine Brox (2019) has described the complicated nature of authorship and participation in Chengdu's Tibetan commercial landscape, which includes not only Tibetans but also Han Chinese sellers and consumers and foreign tourists.

43. According to Wangchuk and other research participants, caterpillar fungus (Tib. *dbyar rtswa dgun 'bu*) generated money for pastoralists in three different ways: by digging it up themselves, by renting out land and allowing others to harvest and sell what they find, or by renting out land, typically to Tibetans or Muslims, who in turn contracted a third party to harvest the fungus for them. Renting out land brings money more quickly and easily but prevents Tibetans from enjoying the potential spoils of an unexpected bumper harvest.

44. In bad years 50,000 yuan was more common. At the time of research, the worst year Wangchuk could remember was the financial crash of 2008. The anticorruption campaign, which limited government officials' purchase of expensive luxury items, had also been difficult.

45. Sivaramakhrishnan and Agrawal (2003, 22) have argued that regional modernities "encompass multiple terrains of localization and point toward the search for patterns generated by socio-political and cultural forces as they act to produce localities. It implies that localities are always produced such that they remain nested in larger networks of relationships best understood as regions."

46. Gidwani and Sivaramakrishnan 2003, 204–5. I am understanding urban development here as a combination of state-led developmental policy and state-regulated market capitalism.

47. The official volume edited by Ren (2013) is exemplary of these various emphases of the Chinese Dream. Elizabeth Economy (2018, 4–5) has stressed that

authorities have distinguished the Chinese Dream from the American Dream by its emphasis on the national collective over the individual.

48. The bilingual phrase was *Zhongguo meng, mi 'grig lam.*

49. Gangshun has traveled through Amdo Tibetan areas advocating his style of entrepreneurialism. Robin (2017) has written, "Gangshun has launched projects and business ventures which, he says, try to combine business, culture and craftiness [Tib. *tshong las, rig gnas* and *las rtsal*], the three indispensable components of any sound business venture according to him." He also circulates organizational advice over social media.

50. The Chinese name for Tsolho is *Hainan zangzu zizhi zhou.*

51. Grant 2017; Brox (2019) connects similar stigmatization in Chengdu to continued fear of Tibetan violence following the March 2008 civil unrest across Tibetan areas. Another concern that Tashi highlighted was that the South Mountain area of Xining where he lived was associated with crimes including opium dealing and kidnapping.

52. Rajan (2015, 149) argues that these empowerment activists' "primary aim is *not* improving the treatment of women, but rather strengthening the Tibetan nationality." While I would hesitate to say Rabten was not genuinely interested in helping further raise the status of women in the Tibetan community, she did argue that women's participation in education and economic development was necessary for all Tibetans' development and adaptation to urban society.

53. These sentiments align with the findings of Adrian Zenz (2014, 182–96) and Andrew Fischer (2013, 275–84), who have suggested that educated and urbanized Tibetans are finding themselves in difficult economic positions because they must compete against better-connected and positioned Han Chinese in both public and private work.

54. Tomba 2014, 89.

55. Fischer and Zenz (2017) argue that a neo-*fenpei* system has been implemented in the TAR and other Tibetan autonomous prefectures and counties, including in Qinghai. The goal is to provide more public positions in order to neutralize unrest among underemployed Tibetan youth after the 2008 uprisings and later self-immolations. They argue that the new program, which favors Chinese-medium educated Tibetans, ultimately promotes further ethnic assimilation.

56. Fischer and Zenz 2017.

57. Teachers also go to rural areas (Zenz 2014). Moreover, as Stuart Wright (2019) has argued in his study of school consolidation, large school compounds have many similarities with towns and are urbanized spaces in their own right.

58. Government officials and civil servants also receive below-market prices on property when their work units coordinate with real estate developers. These deals could shave 10 percent or more off the list prices of apartments. As participants who had received apartments in such a way told me, this is usually the result of an exchange of favors between the development company and a government bureaucracy, members of which contact friends, family, and their social networks about available discounted apartments.

59. Zhaxi 2020, 144–66.

60. Driessen (2018, 78–79) argues that the Chinese state, through administration and classification, "retains and recycles urban-rural binaries, while refusing to perceive of the urban and the rural as a continuum."

61. Van Spengen 2000; T. Harris 2013.

2. Remembering Xining

1. Gu and Lu 2012. Rohlf (2016, 36) discusses a sudden acute interest in early Republican China for assessing the potential of China's northwestern frontiers for economic development, in particular agriculture.

2. The Chinese term used here, *xifan*, can be translated as "western barbarians" or "western aliens" and has been loosely applied to different groups at the western frontier of Inner China over time. By the early twentieth century it was mostly used to describe Amdo Tibetan peoples (Atwood 2015).

3. Victor G. Plymire to his parents, April 13, 1911, item 45, folder 2, box 2, CN 341, Papers of Victor G. Plymire, Billy Graham Center Archives, Wheaton College, IL; Theroux 1989, 394.

4. Theroux 1989, 394; Grenard 1904, 205–6.

5. Gordillo 2014. Maurice Halbwachs (1980) introduced the term "collective memory" to discuss the inseparability of memory and forgetting from participation in affective communities. Scholars including McGranahan (2010) have preferred to use the term "collected memory" in order to stress the power dynamics within affective communities' remembrance practices, such as selective silences embraced for political solidarity.

6. Barnett 2010.

7. Larkin 2013, 238.

8. Makley 2018, passim.

9. Bakhtin 2010. Also see Bhabha (1990) for a discussion of the chronotope and the nation, and Till (2005) for a study of how urban memorials bring the national past into the present.

10. Bakhtin 2010, 90. Xining's history of conquest and reconquest can be likened to the adventure narrative chronotope that Bakhtin uses the "extratemporal hiatus" to elucidate. In Xining's case, the enduring relationship is between the peripheral city and the civilizing center.

11. The deployment of this chronotope is a rhetorical strategy used to diminish the significance of past instability, not to avoid discussing such events altogether.

12. Gaubatz (1996, 20–21) argues that the "frontier of control" is more about political control over trade routes, as opposed to "frontiers of settlement" that are linked to agricultural transformation. She suggests the latter has historically occurred more in southern China. See also Lattimore (1962, 477) for a related discussion of exclusive and inclusive frontiers in the north and south, respectively. Gaubatz focuses on the roles of cities in frontiers of control. But it should be noted that outside of Xining, the valleys of the Huangshui River also have old Chinese agricultural settlements, many of which Jin Yude (2014) discusses in his work.

13. Larkin 2013.

14. Wheatley 1971, 447, 479.

15. A. Wright 1965; Easterling 2014.

16. Gaubatz (1996, 138) explains that Xining deviates from geomantic practices as its east-west road was built to accommodate, facilitate, and control existing trade infrastructure. "Nonetheless," she writes, "the internal structure of the walled city remained geomantically sound, with the most important yamen auspiciously located in the northwest quadrant of the city, adjacent to the central intersection and

facing south, and the main axes of the walled inner area oriented with the cardinal directions."

17. "The former names given by the Ming dynasty to Urumqi and Hohhot were Dihua and Guihua, meaning to 'enlighten and civilize' barbarians, and to 'return to civilization and to pacify' barbarians, respectively, a far cry from the original Mongol meanings of Urumqi and Hohhot as 'fine pasture' and 'blue city' " (Bulag 2002a, 203).

18. Compiling Committee 1993, 11.

19. Horlemann 2012c, 122. The name "Xining" didn't emerge until the thirteenth century under the Song empire.

20. Jin 2014, 2.

21. I wasn't the only one who took the hill to mean something other than lofty—one of the local names for the hill, according to *Old Xining* (Jin 2014, 119), is "false grain heap" (Ch. *huang liang dun*).

22. Jin 2012, 121.

23. R. Harris 2005.

24. Jin 2012, 118; Rachel Harris (2005, 383) writes that the song's "glorious mixture of kitsch and masochism is said to have been inspired by a real-life romantic encounter with a Tibetan herdswoman in Qinghai." Tang Rongyao (2012, 315) writes that this encounter lasted for only three days.

25. The Phoenix Hill tomb, a Sufi site located on top of the city's South Park, also burned down (Li 2008, 94–98). In 1895, armed Muslim rebels based in Duoba, a town west of Xining, unsuccessfully besieged the city, even scaling the walls that separated the Muslim quarter from the rest of the city in order to bombard the Qing urban center (Lipman 1997, 128, 162–64).

26. Tang 2012, 40–44.

27. Bulag 2002b, 43–47.

28. The relationship between the government of Ma Bufang and Tibetan groups was often one of violence, as in his battles for economic and political supremacy against Tibetans in Golok and Yulshul. However, Ma Bufang also invested in education, and Tibetan tribes that allied with him could benefit economically (Horlemann 2012b; Hille, Horlemann, and Nietupski 2015). Fischer (2005, 10) discusses how, under Ma Bufang, Tibetans were excluded from land and forcibly converted to Islam in areas in and around contemporary Xining, including Huangzhong, Xunhua, and Hualong.

29. Jin 2012, 117; Tang 2012, 45–48. The Six Core Tasks (Ch. *liu da zhongxin gongzuo*) and other programs include the various reforms that the authors Jin and Tang reference as accomplishments of administrative and economic modernization (La, Ma, and Ma 2009, 92–93).

30. Cooke 2018.

31. Cooke 2018, 58.

32. Bulag 2002b.

33. La, Ma, and Ma 2009, 109.

34. Rohlf 2013, 169.

35. Gaubatz 2008.

36. The street Wusi Dajie in Xining's Western District commemorates the iconoclastic May Fourth reform movement. The PRC national anthem "March of the Volunteers" is also commemorated with large sculptures of the national flag and open pages of sheet music on July First Avenue.

37. Lipman 1997, 162.

38. Tang 2012, 3. The Queen Mother of the West and her parallel nomadic female chieftain are being located not only in contemporary Qinghai. Jinba Tenzin (2014) explains the competition that has arisen between counties in Sichuan Province to become identified with similar myths of matriarchy. A successful claim can result in lucrative tourist income in a growing market that rewards exotic demonstrations of ethnicity, gender, and cultural practice. See also Schein 2000; Oakes 2000.

39. Plaques (themselves dated between 2006 and 2009) on the tree trunks stated that the trees were 231 years old. Xining's downtown administrative center was redeveloped in 1745, so the trees could have been planted during or after this period (Gaubatz 1996, 60). Zhao (2014), however, gives an earlier date of the trees' planting, 1722. For more information on this period of Qing political establishment in what was then Gansu, as well as the development of Xining, see Perdue 2005, 314–23, and Bulag 2002b, 35–39.

40. Zhao 2014. Rather than offer a unitary story of the trees' provenance, the article entertains historical and mythic origin stories, recognizing the Qing origins of the West Gate Avenue trees.

41. Qinghai News Network 2015.

42. Warner (2011) has shown that there are many Tibetan folktales surrounding Princess Wencheng in eastern Tibet that differ from accounts commemorated at sites such as Sun and Moon Mountain. These tales are often very local in nature and do not map neatly onto one specific route to Lhasa.

43. Makley 2018.

44. Gruschke 2001, 27, citing Schram 2006.

45. The three great Tibetan polymaths (Tib. *mkhas pa mi gsum*) are Gtsang rab gsal, G.yo dge 'byung, and Dmar shAkya mu ne (Brag dgon pa dkon mchog bstan pa rab rgyas 2015). Tuttle (2011, 156) argues that emphasis in Tibetan historical geographies on the polymaths' flight from Central Tibet and later Amdo is a narrative feature that focuses on events that influence "what happened" in Central Tibet, thereby keeping the narrative on Central Tibet rather than Amdo. *The Oceanic Book* does, however, emphasize an Amdo regional history and geography separate, though not divorced, from that of Central Tibet.

46. Wylie 1962, 109.

47. The Four Northern Monasteries (Tib. *byang gi dgon chen bzhi*) are Chu Zang, Sha Khung, Dagon Lung, and Ser Khok. One of them is in Xining, but they are all within the valleys of Tsongkha. Some of my friends included Kumbum, which is in Xining, as one of the Four Northern Monasteries and excluded Ser Khok. For a detailed map of Tsongkha monasteries see Ryavec 2015, 147–49.

48. Its leaves are used to make a tea for reducing pain during childbirth (Chen and Xianba 2003, 118, 133). The leaves are also famous for bearing Tibetan characters; accounts of them were popular with foreign travelers such as Rockhill (1891) and Huc (1900).

49. Gardner 2009. Kongtrül's (Tib. *kong sprul*) "Twenty-Five Great Sites of Kham" is a sectarian document that was doubly anti-imperial, against both the Ganden Podrang and the Qing. The gazetteer elided Gelug religious sites and Chinese places, deprovincializing Kham and highlighting its cultural independence and historical uniqueness.

50. McGranahan 2019, 526.

51. Jin 2012, 5. According to this account, in the vicinity of the current Mojia Street the family also divined a place to build a residence and constructed a family hall.

52. Jin 2012, 17. There is even a greater history of geopolitical circulation here, as the "boiled tea" pilgrimage and trade route between Mongolia and Tibet called *mang ja* also passed through Xining City (Perdue 2005, 266).

53. This civilizing project is perhaps most famous in the case of Songten Gampo's concentric construction of Buddhist structures centered on an untamed demoness's heart in Lhasa and reaching out to eastern Tibet, where her right hand lies supine over the land (Gyatso 1987; Schwartzberg 1994, 613). Martin Mills (2007, 7) argues that though the divining practices used to tame the demoness stem from Chinese geomantic traditions, they also became part of the early Tibetan empire's political and religious project. Rather than these practices suggesting Chinese cultural dominance, however, there is "a pronounced incorporation of geomantic relations with the landscape into the structuring of Buddhist ritual life." On a less pronounced scale, Tibetan lamas have served as taming agents throughout Tibet, not only by using rituals to subdue the wild landscape and the demons within it, but also by bringing Buddhist teachings to their disciples and the lay population (Samuel 1993, 220).

54. Lha mo sgrol ma (2011, 54) remarks on the noise of the valley, which was once more fertile and filled with trees. Shes reb rgan po'i 'bel gtam (2013, 106) argues that the name is composed of parts of two surnames: the *zi* from *nyi ldong ser bo zi na* and the *ling* from *sa ldong gro bo gon ling*. Thanks to Duojie Zhaxi for bringing to my attention these works and others on the origins of Tsongkha place names.

55. rDo sbis bshal sgrub 2008, 2009.

56. During my fieldwork, Amdo area maps, including those of Dobi Shadru, as well as maps of the greater Tibetan cultural region and the Tibetan empire, would often circulate on Weixin. See Grant (2017) on the role of viral social media in Tibetan representational politics.

57. (Tib. *mdo ba mkhar 'og ma*).

58. (Tib. *g.yu khang*); Horlemann 2012c, 129n42, 133n64.

59. Tibetan sources refer to the polity as *shar tsong kha'i bstan po* or *rgyal po*, which has led to English-language sources calling it a kingdom. Song empire sources refrain from using such terms and refer only to the lands of the Tibetans (Ch. *tubo*) or western barbarians (Ch. *xifan*) (Horlemann 2005, 5).

60. The urban population consisted of Tibetans, Turkic peoples, and Qiang, as well as Chinese who had settled in the region in earlier times. Descriptions of the city come mostly from Chinese Song period sources (Gaubatz 1996, 57–58; Horlemann 2005, 21n77).

61. Under the thirteenth Five-Year Plan, Xining was to become "one core, two cities" (Ch. *yixin shuangcheng*) with a green core (Ch. *lüxin*) that contains 217 square kilometers of forest (Zhang Xiaorong 2018). In this scheme, Duoba is slated to become a large urban center that balances out Xining's Great Crossing downtown. When I visited in the summer of 2018 it remained relatively undeveloped; but new construction there, called Qingtang Small Town, a project from Huasheng Real Estate, loomed over surrounding roads and buildings. This housing development has adopted the ancient Chinese transcription of the Tsongkha kingdom city. The

commercial use of the aesthetically rich name of Qingtang, meaning "Turquoise Exquisiteness," is what Uradyn Bulag has called "folkloric enhancement." This practice appropriates ethnic toponyms as appealing names that can be used in commercial branding (Bulag 2002a, 220).

62. The Ming mock-up wall and the maps also serve to commemorate the Xining walls that were destroyed under the PRC as the city developed. During her fieldwork in the late 1980s, Piper Gaubatz (1996) drew maps of remaining sections of Ming-era walls. Another public heritage site for that old wall is the reconstructed North Gate north of the Great Crossing.

63. Huc 1900, 325.

64. Horlemann (2012a, 120–22) also notes the importance of Mongols and Muslims in historical Tongkor. Like that of Xining proper, the town's history is irreducible to any one group.

65. Massumi 1992, 27–37.

66. Rose-Redwood 2008, 432.

3. Civilized City

1. Amin and Thrift 2016, 179–80.

2. Cartier 2013; Oakes 2017.

3. Cartier 2013, 283.

4. For reasons including economic development, geopolitics, and nation building, these projects can be aimed at a combination of global, regional, and domestic audiences (Koch 2018; Bogaert 2018; Ong 2011a).

5. Ong 2007, 2011b.

6. See Cartier (2013) on civilized city competitions, which are discussed in further detail in this chapter. In discussing China's eco-cities, Pow and Neo (2015, 134) note the terminology of modeling and borrowing in contemporary Chinese urban policy making: "We have often encountered Chinese officials using terms such as *mofan* (exemplar), *dianxing* (typical), *bangyang* (model), *biaozhun* (standard) to describe their urban environmental projects," and also "*shifan* project, literally a successful demonstration project that is set to be replicated throughout other parts of China." Xining is itself a *shifan* project in regard to ethnic relations, as discussed in the introduction.

7. Pow and Neo 2015; Hoffman 2011. This can also include the circulation of practices for controlling China's *shaoshu minzu* (cf. Zenz 2019).

8. Dean 2010; Ong 2007.

9. These competitions have historical basis in China. Carolyn Cartier (2013) argues that the images and language used in the national Civilized City competition hark back to the Communist Party's promotion of "model" sites during the Maoist period. See also Bakken (2000) for a discussion of the broader history in China of learning by following exemplary models.

10. Foucault 1990, 139; 2007.

11. Tomba 2014; Bray 2008.

12. Foucault 1990, 139.

13. See Foucault (1977) for the anatamo-political distinction between discipline-blockade, in which authorities obstruct and control subjects through bodily

intervention, and discipline-mechanism, in which subjects come to monitor and discipline their own behavior.

14. Foucault 1990, 139.

15. Foucault 1990, 139; 2003, 246; 2007, 21.

16. Bray 2008.

17. Zhang 2018; Chinese Civilization Network 2017.

18. Anagnost 1997.

19. Barabantseva 2009, 247–50. See also Cartier (2015) on the territorial urbanization and administrative hierarchy.

20. Thompson 1963; Zhang 2010.

21. Zhang 2010, 5–8; Pow 2007. Meanwhile, poorer urban residents obtain limited welfare benefits from state-created community districts (Ch. *shequ*) that share important governmental and discursive continuities with the socialist past (Tomba 2014).

22. Tomba 2014, 593.

23. Anagnost 2008, 501; Tomba 2014. The goal is not to allow the emergence of a potentially antagonist class (Ch. *jieji*) but to cultivate a putatively socially harmonious stratification (Ch. *jieceng*). While the official term is "stratum," English-language scholarship usually translates *zhongchan jieceng* as "middle class" rather than "middle stratum" to avoid awkwardness of usage.

24. Few of my participants confidently self-identified as "middle class" (Ch. *zhongchan jieceng*) and instead positioned themselves as just below the middle average (Ch. *zhongdeng pianxia*). Others didn't use this terminology at all.

25. Cartier 2015.

26. Xining Yearbook Compiling Committee 2015, n.p. The Shanghai Tongji University Urban Planning and Design Research Institute published these maps in August 2013. Several county towns were also indicated to serve as anchors in Xining's administered counties (Ch. *xian*).

27. Brox 2017.

28. S. Wright 2019, 134–46; Zenz 2014, 38–39. Zenz (2014, 129) also remarks on the dilemma of "traditionalist-minded" urban Tibetan parents of either sending their children away to boarding schools like those in Trika, where the parents would be unable to frequently see their children, or of keeping their children with them in urban centers for Chinese-medium education.

29. Zhang 2010.

30. Cartier 2013, 279.

31. Qinghai Xining Civilized City Office 2010.

32. This notice can be found online shared on several government-related websites and media organs. It was also posted in restaurants and businesses across the city in 2017 (Leading Work Office for Create a National Civilized Xining City 2017).

33. See Foucault 1977.

34. Naughton 1988.

35. Pow and Neo 2015.

36. Hoffman 2011; Pow and Neo 2015.

37. Hoffman 2011, 56; Pow 2018, 875–76.

38. Pow 2018, 866.

39. Zhang 2018.

40. *Qinghai Daily* 2017b; State Council Information Office 2018. See also Sun 2012.

41. New Lake District is united by two "ecological axes" (Ch. *shengtai zhou*) formed by the subdistrict's rivers, man-made beaches, and footpaths (Qinghai News Network 2009).

42. Pow and Neo 2015, 134. This is one of the terms used by officials to describe replicable sites that have either copied or will hopefully be copied by other urban places.

43. Oakes 2017.

44. Oakes 2016, 752.

45. Xiao 2012.

46. Zhang 2008. At the time of writing this article, Zhang was deputy mayor of the Xining Municipal People's Government.

47. Zhang 2008.

48. Zhang 2008, 3.

49. Zhang 2008, 3.

50. Zhang 2008, 2.

51. According to Paul Wheatley (1971, 442), ancient early Chinese Daoist texts gave the ur-form of the Chinese city as located in the mythical Kunlun Mountains, where the Queen Mother of the West has her abode. This fits quite well with recent efforts to resource Xining as a Chinese urban civilizational space.

52. Xining Municipal Government 2016.

53. Qinghai News Network 2009.

54. Xining Municipal Government 2016.

55. Grant 2018a; Winter 2019.

56. Zhang 2018.

57. China News Network 2014.

58. *Xining Evening Post* 2012.

59. See Weiner 2020.

60. Also known in Chinese as the Sanjiangyuan, the three rivers source area is today the center of a large national ecological protection zone that has displaced Tibetan pastoralists in the name of environmental protection. The three rivers are the Yangtze, Yellow, and Mekong.

61. Sohu 2016.

62. Zhang 2018. This vision includes not only a "toilet revolution" to clean up villages, but also the creation of tourism opportunities to turn their natural endowment of waters and mountains into lucrative resources.

63. The influential writings on intra-urban place valuation in capitalist cities by Harvey (1989, 250) and Massey (1994, 122) are heavily tied to the language and logic of Western class divisions. Applying their theories to contexts of the Global South requires paying attention not only to different histories of capitalism, but also to different regional modernities and social values.

4. Uncivilized City

1. Agnew 2003, 36. Massey (2005) has offered an important critique of how binary distinctions in core-periphery theorizations obscure the complex realities of global spatial interaction and work to fix unequal power relations to these imagined poles.

2. Koch 2018, 44.

3. Barabantseva 2009; Yeh 2013a; Cliff 2016.

4. Ortner 1995; Raymond Williams (1977, 55) in his examination of Marxist concepts refers to "a system of illusory beliefs—false ideas or false consciousness—which can be contrasted with true or scientific knowledge." False consciousness works to distort a clear picture of existing class relations.

5. Yeh 2013a, 222–24. Tibetans were also skeptical about the motivations of the officials and critical of the style and the quality of the building material of the housing. Yeh (2013a, 267) argued that, in participating in the Comfortable Housing program, "Tibetans exercise agency in a way that appears to contradict their assumed interests, demonstrating that subject positions have multiple, not singular, interests." The overdetermined nature of material and social phenomena makes it difficult to reduce Tibetans' interests or desires to any one factor.

6. Ghertner 2015, 125.

7. Ghertner 2015, 157.

8. Yeh 2013a, 10–14, quote on 25. Antonio Gramsci (1971, 323–23, 419–21) wrote that commonsense is the unreflective practical activity of the "active man-in-the-mass"; this activity is shaped by both historical legacies and contemporaneous class realities. Gramsci contrasted commonsense with good sense, a self-conscious critical examination of commonsense that allows challenges to commonsense and the social order from which it has emerged.

9. Yeh 2013a, 11, 102.

10. Douglas 2002, 3.

11. Kristeva 1982; Lagerspetz 2018, 120–21.

12. Lagerspetz (2018, 109) refers to a "myth of abjection," writing of Kristeva, "The whole enterprise must reasonably be treated as a feature of *Western* cultural self-understanding. The savage and the primitive, like the neurotic and the infant, came in handy for Europeans as mirrors in which they wished (not) to see themselves, or perhaps simply as screens on which they could project their secret desires and fears."

13. Lagerspetz 2018, 124, 155.

14. Fischer 2005, 23.

15. Fischer 2005.

16. In regular speech, *sem* is often used in expressions referring to mental and emotional states and is often translated as "mind." From a Buddhist perspective, *sem* also has importance in karmic registers. Adams (cf. 1998, 89–90) has written that it manifests as the physical and ethical expression of a collectivity of bodies accumulated from past lives. As Caple (2019, 185n1) has pointed out, Tibetans often motion to their physical heart when referring to *sem* though the term shouldn't be taken as limited to the heart.

17. Caple 2019, 85–105, 116. Kumbum (Tib. *sku 'bum*) and Rongwo (Tib. *rong bo*) are both located in Amdo. The former is today a notorious example of purported moral decline facilitated by heavy tourism and urbanization.

18. Kristeva 1982; Ghertner 2015.

19. See also Sibley (1995), who has applied Lacanian psychoanalysis to social processes of spatial boundary making.

20. Barabantseva 2009; Yeh 2013a.

21. Prejudices against Muslims in this regard, though very widespread among Tibetans, were particularly strong among Tibetans from Xunhua, where there is a large Salar Muslim community.

22. At the same time, fast and inexpensive Muslim noodle restaurants were also popular among Tibetans and other ethnic groups. As Fischer (2005) has suggested, dispositions toward Muslims and Muslim restaurants mix social, economic, and religious attitudes and practices that are not always consistent. At times, my Tibetan friends expressed suspicion of the food even while we were eating it.

23. Conventionally, butchers were included among unclean peoples (Tib. *mi btsog pa*) who were socially stigmatized and unable to become monks (Kolås 2003, 188).

24. Kabzung and Yeh 2016; Barstow 2017.

25. Ptáčková 2011, 9.

26. Fischer 2005; Ekvall 1939.

27. The influential ethnic policy reform thinker Hu Angang and his colleague Hu Lianhe have written about the importance of the "openness and inclusivity" (Ch. *kaifang baorongxing*) through which China has absorbed outside and internal difference while also strengthening its shared national identity (Hu and Hu 2011, 6; Leibold 2013, 19–21). Xi Jinping (2014) has used the term in Belt and Road Initiative discourse. Xining City's guidelines for the thirteenth Five Year Plan, using the language of openness and inclusivity, have discussed Xining's urban cultural development in terms of Belt and Road Initiative development (Xining Municipal People's Government 2017).

28. Zhang 2008.

29. Wang Guoli 2012; Ma Jinyuan 2014. The Chinese term for the motto is *baorong chengxin, wushi chuangxin*. Cities across China commonly use *baorong* in their mottos, but I argue that in the ethnic and religious context of Xining, it has taken on a unique significance.

30. Adams 1998, 89.

31. Yeh 2013a, 171–73, 182–83. One concern was that pursuing wealth could lead to slaughtering livestock for income.

32. Caple 2019, 95–96.

33. Janes 1995, 10; Caple 2019, 95; Adams 1998, 89.

34. Ghertner (2015, 125–27) makes the case for an aesthetic "hegemony of form" that is "more imageric and sensory than ideational." While contemporary Chinese urbanism invokes clear images, they can be interpreted in different ways.

35. Lama Jabb 2015, 136. The name of the group in Tibetan is *bod kyi snyan ngag pa'i mi rab gsum pa*.

36. Lama Jabb 2015, 136–37.

37. Lama Jabb 2015, 157–63, quote on 162.

38. Gayley 2013, 249.

39. Gayley 2013, 252, 264–65.

40. Gayley 2013, 263–64.

41. Kabzung and Yeh 2016, 124–28.

42. Gayley 2016. Controversy has included violence in towns that have agreed to abide by Larung Gar's ethical guidelines, the "ten new virtues" that proscribe evil deeds. Some Tibetan bloggers have shared images of monks punishing villagers who violated the guidelines. These critics argue that the *khenpos* are exercising a despotic

power upon their followers, comparing it to the violent conformism of the Cultural Revolution.

43. Kyabchen Dedrol note dated March 5, 2018. Also available at http://www.shambalanews.com/tib/various/1620-2018-03-07-05-59-03.

44. Kyabchen Dedrol note dated March 6, 2018. Also available at https://freewechat.com/a/MzI0Mjc1ODc4NA==/2247486840/2.

45. Lama Jabb 2015, 166.

46. High Peaks Pure Earth 2018.

47. Mauss 1973, 75–76.

48. Bourdieu 1990.

49. Bourdieu (1990, 54) highlighted the "disproportionate weight of early experiences" on these dispositions.

50. As scholars including Eveline Washul (2018) and Elisa Cencetti (2015) have shown, urban migration and changing access to and use of traditional lands have changed conceptions of home areas, including *yul* and *pha yul*, among Tibetan communities. These notions will doubtless continue to change as more Tibetans are born in urban areas.

51. Zenz 2014, 98; Yang 2017, 75–79. These language tracks are not available in all places at all educational levels. Primary schools in Tibetan autonomous administrations may only have Tibetan-only medium (Ch. *zangdan*) education and lack Tibetan-plus medium (Ch. *zangjia*), while options for both may be available at secondary schools located in county towns. Qinghai has more Tibetan-only medium choices than can be found in the Tibetan Autonomous Region, but Xining itself only has Tibetan-medium education at the tertiary level, that is, at Qinghai Minzu University.

52. M. Yang 2017, 77.

53. Rancière 2004, 8.

54. Rancière 2004, 46, 59–61.

55. Emily Yeh 2013a, 181.

56. Shakya 2000; Zenz 2014; Gayley 2016; Yü 2013.

57. Rancière 2009, 55–58.

58. Rancière 1999, 30.

5. Building a Tibetan Xining

1. Jessop, Brenner, and Jones 2008.

2. Leitner, Sheppard, and Sziarto 2008, 157. This definition is a modification of the concept as formulated by Sidney Tarrow, Charles Tilly, and other scholars of social movements (cf. Tarrow 2013).

3. Though restrictions codified in territories may restrict what people do within them, territories change over time, and their restrictions may be only inconsistently enforced (Delaney 2005).

4. Wu and He 2018, 192; Bulag 2002b.

5. Leibold 2015, 2019.

6. Mullaney 2012, 3.

7. Mullaney (2012) on this point cites the American legal scholar Barbara Flagg (1993).

8. A telling sign is research participants' discussion of "turning Han," or *hanhua*, and Xi Jinping–era official discourse of "turning Chinese," or *zhongguo hua* (Leibold 2019). In practice, Tibetans in my research have not perceived the results of national efforts in this register as contributing toward the creation or consolidation of a shared national identity, but as promoting a Han (Tib. *rgya rig*) or Chinese (Tib. *rgya mi*) identity at the expense of a Tibetan one.

9. Yiftachel and Yacobi 2003.

10. Weizman 2007, 26.

11. Weizman 2007, 26.

12. Sarah Cook (2017) has argued that the central state under Xi Jinping has pushed for the sinicization of religions that it has viewed as having foreign elements, including Tibetan Buddhism and what the state considers heterodox Islam. Foreignness is seen as a potential threat to regime stability.

13. Tuan 1980, 6.

14. Tuan 1977, 11.

15. Whatmore 2006, 604.

16. Bennett 2010, 25.

17. Deleuze and Guattari 1987, 20.

18. Andrea Brighenti (2010a, 2010b) has argued that symbolic inscriptions such as graffiti create a communicative realm of the visible in which unauthorized communication overlaps and coexists with authorized messaging. As long as an urban social group is able to create such unauthorized or overlooked inscriptions, its everyday practices can serve as a communicative media for those within the group. In this way, places and municipal territory interpenetrate.

19. Deleuze 1993, 99–100.

20. Hsing 2006; Bray 2005.

21. In practice, *shequ* may have very different roles. They have promoted and facilitated self-responsibility among middle-class property owners through local elections and provided laid-off workers in China's rust belt welfare and supplementary work. Bray 2008; Tomba 2014.

22. Makley 2013, 685; Tynen 2020.

23. Grant 2018b.

24. Xining's housing communities in newly developed parts of the city were in line with urban policy planners' and developers' imaginations about the environment of a typical urban resident: the ideal stability-seeking Chinese citizen with implicitly Han characteristics. As Li Zhang (2010) has shown, in twenty-first-century Kunming, "concept" designs for housing communities have become popular as new urban developers seek to cater to a diversified clientele. The results include housing and shared space designed in reimagined articulations of environmentalism, vernacular and ethnic architecture, Western styles, and those linked to distinct Chinese traditions, such as Daoism.

25. Brighenti (2010a, 323) calls shared spaces "surface[s] of inscription for stratified, crisscrossing, and overlapping traces."

26. Makley (2018, 57) notes the particular sensorial importance of the offering scarf (Tib. *kha btags*) as "perhaps the most ubiquitously exchanged and displayed of the 'five offerings of sensory enjoyment' [Tib. *'dod yon sna lnga*]. Those are the five icons of the most compelling attractions to each of the five senses of higher beings,

including deities and (peaceful) Buddhas (sight/mirror, sound/musical instrument, smell/incense, taste/fruit, touch/scarf)."

27. Because of its length of over six hundred meters and fine detail, this *tangka* was famous in the region and is an accessible Tibetan site in Xining's North District. It was also part of the Arura Group, which Sienna Craig (2011, 358) has called "China's largest Tibetan medical enterprise."

28. Williams 1977.

29. Lefebvre 2004, 18.

30. Zhang 2016, 79.

31. Makley 2018; Caple 2019.

32. For instance, see Duojie Zhaxi (2020) for a discussion of the importance among village members of meeting at *mani khorlo* for sharing information about neighbors and relatives.

33. Ma Xiaodong 2007; Tan, Kwan, and Chen 2020. These studies take a behavioral perspective that sees areal dissimilarity as an important cause of social problems. Therefore, creating environments in which ethnic groups live among and encounter more Han over the course of their days is seen as a solution in and of itself.

34. Ma Xiadong 2007, 69. Ma does not promote the immediate removal of all ethnic differences. Rather, he takes a long view on ethnic assimilation, stressing the importance of *minzu* establishment principles, such as the importance of publicizing ethnic groups' legal rights (see Leibold 2013).

35. Xining Municipal People's Government 2014; Provincial Ethnic and Religious Affairs Committee 2009. Similar restrictions had been in place since the early 1990s (Qinghai Province Standing Committee 1992). During my fieldwork, China's Religious Affairs Bureau (Ch. *zongjiaoju*) operated at subnational territorial scales, where it regulated religious groups and registered large religious structures such as temples. (Potter 2003; Leung 2005). In 2018, the United Front Work Department absorbed the Religious Affairs Bureaus.

36. Quoted from chapter 3, article 12, of Xining Municipality Measures for Religious Affairs Management (Xining Municipal People's Government 2014).

37. Barnett 2013, 90.

38. Xining Municipal People's Government 2011, 5; Xining Financial Information Network 2013.

39. Xu, Kou, and Wall 2018.

40. The government did repay them for the lost value of the destroyed platform. This money was used to rebuild the structure after permission was secured.

41. Yiftachel and Yacobi 2003, 690.

42. Ma Xiaodong 2007; Zhang 2016.

43. Lhudrub Dorje, the cinematographer for "City," also filmed this video (High Peaks Pure Earth 2018).

44. Yeh 2013b; Gagné 2019.

45. Scott 2017, 78.

46. Virtanen 2008, 252–54.

47. Holler 2002, 215.

48. Zhang 2010.

49. Jacobs 2015.

50. Simone 2010, 225.

51. McFarlane 2011, 658, 668.

Conclusion

1. In his 2015 BBC interview about the popularity of the photos, Phuntsok argues, "Maybe we represented thousands of young people from ethnic minorities, who left their hometowns to pursue a 'modern life' but chose to return to tradition after feeling a void in the heart. . . . As we fight for our dreams, some of us get lost. So we wanted to say with the photos: stick to your beliefs."

2. Yü 2013, 168. Dan Smyer Yü has argued that Tibetan subalterns in China have either maintained an inner sense of spiritual civilization (Buddhism) while also pursuing an outer sense of technical modernity, akin to the position of Indian nationalists in the context of postcolonialism (see Chatterjee 1993), or have been antitraditionalist and sought a new ground for a Tibetan identity.

3. Agnew 1987, 40–41. While this statement was made in specific reference to Fascist Italy and Nazi Germany, it could also be extended to authoritarian states that suppress "place-based political life," such as China.

4. Simone 2010, 33.
5. Ghertner 2015, 20.
6. Graham 2008; Fregonese 2020.
7. Rokem and Boano 2017.
8. Koch 2018.
9. Koch 2018, 154.
10. Keobountham 2020; Cain 2014.
11. Moser 2018, 638.
12. Datta 2019.
13. See McDuie-Ra and Chettri (2020) for a discussion of how contemporary state-led urbanization assembles and works to remake subjectivities in India's Himalayan frontiers.

Afterword

1. Leibold 2019.
2. See Greitens, Lee, and Yazici 2020; Wasserstrom 2020.
3. Lam 2020.
4. Veg 2016; Wasserstrom 2020.
5. Lee 2020.
6. Stroup 2019.
7. Thum 2020.
8. Bai 2020; Stroup 2021.
9. Zenz 2019; Byler 2018, 2019.
10. J. Ma 2020; Atwood 2020.
11. Makley 2018.
12. Yeh 2021.

References

Adams, Vincanne. 1998. "Suffering the Winds of Lhasa: Politicized Bodies, Human Rights, Cultural Difference, and Humanism in Tibet." *Medical Anthropology Quarterly* 12, no. 1: 74–102.

Agnew, John A. 1987. *Place and Politics: The Geographical Mediation of State and Society*. Boston: Allen & Unwin.

——. 2002. *Place and Politics in Modern Italy*. Chicago: University of Chicago Press.

——. 2003. *Geopolitics: Re-visioning World Politics*. London: Routledge.

Agnew, John A., and Michael Shin. 2017. "Spatializing Populism: Taking Politics to the People in Italy." *Annals of the American Association of Geographers* 107, no. 4: 915–33.

Allen, John. 2016. *Topologies of Power: Beyond Territory and Networks*. London: Routledge.

Amin, Ash, and Nigel Thrift. 2016. *Seeing Like a City*. Cambridge: Polity.

Anagnost, Ann. 1997. "Constructing the Civilized Community." In *Culture and State in Chinese History: Conventions, Accommodations, and Critiques*, edited by Theodore Huters, R. Bin Wong, and Pauline Yu, 346–65. Stanford, CA: Stanford University Press.

——. 2008. "From 'Class' to 'Social Strata': Grasping the Social Totality in Reform-Era China." *Third World Quarterly* 29, no. 3: 497–519. https://doi.org/10.1080/01436590801931488.

Anderson, Ben, Matthew Kearnes, Colin McFarlane, and Dan Swanton. 2012. "On Assemblages and Geography." *Dialogues in Human Geography* 2, no. 2: 171–89. https://doi.org/10.1177/2043820612449261.

Atwood, Christopher P. 2015. "The First Mongol Contacts with the Tibetans." *Revue d'Études Tibétaines* 31:21–45.

——. 2020. "Bilingual Education in Inner Mongolia: An Explainer." *Made in China Journal* (blog), August 30. https://madeinchinajournal.com/2020/08/30/bilingual-education-in-inner-mongolia-an-explainer/.

Bai Shengyi. 2020. "Secret Plan to Sinicize Xining's Mosques Exposed: The CCP Won't Hesitate to Spend up to 26 Million Yuan" [Xining qingzhensi zhongguo hua mimi zhenggai fangan puguang zhonggong buxi chi yu 2600 wan yuan]. *Bitter Winter*, June 25. https://zh.bitterwinter.org/chinese-government-spends-millions-to-rectify-mosques/.

Bakhtin, M. M. 2010. *The Dialogic Imagination: Four Essays*. Austin: University of Texas Press.

Bakken, Børge. 2000. *The Exemplary Society: Human Improvement, Social Control, and the Dangers of Modernity in China*. Cambridge: Oxford University Press.

Barabantseva, V. Elena. 2009. "Development as Localization." *Critical Asian Studies* 41, no. 2: 225–54. https://doi.org/10.1080/14672710902809393.

Barmé, Geremie. 2013. "Engineering Chinese Civilisation." In *Civilising China*, edited by Geremie Barmé and Jeremy Goldkorn, iix–xxix. Canberra: Australian Centre on China in the World.

Barnett, Robert. 2010. *Lhasa: Streets with Memories*. New York: Columbia University Press.

——. 2013. "Restrictions and Their Anomalies: The Third Forum and the Regulation of Religion in Tibet." *Journal of Current Chinese Affairs* 41, no. 4: 45–107.

Barstow, Geoffrey. 2017. *Food of Sinful Demons: Meat, Vegetarianism, and the Limits of Buddhism in Tibet*. New York: Columbia University Press.

Barth, Fredrik. 1969. Introduction to *Ethnic Groups and Boundaries: The Social Organization of Culture Difference*, edited by Fredrik Barth, 9–38. Boston: Little, Brown.

Bauer, Kenneth, and Huatse Gyal, eds. 2015. "Special Issue: Resettlement among Tibetan Nomads In China." *Nomadic Peoples* 19, no. 2.

Bauer, Kenneth, and Yonten Nyima. 2010. "Laws and Regulations Impacting the Enclosure Movement on the Tibetan Plateau of China." *Himalaya: The Journal of the Association for Nepal and Himalayan Studies* 30, no. 1–2: 23–38.

Bennett, Jane. 2010. *Vibrant Matter: A Political Ecology of Things*. Durham, NC: Duke University Press.

Bessho, Yusuke. 2015. "Migration for Ecological Preservation? Tibetan Herders' Decision-Making Process in the Eco-Migration Policy of Golok Tibetan Autonomous Prefecture (Qinghai Province, PRC)." *Nomadic Peoples* 19, no. 2: 189–208.

Bhabha, Homi. 1990. "DissemiNation: Time, Narrative, and the Margins of the Modern Nation." In *Nation and Narration*, edited by Homi Bhabha, 291–322. New York: Routledge.

Blondeau, Ann-Marie, ed. 2008. *Authenticating Tibet: Answers to China's 100 Questions*. Berkeley: University of California Press.

Bogaert, Koenraad. 2018. *Globalized Authoritarianism: Megaprojects, Slums, and Class Relations in Urban Morocco*. Minneapolis: University of Minnesota Press.

Bourdieu, Pierre. 1990. *The Logic of Practice*. Stanford, CA: Stanford University Press.

Brag dgon pa dkon mchog bstan pa rab rgyas. 2015. *The Religious History of Amdo* [MDo Smad Chos 'byung]. Lanzhou, PRC: Gansu Nationalities Press.

Bray, David. 2005. *Social Space and Governance in Urban China: The Danwei System from Origins to Reform*. Stanford, CA: Stanford University Press.

——. 2008. "Designing to Govern: Space and Power in Two Wuhan Communities." *Built Environment* 34, no. 4: 392–407.

Brenner, Neil. 2014. *Implosions/Explosions: Towards a Study of Planetary Urbanization*. Berlin: Jovis.

Brenner, Neil, and Christian Schmid. 2015. "Towards a New Epistemology of the Urban?" *City* 19, no. 2–3: 151–82. https://doi.org/10.1080/13604813.2015.1014712.

Brighenti, Andrea Mubi. 2010a. "At the Wall: Graffiti Writers, Urban Territoriality, and the Public Domain." *Space and Culture* 13, no. 3: 315–32. https://doi.org/10.1177/1206331210365283.

——. 2010b. "On Territorology: Towards a General Science of Territory." *Theory, Culture & Society* 27, no. 1: 52–72. https://doi.org/10.1177/0263276409350357.

Brox, Trine. 2017. "Tibetan Minzu Market: The Intersection of Ethnicity and Commodity." *Asian Ethnicity* 18, no. 1: 1–21. https://doi.org/10.1080/14631369.2015.1013175.

——. 2019. "Landscapes of Little Lhasa: Materialities of the Vernacular, Political and Commercial in Urban China." *Geoforum* 107 (December): 24–33. https://doi.org/10.1016/j.geoforum.2019.10.017.

Brubaker, Rogers. 2004. *Ethnicity without Groups*. Cambridge, MA: Harvard University Press.

Bulag, Uradyn E. 2002a. "From Yeke-Juu League to Ordos Municipality: Settler Colonialism and Alter/Native Urbanization in Inner Mongolia." *Provincial China* 7, no. 2: 196–234.

——. 2002b. *The Mongols at China's Edge*. Lanham, MD: Rowman & Littlefield.

Bum, Tsering. 2018. "Translating Ecological Migration Policy: A Conjunctural Analysis of Tibetan Pastoralist Resettlement in China." *Critical Asian Studies* 50, no. 4: 518–36. https://doi.org/10.1080/14672715.2018.1515028.

Byler, Darren. 2018. "China's Government Has Ordered a Million Citizens to Occupy Uighur Homes. Here's What They Think They're Doing." ChinaFile, October 24. https://www.chinafile.com/reporting-opinion/postcard/million-citizens-occupy-uighur-homes-xinjiang.

——. 2019. "Uyghur Love in a Time of Interethnic Marriage." SupChina, August 7. https://supchina.com/2019/08/07/uyghur-love-in-a-time-of-interethnic-marriage/.

Cai Yifei and Zhang Yuhua. 2015. "Changes in Methodology for Measuring China's Urban Demography and Directions for Adjustment" [Zhongguo chengzhen renkou tonji fangfa bianqian ji tiaozheng fangxiang]. *Regional Economic Review*, no. 6: 32–39.

Cain, Allan. 2014. "African Urban Fantasies: Past Lessons and Emerging Realities." *Environment and Urbanization* 26, no. 2: 561–67. https://doi.org/10.1177/0956247814526544.

Calvino, Italo. 2013. *Invisible Cities*. Boston: Houghton Mifflin Harcourt.

Caple, Jane E. 2019. *Morality and Monastic Revival in Post-Mao Tibet*. Honolulu: University of Hawai'i Press.

Cartier, Carolyn. 2013. "Building Civilised Cities." In *China Story Yearbook 2013: Civilising China*, edited by Geremie R. Barmé and Jeremy Goldkorn, 258–85. Canberra: Australian Centre on China in the World. https://www.thechinastory.org/yearbooks/yearbook-2013/chapter-5-building-civilised-cities/.

——. 2015. "Territorial Urbanization and the Party-State in China." *Territory, Politics, Governance* 3, no. 3: 294–320.

Cencetti, Elisa. 2015. "Pha Yul: An Analysis of Grassland Management Policies in Amdo-Qinghai." *Nomadic Peoples* 19:303–23.

Chan, Kam Wing. 2010. "Fundamentals of China's Urbanization and Policy." *China Review* 10, no. 1: 63–93.

——. 2014. "China's Urbanization 2020: A New Blueprint and Direction." *Eurasian Geography and Economics* 55, no. 1: 1–9.

Chan, Kam Wing, and Yanning Wei. 2019. "Two Systems in One Country: The Origin, Functions, and Mechanisms of the Rural-Urban Dual System in China."

Eurasian Geography and Economics 60, no. 4: 422–54. https://doi.org/10.1080/15387216.2019.1669203.

Chan, Kam Wing, and Ying Hu. 2003. "Urbanization in China in the 1990s: New Definition, Different Series, and Revised Trends." *China Review* 3, no. 2: 49–71.

Chatterjee, Partha. 1993. *The Nation and Its Fragments: Colonial and Postcolonial Histories*. Princeton, NJ: Princeton University Press.

Chen Yayan and Xianba. 2003. *Sacred Land of the Gelug—Kumbum Monastery and Lusha'er Town* [*Huangjiaoshendi—taersi lushaerzhen*]. Xi'an, PRC: Sanqin.

China News Network. 2014. "Work on the Xining Train Station Comprehensive Transformation Project Has Been Completed" [Qinghai xining huochezhan zonghe gaizao xiangmu wancheng]. China News Network, December 23. http://www.chinanews.com/df/2014/12-23/6903849.shtml.

Chinese Civilization Network. 2017. "List of the Fifth National Civilized City Awardees and Cities That Have Retained the Honorable Designation of National Civilized City through Reexamination" [Diwu jie quanguo wenming chengshi mingdan he fucha queren jixu baoliu rongyu chenghao de wangjie quanguo wenming chengshi mingdan]. People's Daily Network, November 14. http://politics.people.com.cn/n1/2017/1114/c1001-29645517.html.

Chu, Julie Y. 2014. "When Infrastructures Attack: The Workings of Disrepair in China." *American Ethnologist* 41, no. 2: 351–67. https://doi.org/10.1111/amet.12080.

Cliff, Tom. 2016. *Oil and Water*. Chicago: University of Chicago Press.

Compiling Committee. 1993. *Xining City Gazetteer Urban Establishment and Construction Annals* [*Xining shi zhi chengshi jianshe zhi*]. Vol. 4 (53 vols.). Xi'an, PRC: Shaanxi People's Press.

Cook, Sarah G. 2017. *The Battle for China's Spirit: Religious Revival, Repression, and Resistance under Xi Jinping*. Freedom House Special Report. New York: Freedom House; Rowman & Littlefield.

Cooke, Susette. 2018. "Telling Stories in a Borderland: The Evolving Life of Ma Bufang's Official Residence." In *Chinese Heritage in the Making: Experiences, Negotiations and Contestations*, edited by Marina Svensson and Christina Maags, 41–66. Amsterdam: Amsterdam University Press.

Craig, Sienna R. 2011. "'Good' Manufacturing by Whose Standards? Remaking Concepts of Quality, Safety, and Value in the Production of Tibetan Medicines." *Anthropological Quarterly* 84, no. 2: 331–78. https://doi.org/10.1353/anq.2011.0027.

Cramer, Katherine J. 2016. *The Politics of Resentment: Rural Consciousness in Wisconsin and the Rise of Scott Walker*. Chicago: University of Chicago Press.

Das, Veena, and Deborah Poole, eds. 2004. *Anthropology in the Margins of the State*. School of American Research Advanced Seminar Series. Santa Fe, NM: School of American Research.

Datta, Ayona. 2019. "Postcolonial Urban Futures: Imagining and Governing India's Smart Urban Age." *Environment and Planning D: Society and Space* 37, no. 3: 393–410. https://doi.org/10.1177/0263775818800721.

Dean, Mitchell. 2010. *Governmentality: Power and Rule in Modern Society*. London: Sage.

DeLanda, Manuel. 2006. *A New Philosophy of Society: Assemblage Theory and Social Complexity*. London: A&C Black.

Delaney, David. 2005. *Territory: A Short Introduction*. Oxford: Blackwell.

Deleuze, Gilles. 1993. *The Fold: Leibniz and the Baroque*. Minneapolis: University of Minnesota Press.

Deleuze, Gilles, and Félix Guattari. 1983. *Anti-Oedipus: Capitalism and Schizophrenia*. Minneapolis: University of Minnesota Press.

——. 1987. *A Thousand Plateaus: Capitalism and Schizophrenia*. Minneapolis: University of Minnesota Press.

Dirlik, Arif. 1975. "The Ideological Foundations of the New Life Movement: A Study in Counterrevolution." *Journal of Asian Studies* 34, no. 4: 945–80. https://doi.org/10.2307/2054509.

Dittmer, Jason. 2017. *Diplomatic Material: Affect, Assemblage, and Foreign Policy*. Durham, NC: Duke University Press.

Douglas, Mary. 2002. *Purity and Danger: An Analysis of Concepts of Pollution and Taboo*. London: Routledge.

Driessen, Miriam. 2018. "Rural Voids." *Public Culture* 30, no. 1: 61–84. https://doi.org/10.1215/08992363-4189167.

Duara, Prasenjit. 2001. "The Discourse of Civilization and Pan-Asianism." *Journal of World History* 12, no. 1: 99–130. https://doi.org/10.1353/jwh.2001.0009.

Easterling, Keller. 2014. *Extrastatecraft: The Power of Infrastructure Space*. New York: Verso Books.

Economy, Elizabeth C. 2018. *The Third Revolution: Xi Jinping and the New Chinese State*. New York: Oxford University Press.

Ekvall, Robert Brainerd. 1939. *Cultural Relations on the Kansu-Tibetan Border*. Chicago: University of Chicago Press.

Elias, Norbert. 2000. *The Civilizing Process: Sociogenetic and Psychogenetic Investigations*. Hoboken, NJ: Wiley.

Fairbank, John King, ed. 1968. "A Preliminary Framework." In *The Chinese World Order: Traditional China's Foreign Relations*, 1–19. Cambridge, MA: Harvard University Press.

Ferguson, James. 1999. *Expectations of Modernity: Myths and Meanings of Urban Life on the Zambian Copperbelt*. Berkeley: University of California Press.

Fischer, Andrew M. 2005. "Close Encounters of an Inner-Asian Kind: Tibetan-Muslim Coexistence and Conflict in Tibet, Past and Present." International Institute of Social Studies of Erasmus University (ISS). September 1. http://repub.eur.nl/pub/21673/.

——. 2013. *The Disempowered Development of Tibet in China: A Study in the Economics of Marginalization*. Studies of the Weatherhead East Asian Institute. Lanham, MD: Lexington Books.

Fischer, Andrew M., and Adrian Zenz. 2017. "The Limits to Buying Stability in Tibet: Tibetan Representation and Preferentiality in China's Contemporary Public Employment System." *China Quarterly* 234 (December): 527–551. https://doi.org/10.1017/S0305741017001710.

Fiskesjö, Magnus. 1999. "On the 'Raw' and the 'Cooked' Barbarians of Imperial China." *Inner Asia* 1, no. 2: 139–68.

Flagg, Barbara J. 1993. "'Was Blind, but Now I See': White Race Consciousness and the Requirement of Discriminatory Intent." *Michigan Law Review* 91:953–1017. https://doi.org/10.2307/1289678.

Foucault, Michel. 1977. *Discipline and Punish: The Birth of the Prison*. New York: Vintage Books.

——. 1990. *The History of Sexuality: An Introduction*. New York: Vintage Books.

——. 2003. *Society Must Be Defended: Lectures at the Collège de France, 1975–76*. New York: Picador.

——. 2007. *Security, Territory, Population: Lectures at the Collège de France, 1977–78*. New York: Picador.

Fregonese, Sara. 2020. *War and the City: Urban Geopolitics in Lebanon*. London: I. B. Tauris.

Fukuzawa, Yukichi. 2008. *An Outline of a Theory of Civilization*. New York: Columbia University Press.

Gagné, Karine. 2019. "Deadly Predators and Virtuous Buddhists: Dog Population Control and the Politics of Ethics in Ladakh." *Himalaya: The Journal of the Association for Nepal and Himalayan Studies* 39, no. 1: Article 6.

Gardner, Alexander. 2009. "The Twenty-Five Great Sites of Khams: A Narrative Map of an Imperiled Place." In *Studies on the History of Eastern Tibet*, 97–132. Leiden: Brill.

Gaubatz, Piper. 1996. *Beyond the Great Wall: Urban Form and Transformation on the Chinese Frontiers*. Stanford, CA: Stanford University Press.

——. 2008. "Commercial Redevelopment and Regional Inequality in Urban China: Xining's Wangfujing?" *Eurasian Geography and Economics* 49, no. 2: 180–99. https://doi.org/10.2747/1539-7216.49.2.180.

Gayley, Holly. 2013. "Reimagining Buddhist Ethics on the Tibetan Plateau." *Journal of Buddhist Ethics* 20:247–86.

——. 2016. "Controversy over Buddhist Ethical Reform: A Secular Critique of Clerical Authority in the Tibetan Blogosphere." *Himalaya: The Journal of the Association for Nepal and Himalayan Studies* 36, no. 1.

Ghertner, D. Asher. 2015. *Rule by Aesthetics: World-Class City Making in Delhi*. Oxford: Oxford University Press.

Gidwani, Vinay. 2008. *Capital, Interrupted: Agrarian Development and the Politics of Work in India*. Minneapolis: University of Minnesota Press.

Gidwani, Vinay, and K. Sivaramakrishnan. 2003. "Circular Migration and the Spaces of Cultural Assertion." *Annals of the Association of American Geographers* 93, no. 1: 186–213. https://doi.org/10.1111/1467-8306.93112.

Goldstein, Melvyn C., Geoff Childs, and Puchung Wangdui. 2008. "'Going for Income' in Village Tibet: A Longitudinal Analysis of Change and Adaptation, 1997–2007." *Asian Survey* 48, no. 3: 514–34.

Goldstein, Melvyn C., and Matthew Kapstein, eds. 1998. *Buddhism in Contemporary Tibet: Religious Revival and Cultural Identity*. Berkeley: University of California Press.

Goodman, David S. G. 2004. "The Campaign to 'Open Up the West': National, Provincial-Level and Local Perspectives." *China Quarterly* 178:317–34.

Gordillo, Gastón R. 2014. *Rubble: The Afterlife of Destruction*. Durham, NC: Duke University Press.

Graham, Stephen. 2008. *Cities, War, and Terrorism: Towards an Urban Geopolitics*. Hoboken, NJ: John Wiley & Sons.

Gramsci, Antonio. 1971. *Selections from the Prison Notebooks of Antonio Gramsci*. Translated by Geoffrey Nowell-Smith. New York: International.

Grant, Andrew. 2017. "'Don't Discriminate against Minority Nationalities': Practicing Tibetan Ethnicity on Social Media." *Asian Ethnicity* 18, no. 3: 371–86. https://doi.org/10.1080/14631369.2016.1178062.

——. 2018a. "China's Double Body: Infrastructure Routes and the Mapping of China's Nation-State and Civilization-State." *Eurasian Geography and Economics* 59, no. 3–4: 378–407. https://doi.org/10.1080/15387216.2019.1571370.

——. 2018b. "Channeling Xining: Tibetan Place-Making in Western China during the Era of Commodity Housing." *Annals of the American Association of Geographers* 108, no. 5: 1457–71. https://doi.org/10.1080/24694452.2018.1446821.

——. 2018c. "Hyperbuilding the Civilized City: Ethnicity and Marginalization in Eastern Tibet." *Critical Asian Studies* 50, no. 4: 537–55. https://doi.org/10.1080/14672715.2018.1514270.

Greitens, Sheena Chestnut, Myunghee Lee, and Emir Yazici. 2020. "Counterterrorism and Preventive Repression: China's Changing Strategy in Xinjiang." *International Security* 44, no. 3: 9–47. https://doi.org/10.1162/isec_a_00368.

Grenard, Fernand. 1904. *Tibet: The Country and Its Inhabitants*. London: Hutchinson.

Gros, Stéphane. 2019. "Frontier (of) Experience." In *Frontier Tibet: Patterns of Change in the Sino-Tibetan Borderlands*, edited by Stéphane Gros, 41–83. Amsterdam: Amsterdam University Press.

Gruschke, Andreas. 2001. *The Cultural Monuments of Tibet's Outer Provinces: The Qinghai Part of Amdo*. Bangkok: White Lotus.

Gu Zhizhong and Yi Lu. 2012. *Onwards to Qinghai* [*Dao qinghai qu*]. Beijing: Chinese Youth Press.

Guattari, Félix. 2009. "Balance Sheet for 'Desiring-Machines.'" In *Chaosophy: Texts and Interviews 1972–1977*, edited by Sylvère Lotringer, 90–115. Semiotext(e) Foreign Agents Series. Los Angeles: Semiotext(e).

Gyal, Huatse. 2015. "The Politics of Standardising and Subordinating Subjects: The Nomadic Settlement Project in Tibetan Areas of Amdo." *Nomadic Peoples* 19, no. 2: 241–60. https://doi.org/10.3197/np.2015.190206.

——. 2019. "'I Am Concerned with the Future of My Children': The Project Economy and Shifting Views of Education in a Tibetan Pastoral Community." *Critical Asian Studies* 51, no. 1: 12–30. https://doi.org/10.1080/14672715.2018.1544500.

Gyatso, Janet. 1987. "Down with the Demoness: Reflections on a Feminine Ground in Tibet." *Tibet Journal* 12, no. 4: 38–53.

Halbwachs, Maurice. 1980. *The Collective Memory*. New York: Harper & Row.

Harrell, Stevan. 1994. "Introduction: Civilizing Projects and the Reaction to Them." In *Cultural Encounters on China's Ethnic Frontiers*, edited by Stevan Harrell, 3–36. Studies on Ethnic Groups in China. Seattle: University of Washington Press.

Harris, Rachel. 2005. "Wang Luobin: Folk Song King of the Northwest or Song Thief? Copyright, Representation, and Chinese Folk Songs." *Modern China* 31, no. 3: 381–408. https://doi.org/10.1177/0097700405276354.

Harris, Tina. 2013. *Geographical Diversions: Tibetan Trade, Global Transactions*. Athens: University of Georgia Press.

Harvey, David. 1989. *The Urban Experience*. Baltimore: Johns Hopkins University Press.

Henderson, John B. 2010. "Nonary Cosmography in Ancient China." In *Geography and Ethnography: Perceptions of the World in Pre-modern Societies*, edited by Kurt A. Raaflaub and Richard J. A. Talbert, 64–73. Hoboken, NJ: John Wiley & Sons.

High Peaks Pure Earth. 2018. "Music Video: 'City' by Lobsang Nyima." *High Peaks Pure Earth* (blog), August 16. https://highpeakspureearth.com/2018/music-video-city-by-lobsang-nyima/.

Hille, Marie-Paule, Bianca Horlemann, and Paul K. Nietupski. 2015. *Muslims in Amdo Tibetan Society: Multidisciplinary Approaches*. Lanham, MD: Lexington Books.

Hillman, Ben. 2013. "The Causes and Consequences of Rapid Urbanisation in an Ethnically Diverse Region: Case Study of a County Town in Yunnan." *China Perspectives*, no. 3: 25–32.

——. 2014. *Patronage and Power: Local State Networks and Party-State Resilience in Rural China*. Stanford, CA: Stanford University Press.

Hillman, Ben, and Gray Tuttle, eds. 2016. *Ethnic Conflict and Protest in Tibet and Xinjiang: Unrest in China's West*. New York: Columbia University Press.

Ho, Peter. 2001. "Who Owns China's Land? Policies, Property Rights and Deliberate Institutional Ambiguity." *China Quarterly* 166 (June): 394–421. https://doi.org/10.1017/S0009443901000195.

Hoffman, Lisa. 2011. "Urban Modeling and Contemporary Technologies of City-Building in China: The Production of Regimes of Green Urbanisms." In *Worlding Cities*, 55–76. Chichester, UK: John Wiley & Sons. https://doi.org/10.1002/9781444346800.ch2.

Holler, David. 2002. "The Ritual of Freeing Lives." In *Religion and Secular Culture in Tibet*, edited by Henk Blezer, 207–26. Leiden: Brill.

Horlemann, Bianca. 2005. "On the Origin of Jiaosiluo, the Founder of the Tsong Kha Tribal Confederation in 11th Century Amdo." *Zentralasiatische Studien* 34:127–54.

——. 2012a. "Tibetan Nomadic Trade, the Chinese 'Xiejia' System and the Sino-Tibetan Border Market in Stong 'Khor/Dan'gaer in 19th/20th Century A Mdo." In *Studies on the History and Literature of Tibet and the Himalaya*, edited by Roberto Vitali, 109–42. Kathmandu: Vajra.

——. 2012b. "Tibetans and Muslims in Northwest China: Economic and Political Aspects of a Complex Historical Relationship." *Asian Highlands Perspectives* 21:141–86.

——. 2012c. "Buddhist Sites in Eastern Amdo/Longyou from the 8th to the 13th Centuries." In *Proceedings of the Tenth Seminar of the IATS, 2003*, edited by Cristina Scherrer-Schaub, 119–57. Leiden: Brill.

Hsing, You-Tien. 2006. "Land and Territorial Politics in Urban China." *China Quarterly* 187 (September): 575–91. https://doi.org/10.1017/S0305741006000385.

——. 2010. *The Great Urban Transformation: Politics of Land and Property in China*. Oxford: Oxford University Press.

Hu Angang and Hu Lianhe. 2011. "Second Generation Minzu Policy: Promoting Organic Ethnic Blending and Prosperity" [Di er dai minzu zhengce: cujin minzu jiaorong yiti he fanrong yiti]. *Xinhua Wengao* 24:1–6.

Huc, Évariste Régis. 1900. *Travels in Tartary, Thibet and China*. Chicago: Open Court.

Jacobs, Andrew. 2015. "Once-Prized Tibetan Mastiffs Are Discarded as Fad Ends in China." *New York Times*, April 17, sec. World. https://www.nytimes.com/2015/04/18/world/asia/once-prized-tibetan-mastiffs-are-discarded-as-fad-ends-in-china.html.

Janes, Craig R. 1995. "The Transformations of Tibetan Medicine." *Medical Anthropology Quarterly* 9, no. 1: 6–39. https://doi.org/10.1525/maq.1995.9.1.02a00020.

Jessop, Bob, Neil Brenner, and Martin Jones. 2008. "Theorizing Sociospatial Relations." *Environment and Planning D: Society and Space* 26:389–401.

Jin Yude. 2012. *Old Xining* [*Lao Xining*]. Vol. 1. Xining, PRC: Qinghai People's Press.

——. 2014. *Old Xining* [*Lao Xining*]. Vol. 2. Xining, PRC: Qinghai People's Press.

Jinba Tenzin. 2014. *In the Land of the Eastern Queendom: The Politics of Gender and Ethnicity on the Sino-Tibetan Border*. Seattle: University of Washington Press.

Kabzung, and Emily T. Yeh. 2016. "Slaughter Renunciation in Tibetan Pastoral Areas: Buddhism, Neoliberalism, and the Ironies of Alternative Development." In *Ghost Protocol: Development and Displacement in Global China*, edited by Carlos Rojas and Ralph A. Litzinger, 109–30. Durham, NC: Duke University Press.

Kapstein, Matthew. 2004. "A Thorn in the Dragon's Side." In *Governing China's Multiethnic Frontiers*, edited by Morris Rossabi, 230–69. Seattle: University of Washington Press.

——. 2006. *The Tibetans*. Malden, MA: Blackwell.

Keobountham, Sivilay. 2020. "The Production of Urban Space in Vientiane: From Colonial to Neoliberal Times (1893–2020)." *Open Access Library Journal* 07:e6696. https://doi.org/10.4236/oalib.1106696.

Koch, Natalie. 2018. *The Geopolitics of Spectacle: Space, Synecdoche, and the New Capitals of Asia*. Ithaca, NY: Cornell University Press.

Kolås, Åshild. 2003. "'Class' in Tibet: Creating Social Order before and during the Mao Era." *Identities* 10, no. 2: 181–200. https://doi.org/10.1080/10702890304327.

Kolås, Åshild, and Monika P. Thowsen. 2005. *On The Margins Of Tibet: Cultural Survival on the Sino-Tibetan Frontier*. Seattle: University of Washington Press.

Kristeva, Julia. 1982. *Powers of Horror*. New York: Columbia University Press.

La Bingde, Ma Wenhui, and Ma Xiaoqin. 2009. *History of the Hui Nationality of Qinghai* [*Qinghai huizu shi*]. Beijing: Nationalities' Press.

Lagerspetz, Olli. 2018. *A Philosophy of Dirt*. London: Reaktion Books.

Lam, Tong. 2010. "Policing the Imperial Nation: Sovereignty, International Law, and the Civilizing Mission in Late Qing China." *Comparative Studies in Society and History* 52, no. 4: 881–908. https://doi.org/10.1017/S0010417510000496.

Lam, Willy Wo-Lap. 2020. "Beijing Imposes Its New 'National Security' Law on Hong Kong." *Jamestown Foundation* (blog). July 3. https://jamestown.org/program/jamestown-early-warning-brief-beijing-imposes-its-new-national-security-law-on-hong-kong/.

Lama Jabb. 2015. *Oral and Literary Continuities in Modern Tibetan Literature: The Inescapable Nation*. Lanham, MD: Lexington Books.

Larkin, Brian. 2013. "The Politics and Poetics of Infrastructure." *Annual Review of Anthropology* 42, no. 1: 327–43. https://doi.org/10.1146/annurev-anthro-092412-155522.

Lattimore, Owen. 1962. "The Frontier in History." In *Studies in Frontier History, Collected Papers 1928–1958*, 469–91. London: Oxford University Press.

——. 1980. "The Periphery as a Locus of Innovation." In *Centre and Periphery: Spatial Variation in Politics*, edited by Jean Gottmann, 205–8. Beverly Hills, CA: Sage.

Leading Work Office for Create a National Civilized Xining City. 2017. "Create a Nationwide Civilized City. Build Together a Harmonious and Happy Xining" [Chuangjian quanguo wenming chengshi gongjian hexie xingfu xining]. June 6. http://difang.gmw.cn/roll2/2017-06/06/content_118794973.htm.

Lee, Ching Kwan. 2020. "Hong Kong: Global China's Restive Frontier." Presented at the University of Colorado Center for Asian Studies, Boulder, CO, September 16.

Lefebvre, Henri. 2003. *The Urban Revolution*. Minneapolis: University of Minnesota Press.

——. 2004. *Rhythmanalysis: Space, Time and Everyday Life*. London: Continuum.

Lefebvre, Henri, and Donald Nicholson-Smith. 1991. *The Production of Space*. Malden, MA: Blackwell.

Leibold, James. 2013. "Ethnic Policy in China: Is Reform Inevitable?" *East-West Center Policy Studies* 68.

——. 2015. "China's Ethnic Policy under Xi Jinping." *Jamestown* 15, no. 20. https://jamestown.org/program/chinas-ethnic-policy-under-xi-jinping/.

——. 2019. "Planting the Seed: Ethnic Policy in Xi Jinping's New Era of Cultural Nationalism." *China Brief* 19, no. 22. https://jamestown.org/program/planting-the-seed-ethnic-policy-in-xi-jinpings-new-era-of-cultural-nationalism/.

Leitner, Helga, Eric Sheppard, and Kristin M. Sziarto. 2008. "The Spatialities of Contentious Politics." *Transactions of the Institute of British Geographers* 33, no. 2: 157–72. https://doi.org/10.1111/j.1475-5661.2008.00293.x.

Leung, Beatrice. 2005. "China's Religious Freedom Policy: The Art of Managing Religious Activity." *China Quarterly* 184 (December): 894–913. https://doi.org/10.1017/S030574100500055X.

Levine, Nancy E. 1987. "Caste, State, and Ethnic Boundaries in Nepal." *Journal of Asian Studies* 46, no. 1: 71–88. https://doi.org/10.2307/2056667.

——. 1999. "Cattle and the Cash Economy: Responses to Change among Tibetan Nomadic Pastoralists in Sichuan, China." *Human Organization* 58, no. 2: 161–72. https://doi.org/10.17730/humo.58.2.u7325778028243h2.

——. 2021. "Practical Kinship: The Centrality of Siblings in Pastoralist Life." *Inner Asia* 23, no. 1: 79–102. https://doi.org/10.1163/22105018-12340163.

Lha mo sgrol ma. 2011. "A Brief Discussion about the Progress of Tibetan People of Tsongkha" [Nga kha bod pa'i byung 'phel mdo tsam dpyad pa]. *Rtser rnyeg*, no. 2: 48–56.

Li Xinghua. 2008. "Research into Islam in Xining" [Xining yisilanjiao yanjiu]. *Journal of Hui Minority Studies*, no. 4: 79–100.

Lin, George C. S., and Samuel P. S. Ho. 2005. "The State, Land System, and Land Development Processes in Contemporary China." *Annals of the Association of American Geographers* 95, no. 2: 411–36. https://doi.org/10.1111/j.1467-8306.2005.00467.x.

Lipman, Jonathan Neaman. 1997. *Familiar Strangers: A History of Muslims in Northwest China*. Seattle: University of Washington Press.

Liu Zuyu, Yang Weifeng, Yan Haowen, Wu Xiaosuo, and Huang Yuhan. 2019. "Evolution of Impervious Surface Pattern in Xining City Based on Landsat Imagery" [Zhenyu landsat yingxiang de xining shi bu toushui mian geju yanbian guocheng]. *Science Technology and Engineering* 19, no. 33: 55–60.

Ma Jinyuan. 2014. "Moulding the Humanistic Spirit of Xining City" [Suzao xining chengshi de renwen jingshen]. Xining Civilization Network. http://xn.wenming.cn/corpus/cd/cdbz/201407/t20140702_1242843.htm.

Ma, Josephine. 2020. "Inner Mongolia Doubles Down on Teaching Key Subjects in Mandarin." *South China Morning Post*, September 3. https://www.scmp.com/news/china/politics/article/3100112/inner-mongolia-doubles-down-chinas-plan-teach-key-subjects.

Ma, Laurence J. C. 2005. "Urban Administrative Restructuring, Changing Scale Relations and Local Economic Development in China." *Political Geography* 24, no. 4: 477–97. https://doi.org/10.1016/j.polgeo.2004.10.005.

Ma, Rong. 2007. "A New Perspective in Guiding Ethnic Relations in the Twenty-First Century: 'De-Politicization' of Ethnicity in China." *Asian Ethnicity* 8, no. 3: 199–217. https://doi.org/10.1080/14631360701594950.

Ma Xiaodong. 2007. "Research into the Influence of Residential Patterns on Ethnic Relations and Potential Countermeasures" [Juzhu geju dui minzu guanxi de yingxiang ji duice yanjiu]. *Journal of the Second Northwest University for Nationalities Philosophy and Social Sciences Edition* 73, no. 1: 66–69.

Makley, Charlene. 2007. *The Violence of Liberation: Gender and Tibetan Buddhist Revival in Post-Mao China*. Berkeley: University of California Press.

——. 2013. "The Politics of Presence: Voice, Deity Possession, and Dilemmas of Development among Tibetans in the People's Republic of China." *Comparative Studies in Society and History* 55, no. 03: 665–700. https://doi.org/10.1017/S0010417513000285.

——. 2018. *The Battle for Fortune*. Ithaca, NY: Cornell University Press.

Massey, Doreen B. 1994. *Space, Place, and Gender*. Minneapolis: University of Minnesota Press.

——. 2005. *For Space*. London: Sage.

Massumi, Brian. 1992. *A User's Guide to Capitalism and Schizophrenia: Deviations from Deleuze and Guattari*. Cambridge, MA: MIT Press.

Mauss, Marcel. 1973. "Techniques of the Body." *Economy and Society* 2, no. 1: 70–88.

Mazlish, Bruce. 2001. "Civilization in a Historical and Global Perspective." *International Sociology* 16, no. 3: 293–300. https://doi.org/10.1177/026858001016003003.

McDuie-Ra, Duncan, and Mona Chettri. 2020. "Concreting the Frontier: Modernity and Its Entanglements in Sikkim, India." *Political Geography* 76:102089. https://doi.org/10.1016/j.polgeo.2019.102089.

McFarlane, Colin. 2011. "The City as Assemblage: Dwelling and Urban Space." *Environment and Planning D: Society and Space* 29, no. 4: 649–71. https://doi.org/10.1068/d4710.

McGranahan, Carole. 2010. *Arrested Histories: Tibet, the CIA, and Memories of a Forgotten War*. Durham, NC: Duke University Press.

——. 2019. "Chinese Settler Colonialism: Empire and Life in the Tibetan Borderlands." In *Frontier Tibet: Patterns of Change in the Sino-Tibetan Borderlands*, edited by Stéphane Gros, 517–40. Amsterdam: Amsterdam University Press.

Mills, Martin. 2007. "Re-Assessing the Supine Demoness: Royal Buddhist Geomancy in the Srong Btsan Sgam Po Mythology." *Journal of the International Association of Tibetan Studies* 3 (December): 1–47.

Moser, Sarah. 2018. "Forest City, Malaysia, and Chinese Expansionism." *Urban Geography* 39, no. 6: 935–43. https://doi.org/10.1080/02723638.2017.1405691.

Mullaney, Thomas. 2011. *Coming to Terms with the Nation: Ethnic Classification in Modern China*. Berkeley: University of California Press.

——. 2012. "Introduction and Prolegomenon." In *Critical Han Studies: The History, Representation, and Identity of China's Majority*, edited by Thomas S. Mullaney, James Leibold, Stéphane Gros, and Eric Vanden Bussche, 1–20. Global, Area, and International Archive 4. Berkeley: University of California Press.

Naughton, Barry. 1988. "The Third Front: Defence Industrialization in the Chinese Interior." *China Quarterly* 115 (September): 351–86.

Needham, Joseph. 1959. *Science and Civilisation in China*. Vol. 3, *Mathematics and the Sciences of the Heavens and the Earth*. London: Cambridge University Press.

Oakes, Tim. 2000. "China's Provincial Identities: Reviving Regionalism and Reinventing 'Chineseness.'" *Journal of Asian Studies* 59, no. 3: 667–92.

——. 2016. "Villagizing the City: Turning Rural Ethnic Heritage into Urban Modernity in Southwest China." *International Journal of Heritage Studies* 22, no. 10: 751–65. https://doi.org/10.1080/13527258.2016.1212387.

——. 2017. "Happy Town: Cultural Governance and Biopolitical Urbanism in China." *Environment and Planning A* 51, no. 1: 244–62. https://doi.org/10.1177/0308518X17693621.

Ong, Aihwa. 2007. "Neoliberalism as a Mobile Technology." *Transactions of the Institute of British Geographers* 32, no. 1: 3–8. https://doi.org/10.1111/j.1475-5661.2007.00234.x.

——. 2011a. "Hyperbuilding: Spectacle, Speculation, and the Hyperspace of Sovereignty." In *Worlding Cities: Asian Experiments and the Art of Being Global*, edited by Ananya Roy and Aihwa Ong, 205–26. Chichester, UK: John Wiley & Sons.

——. 2011b. "Introduction: Worlding Cities, or the Art of Being Global." In *Worlding Cities: Asian Experiments and the Art of Being Global*, edited by Ananya Roy and Aihwa Ong, 1–25. Chichester, UK: John Wiley & Sons.

Ortner, Sherry B. 1995. "Resistance and the Problem of Ethnographic Refusal." *Comparative Studies in Society and History* 37, no. 01: 173–93. https://doi.org/10.1017/S0010417500019587.

People's Government of Xining City Chengdong District [Xiningshi chengdongqu renmin zhengfu]. 2013. "Announcement on the Resettlement Compensation Plan for the Urban Resident Houses in Minxiang and Qinfenxiang Areas as Part of the Xining Railway Station Comprehensive Reconstruction Project" [Xining huoche zhan zonghe gaizao xiangmu wei min xiang qinfen xiang pianqu chengshi jumin fangwu qianbian anzhi buchang fang'an de tonggao].

Perdue, Peter C. 2005. *China Marches West: The Qing Conquest of Central Eurasia*. Cambridge, MA: Belknap Press of Harvard University Press.

Polanyi, Karl. 2001. *The Great Transformation: The Political and Economic Origins of Our Time*. 2nd Beacon paperback ed. Boston: Beacon.

Potter, Pitman B. 2003. "Belief in Control: Regulation of Religion in China." *China Quarterly* 174 (June): 317–37. https://doi.org/10.1017/S0009443903000202.

Pow, C. P. 2007. "Securing the 'Civilised' Enclaves: Gated Communities and the Moral Geographies of Exclusion in (Post-)Socialist Shanghai." *Urban Studies* 44, no. 8: 1539–58. https://doi.org/10.1080/00420980701373503.

——. 2018. "Building a Harmonious Society through Greening: Ecological Civilization and Aesthetic Governmentality in China." *Annals of the American Association of Geographers* 108, no. 3: 864–83. https://doi.org/10.1080/24694452.2017.1373626.

Pow, C. P., and Harvey Neo. 2015. "Modelling Green Urbanism in China." *Area* 47, no. 2: 132–40. https://doi.org/10.1111/area.12128.

Provincial Ethnic and Religious Affairs Committee. 2009. "Regulations on Religious Affairs for Qinghai Province" [Qinghai sheng zongjiao shiwu tiaolie]. http://www.qh.gov.cn/mzfw/system/2012/09/17/010007470.shtml.

Ptáčková, Jarmila. 2011. "Sedentarisation of Tibetan Nomads in China: Implementation of the Nomadic Settlement Project in the Tibetan Amdo Area; Qinghai and Sichuan Provinces." *Pastoralism: Research, Policy and Practice* 1, no. 4: 1–11. https://doi.org/10.1186/2041-7136-1-4.

——. 2015. "Hor—a Sedentarisation Success for Tibetan Pastoralists in Qinghai?" *Nomadic Peoples* 19, no. 2: 221–40.

——. 2020. *Exile from the Grasslands: Tibetan Herders and Chinese Development Projects*. Seattle: University of Washington Press.

Qinghai Daily. 2017a. "Xining Successfully Established as a Demonstration City for the Progress of Ethnic Unity" [Xining shi chenggong chuangjian quanguo minzu tuanjie jinbu shifan shi]. Qinghai News Network. http://www.qhnews.com/newscenter/system/2017/12/28/012508144.shtml.

——. 2017b. "The Water Ecological City Construction Test Site Passes Provincial Joint Inspection" [Shui shengtai wenming chengshi jianshe shidian tongguo shengbu lianhe yanshou]. People's Government of Qinghai Province, December 30. http://www.qh.gov.cn/zwgk/system/2017/12/30/010291565.shtml.

Qinghai News Network. 2009. "Special Report: Xining's New Lake District Unfolds at a Magnificent Scale in 2008" [Tegao: 2008 bolanzhuangkuo xining haihu xinqu]. Sina News Center, January 19. http://news.sina.com.cn/o/2009-01-19/111315057092s.shtml.

——. 2015. "Across the Straights Public Ceremony for the Ancestor Mysterious Lady of the Nine Heavens" [Haixia liang'an gongji yuanzu jiutian xuan nü dadian]. Phoenix News. http://ah.ifeng.com/news/wangluo/detail_2015_10/19/4461010_0.shtml.

Qinghai People's Congress. 2014. "Explanation of the Qinghai Provincial Urban System Plan for 2014–2030" [Qinghaisheng chengzhentixi guihua (2013–2014 nian) de shuoming]. http://www.qhrd.gov.cn/html/1501/11715.html.

——. 2019. "State Council Official Ratification: Huangzhong County of Qinghai Province Re-established as a Municipal District" [Guowuyuan zhengshi pizhun: qinghai sheng huangzhong xian che xian shequ she].

Qinghai Province Standing Committee. 1992. "Qinghai Province Venue for Religious Activity Management Regulation" [Qinghaisheng zongjiao huadong changsuo guanli guiding]. http://www.law-lib.com/lawhtm/1992/22735.htm.

Qinghai Provincial Bureau of Statistics. 2017. *Qinghai Statistical Yearbook 2017* [*Qinghai tongji nianjian 2017*]. Beijing: China Statistics.

Qinghai Ramadan Industrial Trading Company [Qinghai laimaidan gongshangmao youxian gongsi]. 2013. "Relocation Notice" [Banqian tongzhi].

Qinghai Xining Civilized City Office. 2010. "Xining's 'Three Strengthenings' Will Push Forward the Construction of a National Civilized City" [Xining 'san ge qianghua' tuijin chuangjian quanguo wenming chengshi gongzuo]. http://www.wenming.cn/syjj/dfcz/201010/t20101026_1085.shtml.

Rajan, Hamsa. 2015. "The Discourse of Tibetan Women's Empowerment Activists." *Revue d'Études Tibétaines*, no. 33: 127–53.

Rancière, Jacques. 1999. *Disagreement: Politics and Philosophy*. Minneapolis: University of Minnesota Press.

——. 2004. *The Politics of Aesthetics*. New York: Continuum.

——. 2009. *The Emancipated Spectator*. New York: Verso.

rDo sbis bshal sgrub. 2008. "The Regime of Jiaoluosi during the Song Dynasty" [Song dai jiaosiluo zhengquan]. *Tso Ngon Tibetan Research* [*Mtsho sngon bod rags pa*], no. 2: 23.

——. 2009. "Discussion of History Related to the Tsongkha Kingdom Palace" [Tsong kha rgyal po'i pho brang dang 'brel yod kyi lo rgyus rags gleng]. *Amdo Research* [*Mdo smad zhib 'jug*], no. 4: 1–8.

Ren Zhongwen, ed. 2013. *Thoroughly Study Comrade Xi Jinping's Important Discourse on the Realization of the Dream of the Zhonghua Nationality's Great Renewal* [*Shenru xuexi xi jinping tongzhi guanyu shixian zhonghua minzu weida fuxing de zhongguo meng zhongyao lunshu*]. Beijing: People's Daily Press.

Rinzin Dorjee. 2017. "China's Urbancide in Tibet." Diplomat, March 17. https://thediplomat.com/2017/03/chinas-urbancide-in-tibet/.

Robin, Françoise. 2009. "The 'Socialist New Villages' in the Tibetan Autonomous Region: Reshaping the Rural Landscape and Controlling Its Inhabitants." *China Perspectives* 2009 (3).

——. 2017. "Gangshun and Rise of Capitalism with Tibetan Characteristics." High Peaks Pure Earth. https://highpeakspureearth.com/2017/poem-this-is-how-we-quietly-work-by-gangshun-with-accompanying-essay-by-francoise-robin/.

Roche, Gerald, Ben Hillman, and James Leibold. 2017. "Why Are So Many Tibetans Moving to Chinese Cities?" ChinaFile, June 26. https://www.chinafile.com/reporting-opinion/viewpoint/why-are-so-many-tibetans-moving-chinese-cities.

Roche, Gerald, and Yudru Tsomu. 2018. "Tibet's Invisible Languages and China's Language Endangerment Crisis: Lessons from the Gochang Language of Western Sichuan." *China Quarterly* 233 (March): 186–210. https://doi.org/10.1017/S0305741018000012.

Rockhill, William Woodville. 1891. *The Land of the Lamas: Notes of a Journey through China, Mongolia and Tibet*. New York: Century.

Rohlf, Gregory. 2013. "A Preliminary Investigation of the Urban Morphology of Towns of the Qinghai-Tibet Plateau." In *Chinese History in Geographical Perspective*, edited by Jeff Kyong-McClain and Yongtao Du, 159–77. Lanham, MD: Rowman & Littlefield.

——. 2016. *Building New China, Colonizing Kokonor: Resettlement to Qinghai in the 1950s*. Lanham, MD: Lexington Books.

Rokem, Jonathan, and Camillo Boano. 2017. *Urban Geopolitics: Rethinking Planning in Contested Cities*. London: Routledge.

Rokem, Jonathan, Sara Fregonese, Adam Ramadan, Elisa Pascucci, Gillad Rosen, Igal Charney, Till F. Paasche, and James D. Sidaway. 2017. "Interventions in Urban Geopolitics." *Political Geography* 61 (November): 253–62. https://doi.org/10.1016/j.polgeo.2017.04.004.

Rose-Redwood, Reuben S. 2008. "From Number to Name: Symbolic Capital, Places of Memory and the Politics of Street Renaming in New York City." *Social & Cultural Geography* 9, no. 4: 431–52. https://doi.org/10.1080/14649360802032702.

Roy, Ananya, and Aihwa Ong, eds. 2011. *Worlding Cities: Asian Experiments and the Art of Being Global*. Chichester, UK: John Wiley & Sons.

Ryavec, Karl E. 2015. *A Historical Atlas of Tibet*. Chicago: University of Chicago Press.

Samuel, Geoffrey. 1993. *Civilized Shamans: Buddhism in Tibetan Societies*. Washington, DC: Smithsonian Institution.

Sassen, Saskia. 2005. "The Global City: Introducing a Concept." *Global City*, no. 2: 18.

Schein, Louisa. 2000. *Minority Rules: The Miao and the Feminine in China's Cultural Politics*. Durham, NC: Duke University Press.

Schram, Louis M. J. 2006. *The Mongours of the Kansu-Tibetan Frontier*. Xining, PRC: Plateau.

Schwartzberg, Joseph E. 1994. "Maps of Greater Tibet." In *History of Cartography*, vol. 2, *Book 2*, edited by J. B. Harley and David Woodward, 79. Chicago: University of Chicago Press.

Scott, James C. 2017. *Against the Grain: A Deep History of the Earliest States*. Yale Agrarian Studies. New Haven, CT: Yale University Press.

Shakya, Tsering. 1999. *The Dragon in the Land of Snows: A History of Modern Tibet since 1947*. New York: Columbia University Press.

——. 2000. "The Waterfall and Fragrant Flowers: The Development of Tibetan Literature since 1950." *Manoa* 12, no. 2: 28–40. https://doi.org/10.1353/man.2000.0070.

Shes reb rgan po'i 'bel gtam. 2013. "Is the Place Name 'Ziling' a Tibetan Name or a Chinese Name?" [Ziling zhes pa'i sa ming bod skad yin nam ra rgya skad yin]. *Gentle Rain* [*Sbrang char*] 4, no. 106.

Shneiderman, Sara. 2006. "Barbarians at the Border and Civilising Projects: Analyzing Ethnic and National Identities in the Tibetan Context." In *Tibetan Borderlands*, edited by P. Christiaan Klieger, 9–34. Leiden: Brill.

——. 2013. "Himalayan Border Citizens: Sovereignty and Mobility in the Nepal–Tibetan Autonomous Region (TAR) of China Border Zone." *Political Geography* 35 (July): 25–36. https://doi.org/10.1016/j.polgeo.2013.04.001.

Sibley, David. 1995. *Geographies of Exclusion: Society and Difference in the West*. London: Routledge.

Simone, AbdouMaliq. 2010. *City Life from Jakarta to Dakar: Movements at the Crossroads*. London: Routledge.

Sivaramakrishnan, K., and Arun Agrawal. 2003. "Regional Modernities in Stories and Practices of Development." In *Regional Modernities: The Cultural Politics of Development in India*, edited by K. Sivaramakrishnan and Arun Agrawal, 1–61. Stanford, CA: Stanford University Press.

Sohu. 2016. "The Qinghai Wanderer Chen Meng: Creating the Sculpture for the Xining Train Station Square" [Zounan chuangbei qinghairen chen meng: xiujian xining huochezhan guangchang diaosu]. July 18. www.sohu.com/a/106313288_115496.

Solinger, Dorothy J., ed. 2018. *Polarized Cities: Portraits of Rich and Poor in Urban China*. Lanham, MD: Rowman & Littlefield.

State Council. 2008. "Regulations concerning the Statistical Division of the Urban and the Rural" [Tongji shang huafen chengxiang de guiding]. State Council Letter July 12, No. 60.

State Council Information Office. 2018. "Condition of Ecological Civilization Construction on the Qinghai Plateau" [Qinghai gaoyuan shengtai wenming jianshe zhuangkuang]. Xinhua News Network, July 18. http://www.xinhuanet.com/2018-07/18/c_1123141752.htm.

Stroup, David R. 2019. "The De-Islamification of Public Space and Sinicization of Ethnic Politics in Xi's China." Middle East Institute. https://www.mei.edu/publications/de-islamification-public-space-and-sinicization-ethnic-politics-xis-china.

——. 2021. "China: Removing 'Arab-Style' Features from Country's Biggest Mosques the Latest Move in Campaign of Muslim Assimilation." The Conversation. September 28, 2021. http://theconversation.com/china-removing-arab-style-features-from-countrys-biggest-mosques-the-latest-move-in-campaign-of-muslim-assimilation-168799.

Sułek, Emilia. 2011. "Disappearing Sheep: The Unexpected Consequences of the Emergence of the Caterpillar Fungus Economy in Golok, Qinghai, China." *Himalaya: The Journal of the Association for Nepal and Himalayan Studies* 30, no. 1–2: 9–22.

Sułek, Emilia, and Jarmila Ptáčková. 2017. "Mapping Amdo: People and Places in Transition." In *Mapping Amdo: Dynamics of Change*, edited by Jarmila Ptáčková and Adrian Zenz, 9–21. Prague: Oriental Institute.

Sun Aixia. 2012. "The Mysterious Frontier of the 'Concrete Forest'" ["Shuini senlin" li de mijing]. In *The Story of West District* [*Xiqu gushi*], edited by Yan Jinyun and Wang Yuanjing, 167–73. Xining, PRC: Qinghai People's Publishing House.

Tan, Yiming, Mei-Po Kwan, and Zifeng Chen. 2020. "Examining Ethnic Exposure through the Perspective of the Neighborhood Effect Averaging Problem: A Case Study of Xining, China." *International Journal of Environmental Research and Public Health* 17, no. 8: 2872. https://doi.org/10.3390/ijerph17082872.

Tang Rongyao. 2012. *Book of Qinghai* [*Qinghai zhi shu*]. Xining, PRC: Qinghai People's Publishing House.

Tarrow, Sidney. 2013. "Contentious Politics." In *The Wiley-Blackwell Encyclopedia of Social and Political Movements*. Hoboken, NJ: Wiley-Blackwell. https://doi.org/10.1002/9780470674871.wbespm051.

Theroux, Paul. 1989. *Riding the Iron Rooster: By Train through China*. New York: Ivy Books.

Thompson, E. P. 1963. *The Making of the English Working Class*. New York: Vintage Books.

Thum, Rian. 2020. "The Spatial Cleansing of Xinjiang: Mazar Desecration in Context." *Made in China Journal* (blog), August 24. https://madeinchinajournal.com/2020/08/24/the-spatial-cleansing-of-xinjiang-mazar-desecration-in-context/.

Till, Karen E. 2005. *The New Berlin: Memory, Politics, Place*. Minneapolis: University of Minnesota Press. http://www.loc.gov/catdir/toc/cdc051/2004028616.html.

Tomba, Luigi. 2014. *The Government Next Door: Neighborhood Politics in Urban China*. Ithaca, NY: Cornell University Press.

Tuan, Yi-Fu. 1977. *Space and Place: The Perspective of Experience*. Minneapolis: University of Minnesota Press.

——. 1980. "Rootedness versus Sense of Place." *Landscape* 24, no. 1: 3–8.

——. 1982. *Segmented Worlds and Self: Group Life and Individual Consciousness*. Minneapolis: University of Minnesota Press.

Tuttle, Gray. 2011. "Challenging Central Tibet's Dominance of History: The Oceanic Book, a 19th Century Politico-Religious Geographic History." In *Mapping the Modern Tibet*, 135–72. Andiast, Switzerland: International Institute for Tibetan and Buddhist Studies.

——. 2013. "An Overview of Amdo (Northeastern Tibet) Historical Polities." August 29. http://www.thlib.org/places/polities/#iframe=http://places.thlib.org/features/24106/descriptions/1228.

Tynen, Sam. 2020. "State Territorialization through Shequ Community Centres: Bureaucratic Confusion in Xinjiang, China." *Territory, Politics, Governance* 8, no. 1: 7–22. https://doi.org/10.1080/21622671.2019.1643778.

Van Spengen, Wim. 2000. *Tibetan Border Worlds*. London: Kegan Paul International.

Vasantkumar, Chris. 2012. "Han at Minzu's Edges: What Critical Han Studies Can Learn from China's 'Little Tibet.'" In *Critical Han Studies: The History, Representation, and Identity of China's Majority*, edited by Thomas S. Mullaney, James Leibold, Stéphane Gros, and Eric Vanden Bussche, 234–56. Global, Area, and International Archive 4. Berkeley: University of California Press.

Veg, Sebastian. 2016. "Creating a Textual Public Space: Slogans and Texts from Hong Kong's Umbrella Movement." *Journal of Asian Studies* 75, no. 3: 673–702. https://doi.org/10.1017/S0021911816000565.

Virtanen, Riika J. 2008. "Development and Urban Space in Contemporary Tibetan Literature." In *Modern Tibetan Literature and Social Change*, edited by Lauran R. Hartley and Patricia Schiaffini-Vedani, 236–62. Durham, NC: Duke University Press.

Wallenböck, Ute. 2016. "Marginalisation at China's Multi-ethnic Frontier: The Mongols of Henan Mongolian Autonomous County in Qinghai Province." *Journal of Current Chinese Affairs* 45, no. 2. http://journals.sub.uni-hamburg.de/giga/jcca/article/view/967.

Wang, Gungwu. 1984. "The Chinese Urge to Civilize: Reflections on Change." *Journal of Asian History* 18, no. 1: 1–34.

——. 2013. *Renewal: The Chinese State and the New Global History*. Hong Kong: Chinese University Press.

Wang Guoli. 2012. "Xining Spirit: The Humanistic Dimension of Xining's Rapid Development in the New Era" [Xining jingshen: xin shiqi xining kuaisu fazhan de renwen xiangdu]. http://www.cqvip.com/QK/81564X/201205/42029868.html.

Wang, Shiyong. 2014. "Challenges and Opportunities for Tibetan Farmers." *Asian Survey* 54, no. 6: 1113–35. https://doi.org/10.1525/as.2014.54.6.1113.

Warner, Cameron David. 2011. "A Miscarriage of History: Wencheng Gongzhu and Sino-Tibetan Historiography." *Inner Asia* 13, no. 2: 239–64. https://doi.org/10.1163/000000011799297663.

Washul, Eveline. 2018. "Tibetan Translocalities: Navigating Urban Opportunities and New Ways of Belonging in Tibetan Pastoral Communities in China." *Critical Asian Studies* 50, no. 4: 492–517. https://doi.org/10.1080/14672715.2018.1520606.

Wasserstrom, Jeffrey N. 2020. *Vigil: Hong Kong on the Brink*. New York: Columbia Global Reports.

Weiner, Benno. 2020. *The Chinese Revolution on the Tibetan Frontier*. Ithaca, NY: Cornell University Press.

Weizman, Eyal. 2007. *Hollow Land: Israel's Architecture of Occupation*. New York: Verso Books.

Whatmore, Sarah. 2006. "Materialist Returns: Practising Cultural Geography in and for a More-Than-Human World." *Cultural Geographies* 13, no. 4: 600–609. https://doi.org/10.1191/1474474006cgj377oa.

Wheatley, Paul. 1971. *The Pivot of the Four Quarters: A Preliminary Enquiry into the Origins and Character of the Ancient Chinese City*. Chicago: Aldine.

Williams, Raymond. 1976. *Keywords: A Vocabulary of Culture and Society*. New York: Oxford University Press.

——. 1977. *Marxism and Literature*. Oxford: Oxford University Press.

Winter, Tim. 2019. *Geocultural Power: China's Quest to Revive the Silk Roads for the Twenty-First Century*. Chicago: University of Chicago Press.

Wright, Arthur F. 1965. "Symbolism and Function: Reflections on Changan and Other Great Cities." *Journal of Asian Studies* 24, no. 4: 667–79.

Wright, Stuart J. 2019. "Governing Social Change in Amdo: Tibetans in the Era of Compulsory Education and School Consolidation." PhD diss., University of Sheffield.

Wu, Xiaogang, and Guangye He. 2015. "The Evolution of Population Census Undertakings in China, 1953–2010." *China Review* 15, no. 1: 171–206.

——. 2018. "Ethnic Autonomy and Ethnic Inequality: An Empirical Assessment of Ethnic Policy in Urban China." *China Review* 18, no. 2: 185–216.

Wylie, Turrell V. 1962. *The Geography of Tibet according to the 'Dzam-Gling-Rgyas-Bshad*. Rome: Istituto Italiano per il Medio ed Estremo Oriente.

Xi Jinping. 2014. "Xi Jinping's Speech at the China International Friendship Conference and Chinese People's Foreign Friends Association 60th Anniversary Event" [Xi jinping zai zhongguo guoji youhao dahui ji zhonguo renmin dui wai youhao xiehui chengli 60 zhounian jinian huodong shang de jianghua]. Chinese Communist Party News Network, May 15. http://cpc.people.com.cn/n/2014/0516/c64094-25024391.html.

Xiao Dai. 2012. "The Color of West District" [*Chengxibian de Yanse*]. In *The Story of West District* [*Xiqu gushi*], edited by Yan Jinyun and Wang Yuanjing, 1–3. Xining, PRC: Qinghai People's Publishing House.

Xining Evening Post. 2012. "Xining's New Train Station Is the Largest Such Public Benefit Project since the Founding of the PRC" [Xin xining huoche zhan jiangcheng jianguo yilai zuida hui min gongcheng]. Xining government website, May 10. http://www.xining.gov.cn/html/98/253002.html.

Xining Financial Information Network. 2013. "'Spring Action' to Boost Public Awareness of the Law" ["Chunfeng xingdong" zhu tui falü puji]. Xining Financial News Network, April 26. http://xnczj.xining.gov.cn/E_ReadNews.asp?NewsID=759.

Xining Municipal Government. 2016. "Trial Style Guidelines for Xining Urban Construction" [Xiningshi chengshi jianzhu fengmao guize (shixing)]. People's Government of Qinghai Province, October 8. http://www.qh.gov.cn/zwgk/system/2016/10/08/010234694.shtml.

Xining Municipal People's Government. 2011. "Official Gazette of the Xining City People's Government" [Xiningshi renmin zhengfu gongbao]. Xining, PRC: Xining Government.

——. 2014. "Xining Municipality Measures for Religious Affairs Management" [Xining shi zongjiao shiwu guanli banfa]. Chinese Law Online. https://www.66law.cn/tiaoli/8620.aspx.

——. 2017. "'Thirteenth Five-Year Plan' Cultural Development Program of Xining City" [Xining shi "shisanwu" wenhua fazhan guihua]. http://czj.xining.gov.cn/html/4466/318172.html.

Xining Statistical Bureau. 2013. *Xining Statistical Yearbook 2013* [*Xining tongji nianjian 2013*]. Xining, PRC: Qinghai Xinhua Printing House.

——. 2020. "Permanent Population and Urbanization Rates for Xining's Districts and Counties in 2019" [2019 nian xining shi ge xianqu changzhu renkou ji chengzhenhualü]. http://tjj.xining.gov.cn/html/872/340329.html.

——. 2021a. "Communiqué No. 1 of the Seventh National Census of Xining City" [Xining Shi Di Qi Ci Quanguo Renkou Pucha Gongbai Di Yi Hao]. http://tjj.xining.gov.cn/files/202106180901408832.pdf.

——. 2021b. "Communiqué No. 6 of the Seventh National Census of Xining City" [Xining Shi Di Qi Ci Quanguo Renkou Pucha Gongbai Di Liu Hao]. http://tjj.xining.gov.cn/files/202106180910286633.pdf.

Xining Yearbook Compiling Committee, ed. 2015. *Xining City Yearbook 2013–2014* [*Xining nianjian 2013–2014*]. Xining, PRC: Qinghai People's Publishing House.

Xu, Honggang, Lirong Kou, and Geoffrey Wall. 2018. "Retired Tibetan Migrants' Adaptation Experiences in Chengdu, China." *Asian Ethnicity* 19, no. 3: 319–43. https://doi.org/10.1080/14631369.2018.1433527.

Yang, Eveline. 2016. "Tracing the Chol Kha Gsum: Reexaming a Sa Skya-Yuan Period Administrative Geography." *Revue d'Études Tibétaines* 37:551–68.

Yang, Miaoyan. 2017. *Learning to Be Tibetan: The Construction of Ethnic Identity at Minzu University of China*. Lanham, MD: Lexington Books.

Yeh, Emily T. 2005. "Green Governmentality and Pastoralism in Western China: 'Converting Pastures to Grasslands.'" *Nomadic Peoples* 9, no. 1–2: 9–30. https://doi.org/10.3167/082279405781826164.

——. 2009a. "From Wasteland to Wetland? Nature and Nation in China's Tibet." *Environmental History* 14, no. 1: 103–37. https://doi.org/10.1093/envhis/14.1.103.

——. 2009b. "Greening Western China: A Critical View." Themed Issue: Land, Labor, Livestock and (Neo)Liberalism: Understanding the Geographies of Pastoralism and Ranching. *Geoforum* 40, no. 5: 884–94. https://doi.org/10.1016/j.geoforum.2009.06.004.

——. 2013a. *Taming Tibet: Landscape Transformation and the Gift of Chinese Development*. Ithaca, NY: Cornell University Press.

——. 2013b. "Blazing Pelts and Burning Passions: Nationalism, Cultural Politics, and Spectacular Decommodification in Tibet." *Journal of Asian Studies* 72, no. 02: 319–44, https://doi.org/10.1017/S0021911812002227.

——. 2021. "The Cultural Politics of New Tibetan Entrepreneurship in Contemporary China: Valorisation and the Question of Neoliberalism." *Transactions of the Institute of British Geographers*. June 16. https://doi.org/10.1111/tran.12479.

Yeh, Emily T., and Mark Henderson. 2008. "Interpreting Urbanization in Tibet: Administrative Scales and Discourses of Modernization." *Journal of the International Association of Tibetan Studies*, no. 4: 1–44.

Yeh, Emily T., and Charlene Makley. 2019. "Urbanization, Education, and the Politics of Space on the Tibetan Plateau." *Critical Asian Studies* 51, no. 1: 1–11. https://doi.org/10.1080/14672715.2018.1555484.

Yiftachel, Oren, and Haim Yacobi. 2003. "Urban Ethnocracy: Ethnicization and the Production of Space in an Israeli 'Mixed City.'" *Environment and Planning D: Society and Space* 21, no. 6: 673–93. https://doi.org/10.1068/d47j.

Yü, Dan Smyer. 2013. "Subaltern Placiality in Modern Tibet: Critical Discourses in the Works of Shogdong." *China Information* 27, no. 2: 155–72. https://doi.org/10.1177/0920203X13479860.

Zenz, Adrian. 2014. *"Tibetanness" under Threat? Neo-Integrationism, Minority Education and Career Strategies in Qinghai, P.R. China*. Leiden: Global Oriental.

——. 2019. "'Thoroughly Reforming Them towards a Healthy Heart Attitude': China's Political Re-education Campaign in Xinjiang." *Central Asian Survey* 38, no. 1: 102–28. https://doi.org/10.1080/02634937.2018.1507997.

Zhang, Li. 2010. *In Search of Paradise: Middle-Class Living in a Chinese Metropolis*. Ithaca, NY: Cornell University Press.

Zhang Xiaorong. 2008. "Mould the Character of Xining Using the Plateau Landscape Artistic Mood" [Yi gaoyuan shanshui yijing suzao xining chengshi tese]. *Journal of Chongqing Jianzhu University* 30, no. 5: 1–3.

——. 2018. "Zhang Xiaorong: Exploring the 'Secret' of Happy Xining" [Zhang xiaorong: tanxun xinfu xining de "aomi"]. China Civilization Network, August 6. http://www.wenming.cn/zgwmw_ysp/ysp_ft/201809/t20180907_4822059.shtml.

Zhang Yuning. 2016. "Community District Culture in the Process of Urbanization in Western Ethnic Regions" [Xibu minzu diqu chengshihua jinchengzhong de shequ wenhua]. *New Heights* 35, no. 1: 74–79.

Zhao Xinli. 2014. "First Read Xining Communications: Eight Immortal Trees" [Di yi yuedu xiningchuanji: baxian shu]. September 1. http://www.qhnews.com/newscenter/system/2014/09/01/011496651.shtml.

Zhaxi, Duojie. 2019. "Housing Subsidy Projects in Amdo: Modernity, Governmentality, and Income Disparity in Tibetan Areas of China." *Critical Asian Studies* 51, no. 1: 31–50. https://doi.org/10.1080/14672715.2018.1543548.

——. 2020. "Tibetan Farmers in Transition: Urbanization, Development, and Labor Migration in Amdo." Boulder: University of Colorado Press.

Zhong Shang. 2001. "The Emergence of the Xining Tibetan Cultural Style Street" [Xining chuxian zangzu fengqing yi tiaojie]. *China Business Information* Z4:12.

Zhou, Yixing, and Laurence J. C. Ma. 2003. "China's Urbanization Levels: Reconstructing a Baseline from the Fifth Population Census." *China Quarterly* 173 (March): 176–96. https://doi.org/10.1017/S000944390300010X.

Studies of the Weatherhead East Asian Institute, Columbia University

Selected Titles

(Complete list at: weai.columbia.edu/content/publications)

Mobilizing Japanese Youth: The Cold War and the Making of the Sixties Generation, by Christopher Gerteis. Cornell University Press, 2021.

Middlemen of Modernity: Local Elites and Agricultural Development in Modern Japan, by Christopher Craig. University of Hawai'i Press, 2021.

Isolating the Enemy: Diplomatic Strategy in China and the United States, 1953–1956, by Tao Wang. Columbia University Press, 2021.

A Medicated Empire: The Pharmaceutical Industry and Modern Japan, by Timothy M. Yang. Cornell University Press, 2021.

Dwelling in the World: Family, House, and Home in Tianjin, China, 1860–1960, by Elizabeth LaCouture. Columbia University Press, 2021.

Disunion: Anticommunist Nationalism and the Making of the Republic of Vietnam, by Nu-Anh Tran. University of Hawai'i Press, 2021.

Made in Hong Kong: Transpacific Networks and a New History of Globalization, by Peter Hamilton. Columbia University Press, 2021.

China's influence and the Center-periphery Tug of War in Hong Kong, Taiwan and Indo-Pacific, by Brian C.H. Fong, Wu Jieh-min, and Andrew J. Nathan. Routledge, 2020.

The Power of the Brush: Epistolary Practices in Chosŏn Korea, by Hwisang Cho. University of Washington Press, 2020.

On Our Own Strength: The Self-Reliant Literary Group and Cosmopolitan Nationalism in Late Colonial Vietnam, by Martina Thucnhi Nguyen. University of Hawai'i Press, 2020.

A Third Way: The Origins of China's Current Economic Development Strategy, by Lawrence Chris Reardon. Harvard University Asia Center, 2020.

Disruptions of Daily Life: Japanese Literary Modernism in the World, by Arthur M. Mitchell. Cornell University Press, 2020.

Recovering Histories: Life and Labor after Heroin in Reform-Era China, by Nicholas Bartlett. University of California Press, 2020.

Figures of the World: The Naturalist Novel and Transnational Form, by Christopher Laing Hill. Northwestern University Press, 2020.

Arbiters of Patriotism: Right Wing Scholars in Imperial Japan, by John Person. University of Hawai'i Press, 2020.

The Chinese Revolution on the Tibetan Frontier, by Benno Weiner. Cornell University Press, 2020.

Making It Count: Statistics and Statecraft in the Early People's Republic of China, by Arunabh Ghosh. Princeton University Press, 2020.

Tea War: A History of Capitalism in China and India, by Andrew B. Liu. Yale University Press, 2020.

Revolution Goes East: Imperial Japan and Soviet Communism, by Tatiana Linkhoeva. Cornell University Press, 2020.

Vernacular Industrialism in China: Local Innovation and Translated Technologies in the Making of a Cosmetics Empire, 1900–1940, by Eugenia Lean. Columbia University Press, 2020.

Fighting for Virtue: Justice and Politics in Thailand, by Duncan McCargo. Cornell University Press, 2020.

Beyond the Steppe Frontier: A History of the Sino-Russian Border, by Sören Urbansky. Princeton University Press, 2020.

Index

The letter *f* following a page number denotes a figure.

CPSIA information can be obtained
at www.ICGtesting.com
Printed in the USA
LVHW101601060722
722885LV00017B/390/J

9 781501 764097